Small Residential Structures

Professional Edition

Small Residential Structures

Construction Practices and Material Take Off Estimates

Professional Edition

Frank J. Gallo, M.S.C.E., P.E.
Cleveland State University
and
Regis I. Campbell, P.E.
Vice-President
Barber & Hoffman, Inc., Cleveland, Ohio

John Wiley & Sons
New York   Chichester   Brisbane   Toronto   Singapore

Library of Congress Cataloging in Publication Data:

Gallo, Frank J.
   Small residential structures.

   Bibliography: p.
   Includes index.
   1. House construction—Estimates.   I.
Regis I.   II. Title.
TH4812.G34   1984   692'.5   83-16847
ISBN 0-471-88359-X

Printed in the United States of America

10 9 8 7 6 5 4 3 2 1

This book is dedicated to

C. Merrill Barber

Professional Engineer and Architect

whose teaching and example have made many young engineers
and architects, including the authors, aware of their
responsibilities to society and to their professions.

Preface

This book was originally written to give contractors and tradespeople involved in the building industry some insight into the task of determining costs for constructing residential structures. It was intended to be used as a part of a continuing-education-type program that included videotaped lectures of the book's content.

As the book came together, the authors found that the inclusion of information on construction procedures, construction nomenclature, and so forth would make the book particularly useful to others. The resulting product now introduces construction as related to the assembly and the estimating of materials required to erect residential-type structures. The procedures discussed can very readily be adapted to the construction of small commercial structures as well.

We believe that this book will be useful to all individuals in the residential construction field. It is written to be easily understood by anyone having a basic knowledge of mathematics and simple trigonometry. Tables and charts are included to further simplify calculations.

This is not a "costing book," simply because we have found that construction costs vary tremendously throughout the country. As written, the material can be used in every area of the United States. References to published "costing" books that may be used are included for use when the builder is ready to put cost numbers into the estimate.

Small Residential Structures deals with the determining of quantities required as far as the following construction procedures are concerned:

1. Excavation and other earthwork operations.

2. Framing of floors, walls, and roofs.

3. Rough and final finishes needed.

4. Mechanical and electrical systems.

5. Decorating the finished structure.

The materials and procedures discussed have been used by us for many years. In addition, we have called on colleagues to aid us in presenting materials and methods that are truly up-to-date.

Frank J. Gallo
Regis I. Campbell

Acknowledgments

A book of this type needs a large number of "cooks" to make the "broth" come out clear and complete. The authors would not have been able to fulfill their ideas for this book without the help of many "cooks." Chief among these were

Harry G. Anderson, P.E., Office Manager, Barber & Hoffman, Inc., Cleveland, Ohio. Mr. Anderson was responsible for having the illustrations prepared by the Barber & Hoffman staff and also for much of the editing in parts of the text.

Albert Fishman, President, and **Leonard Nyman,** Chief Executive Officer, Drake Construction Co., Cleveland, Ohio. These men provided the impetus to getting the material for this book put down on paper. In addition, they were of tremendous help in developing the Wood Framing sections of the text.

James Hurst, P.E., formerly President, Evans & Associates, Inc., Cleveland, Ohio. Mr. Hurst was of enormous help in the developing of the chapter on Mechanical Systems.

To these, and to the many others who helped us to prepare this volume, we extend our sincerest thanks.

F.J.G.
R.I.C.

Contents

Chapter One Introduction and General Information 2

Introduction to Estimating Costs 3   Costs 6
Basic Computations Needed in Estimating 8
Qualifications of an Estimator 12   Forms Used by Estimators 12

Chapter Two Earthwork Operations 16

Earthwork Computations 17   Earth Movement 19
Excavating and Related Equipment 20
Additional Earthwork Operations 21   Summary 25

Chapter Three Foundation Work 28

Concrete Work 29   Concrete Blocks 34
Brick Walls: Concrete and Burned Clay Elements 35
Wall Exposures and Patterns 37   Masonry Piers 39   Steel Posts 40
Wooden Posts 40   Post Note 40

Chapter Four House Framing 42

Part I Floors 43   Floor-Supporting Structures 43
Summary on Floor Framing 52
Part II Walls and Partitions 54   Exterior Walls 54
Estimating Procedures 57   Additional Framing Needed 58
Sheathing (Covering) the Wall 59
Part III Roofs and Ceilings 62   Ceilings 62   Roof Framing 62
Roof Sheathing 69

Chapter Five Roofing and Exterior Finish Materials 72

Roofing 73   Cornice and Gutter (Fascia) Boards 76
Gutters and Downspouts 76   Windows 77   Exterior Doors 79
Louvers 80   Exterior Wall Finishes 88

Chapter Six   Insulation and Interior Finishes   88

Insulation and Related Factors **89**   Interior Finishes **91**   Summary **98**

Chapter Seven   Decorating   100

Exterior Painting and Staining **101**   Interior Painting and Varnishing **102**
Interior Wall Coverings **104**   Floor Coverings **108**

Chapter Eight   Hardware   116

Rough Hardware **118**   Finish Hardware **125**

Chapter Nine   Mechanical Systems   138

Part I Plumbing 139   Water Distribution **140**   Sewage Disposal **159**
Summary of Part I **165**
Part II Heating, Ventilating, and Air-Conditioning 170   Heating **170**
Economy Tips **171**   Systems **171**   Distribution System **180**
Humidity Control **181**   Ventilation **182**   Filtering **182**   Cooling **182**
Special Installation Considerations **183**

Chapter Ten   Basic Electrical   188

General Discussion **189**   Procedure **190**   Details to Be Noted **196**

Chapter Eleven   Putting It All Together   202

Review of Construction Aspects Covered **203**   Miscellaneous Materials **204**
Labor **210**   Overhead and Profit **210**   Summary **211**
Common Estimating Errors **212**   Summary Sheets **214**   Conclusion **215**
Epilogue **216**

Symbols and Abbreviations   217

Appendixes   220

A. Earthwork **221**   B. Concrete Work **223**   C. Lumber-Related Tables **225**
D. Finish-Related Tables **233**

Glossary   235

Bibliography   243

Index   245

Small Residential Structures

Professional Edition

Chapter One

Introduction and General Information

The purpose of this book is to show the student or the builder many of the factors that influence the cost of a residential structure. In addition, the authors will show how the cost of the structure can be estimated with reasonable accuracy. It is not our intent to make this a "costing book." Costs vary so greatly in different areas of the country that no one book can suit all the markets. This book illustrates typical ways to determine the kinds and quantities of the components needed for a residential structure. With these quantities and local cost figures, the estimator should be able to put together a reasonably accurate estimate of the total cost of a residential structure.

Introduction to Estimating Costs

Estimating costs of construction (even estimating costs of residential properties) is an involved process requiring the use of basic mathematics. In addition, knowledge of construction methods, materials of construction, and local sources of supplies is required in making accurate estimates.

An estimate represents a compilation of the materials needed and the approximate cost of constructing the project. The preparation of an estimate of construction costs is time consuming. In deciding whether or not to bid on a particular project, the estimator must consider the following questions:

Is adequate time available for preparing the estimate properly?

Is the type of work to be done within the scope and experience of the builder's firm?

Does the builder have the labor force, equipment, and knowledge to complete the job in question?

Does the builder's firm have access to the *subcontractors* the builder needs to fulfill the project requirements?

Does the estimator have reliable cost information for the type of work required on this project?

Will the estimate be based on results of previous projects, or will it be based on "costing books" only?

How will the undertaking of this project affect the firm's overall workload?

Can the contractor obtain the necessary *bonding* for the job (if required)?

Can the contractor obtain the required financing for the job?

It is important to establish the cost of a construction project as accurately as possible, because the inability to estimate costs effectively may well result in the failure of the contractor's business. This book will try to cover the costs that the residential builder will need to know to be able to handle most home and other small building projects.

In order to estimate construction costs accurately, one needs to know how to read and interpret *construction documents* (drawings and specifications) and also to be able to understand the principles of construction. The number and type of construction documents will vary with the scope of the project under review. In a typical residential structure, for example, the construction documents will include

1. The contract itself indicating general scope and cost of the project—to be signed by client (owner) and the builder.

2. Complete drawings of the project—minimum drawings required would be
(a) Plans of each separate level—scaled $\frac{1}{4}$ in. = 1 ft 0 in. typically.
(b) Elevations of all walls of the structure—most frequently scaled at $\frac{1}{8}$ in. = 1 ft 0 in.
(c) Cross section(s) of structure indicating basic construction and other details—scales used are $\frac{3}{8}$ in. = 1 ft 0 in., $\frac{1}{2}$ in. = 1 ft 0 in., $\frac{3}{4}$ in. = 1 ft 0 in., and larger.
(d) Drawings of special features of the structure.

3. Specifications—a written document (usually) that details requirements for the structure and will include type, grade, and quality of the materials and labor to be used. There are many sample specifications that can be used to develop the specifications for a particular structure. One widely used sample is the Guide Specifications of the American Institute of Architects. Another is published by the National Society of Professional Engineers.

With larger structures—usually commercial types—the construction documents may include items such as

1. Invitation to bid—publicizing the availability of the project for bidding purposes.

2. Proposal (or bid) form—standardized form on which the contractor is to submit his/her bid.

3. Bond forms required.

Other aids to the designer/builder are "how to" books that detail construction procedures, methods, and so forth. These are provided by many trade organizations such as The American Plywood Association, The Clay Institute, The Portland Cement Association, and so forth. One "bible" used frequently by the authors and others involved in architectural drafting is Ramsey and Sleeper's *Architectural Graphic Standards*.[1]

The ability to estimate and make rapid computations of adequate accuracy is a necessary requirement to being a successful estimator.

In addition to being able to read and understand working drawings and specifications, the estimator must be able to take off quantities of materials and labor needed. Estimates vary in complexity and degree of accuracy. The degree of accuracy needed depends upon the reason for making the estimate. The builder—or the firm's estimator—is best able to prepare whatever type of estimate is needed because he/she knows

1. The firm's resources, equipment, and labor force.

2. The results of previously built structures of a similar type.

3. That each firm can handle only a certain volume of business (the builder or estimator is in the best position to know at what volume the firm is presently operating).

In general, estimates can be broken down into two broad categories: approximate estimates, such as cost of a unit per square foot, cost per room, and so forth, and detailed estimates, such as cost per square foot of masonry wall or cost per board foot of lumber.

Obviously, the detailed estimate is the more accurate but requires a greater degree of skill and, of course, more time. The *material quantity take off* in a detailed estimate should always be developed according to the drawings and specifications for the job. The various sections of the material quantity take off should be kept separate and summarized individually. This will aid in effecting changes or locating errors at a later date. In addition, a recap or summary of each section, or trade, is required. Subsequent chapters will illustrate these summaries.

The material quantity take off should be completed in the same order in which the project will be built—in other words, in a building sequence that is logical for the structure being estimated. All take offs and calculations should be written neatly in pencil, with all totals shown on the extreme right side of the paper. In addition, all final calculations should be underlined. Some estimators use different colors for different types of work. It is important that the material quantity take off and the estimate be prepared accurately and carefully, without errors. Errors tend to result from misreading the specifications and from miscalculations. All work should be double-checked.

It should be noted that major items involved in the cost of a project are

Material quantity take off, counting and tabulating all the individual items and parts that compose the entire structure.

[1] Charles G. Ramsey and Harold R. Sleeper, *Architectural Graphic Standards* (New York: John Wiley & Sons, 1981).

Labor, the cost involved in building the structure according to the plans and specifications.

If the length of time for constructing the project is long, the person preparing the estimate must be aware that material and/or labor costs can escalate during the period of construction. This possibility should be considered before submitting the final cost bid for the project.

After figuring material and labor costs, the estimator must include other items to get a total cost for the project. Among these items are

Licenses and permits.

Equipment purchase or rental along with its fuel and maintenance costs.

Various overhead costs (such as main office expenses, executive and estimator costs, and secretarial office operating costs).

Insurances (such as Social Security and Workmen's Compensation).

Contingencies (risk).

Profit.

To be sure that no items are missed in the estimate, the estimator should use a checklist. Many good checklists are obtainable depending upon the project's size. Remember, use a checklist that permits listing the various operations in the order in which they are to be done on the project. See Figure 1-1 for a sample checklist.

Costs   The cost for any operation requires a knowledge of the costs of all types of construction materials involved in a building project, the cost of labor, a knowledge of up-to-date wage rates, and production rates of the workers on the job. Although much of this information is available in published cost books, it is much better for the estimator to maintain a good cost and production rate record of projects in which the estimator's firm has been involved. This information should be gathered from reports that show

1. The number of units completed.

2. The number of workers employed (by classification or skills).

3. The time required to complete each unit of the work involved.

4. A description of job conditions, climatic conditions, and any other conditions or factors that may have affected the production of labor and the progress of the project.

This information should be broken down into relatively short periods of time, such as days or weeks.

As mentioned previously, this book will not detail many cost factors. The authors will give the reader sources from which these costs can be obtained on a local basis. One publication that is usable in most areas of the country is the

```
                    SAMPLE CHECK LIST

Code Category                      Code Category
1.00  GENERAL CONDITIONS           7.00  MOISTURE PROTECTION
 .10  Permits & Fees                .20  Insulation
 .20  Field Administration          .31  Asphalt
 .21  Supervision                   .52  Roll Roofing
 .22  Layout                        .63  Gutters & Downspouts
 .30  Temporary Utilities
 .38  Temporary Drive              8.00  DOORS & WINDOWS
 .50  Equipment                     .36  Overhead Doors
 .52  Rental Equipment              .52  Aluminum Windows
 .60  Clean-Up                      .70  HARDWARE & SPECIALTIES
                                    .72  Door Operators
2.00  SITEWORK                      .80  Glass & Glazing
 .13  Clearing & Grubbing           .86  Weatherstripping
 .22  Excavating & Backfilling
 .60  Pavement & Walks             9.00  FINISHES
 .61  Asphalt Paving                .17  Stucco
 .80  Landscaping                   .25  Drywall
                                    .31  Ceramic Tile
3.00  CONCRETE WORK                 .52  Acoustical Ceiling Tile
 .21  Wire Mesh                     .66  Resilient Tile Flooring
 .30  Structural Concrete           .67  Rubber Base
 .31  Footers & Pads                .69  Carpeting
                                    .91  Exterior Painting
4.00  MASONRY                       .92  Interior Painting
                                    .95  Wall Coverings
5.00  METALS
                                   10.00  SPECIALTIES
6.00  CARPENTRY                     .30  Fireplaces
 .10  Rough Carpentry               .80  Toilet & Bath Accessories
 .13  Exterior Trim
 .14  Wood Siding                  11.00  EQUIPMENT
 .20  Interior Finish               .93  Kitchen Appliances
 .21  Millwork
 .23  Wood Frames                  15.00  MECHANICAL
 .24  Wood Doors                    .40  PLUMBING
 .41  Cabinets                      .80  H.V.A.C.
 .42  Plastic Laminate Work         .81  Ductwork
 .50  Flooring
                                   16.00  ELECTRICAL
                                    .50  Light Fixtures
```

Figure 1-1. Sample checklist.

Engineering News-Record.[2] This reference is aimed mostly at heavy projects such as roads, bridges, and dams that are undertaken by commercial building contractors and civil engineers. For smaller projects, better results would be obtained from Robert S. Means costing books[3] and Frank R. Walker costing books.[4]

Another point that should be considered by the contractor is that many firms are organized to do a limited number of construction specialties, such as wood framing, concrete and/or masonry work, electrical wiring, and mechanical heating–ventilation–air-conditioning (HVAC). To complete a project, some or all of these specialties will be needed. If the contractor bidding on a project does not

[2] Weekly magazine published by the McGraw-Hill Publishing Company, New York.
[3] Robert S. Means, Inc., Kingston, Mass.
[4] Frank R. Walker, Publishers, Chicago.

have all of these specialties in his/her organization, it would be necessary to subcontract the missing items to specialists in these fields.

The contractor's estimator should become familiar with the material quantity take offs and unit costs of the subcontracting trades that will work on the contractor's project. This capability will gain the respect of the subcontractors. They will, hopefully, give better and more accurate bids for their parts of the project.

Basic Computations Needed in Estimating

One does not have to be an engineer or a mathematician to make accurate estimates, although basic background in figuring areas and volumes of triangular, rectangular, and circular shapes is needed. In addition, the use of a calculator will assure the estimator reasonably accurate computations. The accuracy used in estimating quantities is not required to be of a high order, however, since the materials involved usually cannot (and need not) be established with a high degree of precision during the early stages of the estimate.

The examples in this book have answers that are rounded off. To illustrate our experience in construction, many of the examples will be stated in feet, inches, and fractions since most carpenters, masons, and concrete workers use measuring devices that are graduated in this fashion. If the data are given in feet and inches, convert the data to tenths or hundredths of a foot and round off your answers to tenths or hundredths. Note that the accuracy of the estimate does not have to be any more accurate than to one tenth of the main units. We will also use consistent abbreviations for units. A listing of these will be found at the end of this book.

Example 1-1
Compute the volume of concrete in a footing that is 6 ft² and 16 in. thick (Figure 1-2). The volume is given as volume = width × length × thickness (depth).

Step 1: Change thickness to feet.

$T = \frac{16}{12} = \frac{4}{3}$ ft or 1.33 ft

Step 2: Compute volume in cubic feet.

$V = 6$ ft $\times$ 6 ft $\times$ 1.33 ft

$= 47.88$ ft³ or 48 ft³ rounded off

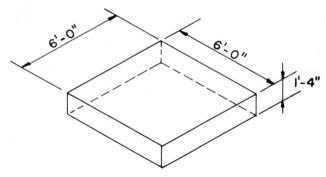

Figure 1-2.

The basic unit used in concrete work is cubic yards (yd^3). To convert the volume found in Step 2, the value must be divided by 27 ft^3/yd^3., since 27 ft^3 equals 1.0 yd^3.

Step 3: Convert 48 ft^3 to cubic yards.

$V = 48$ $ft^3 \div 27$ ft^3/yd^3

   $= 1.78$ yd^3

Answer: Round off to 1.8 yd^3

The precision of earthwork or concrete volumes seldom needs to be more precise than one decimal place as shown. To illustrate this, check into the following variation of Example 1-1.

Example 1-2

Because of tolerances in field work, the footing of Example 1-1 was formed with the following dimensions:

$W = 6$ ft $\frac{1}{2}$ in.

$L = 6$ ft 1 in.

What is the actual volume required?

Step 1: $V = W \times L \times T$

   $= 6.04$ ft $\times$ 6.08 ft $\times \frac{4}{3}$ ft

   $= 36.72 \times 1.33$

$V = 48.84$ ft^3

Step 2: $V = 48.84$ $ft^3 \div 27$ ft^3/yd^3

   $= 1.81$ yd^3

Answer: Round off to 1.8 yd^3

In other words, minor variations in the dimensions may not affect the final usable answer.

In summary, be reasonably accurate in all calculations. Do not be concerned about decimal places beyond tenths. The answer cannot be any better than the field layout and measurements.

Example 1-3

Determine the area of a circle having a 12-ft diameter (Figure 1-3). (Radius is one half the diameter: 6 ft.)

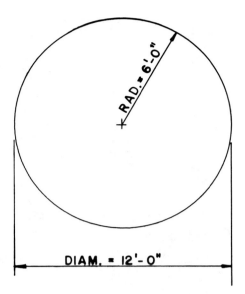

Figure 1-3.

Solution: Area of a circle $= \pi r^2$, where $\pi = 3.14$ (approximately)

$$= 3.14 \times (6)^2 = 3.14 \times (6) \times (6)$$

$$= 3.14 \times 36$$

$$A = 113.04 \text{ ft}^2$$

Answer: Use $A = 114.0$ ft^2

note: Using the given approximate value for π gives an answer that is adequate for most calculations.

Another figure that will be used in estimating quantities is the *triangle,* most generally, the right triangle.

note: You can use multiples of the numbers shown in Figure 1-4.

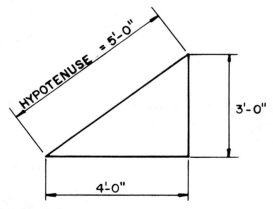

Figure 1-4.

As you can see in Figure 1-4, the length of the diagonal (hypotenuse) is found as follows from the Pythagorean Theorem in trigonometry:

the diagonal = square root of the sum of the squares of the two legs

Example 1-4
Find the length of the diagonal of a triangle whose legs are 3 and 4 ft long.

Solution: $\text{Diagonal}^2 = 3^2 + 4^2$

$$D^2 = 9 + 16$$

$$D^2 = 25$$

$$D = \text{square root of 25 or}$$

Answer: $D = \sqrt{25} = 5$ ft

note: For large values of D^2 use the square root key on your calculator to determine D.

The area of a triangle is found by using the following formula:

area = $\frac{1}{2}$ × base dimension × height dimension at right angles to the base.

Example 1-5
Determine the area of the triangle shown in Figure 1-5.

note: The height is always the perpendicular distance from the base to the peak.

Solution: From basic trigonometry, the area of any triangle is equal to one half the product obtained by multiplying the base (any side) by the height measured at right angles to the base shown in Figure 1-5.

$A = \frac{1}{2}$ base × height

$\quad = \frac{1}{2}\, b \times h$

$\quad = \frac{1}{2} \times 20.0$ ft × 12.5 ft

$\quad = 10.0$ ft × 12.5 ft

Answer: $A = 125.0$ ft^2

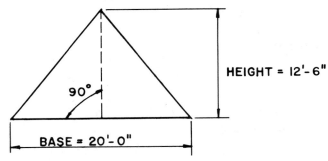

Figure 1-5.

Qualifications of an Estimator

As previously stated, the good estimator need not be a mathematician. However, the estimator should be able to make reasonably accurate computations of volumes, areas, lengths, and so forth. In order to do the job properly, the estimator should be

1. Reasonably intelligent and capable of handling basic computations.

2. Knowledgeable of methods, field construction, and erection procedures.

3. Capable of reading and understanding blueprints.

4. Familiar with the types of licenses and permits needed, and how and where they are obtained.

5. Able to maintain and use records of job costs, labor rates for the area in which the project is to be built, production rates and equipment costs or rental rates, and so forth. This is particularly true with regard to the projects the estimator's firm actually completes.

6. Able to locate suppliers of the needed materials and equipment, as well as labor required for the job being estimated.

7. Familiar with overhead costs, taxes, and insurance rates.

This listing (only partial) shows that math prowess takes a back seat to the organizational and referencing abilities of the estimator.

In many construction firms, the owner will take over this important task. In general, however, the contractor will find that as the size and/or number of projects increases, the need for a formal estimator with all or many of the above-listed qualifications will become more important. The student interested in construction may well find a very satisfying career in the field of estimating.

The primary objective of an estimate is to determine a reasonably accurate cost of a project in a reasonable length of time. Remember that, in general, only the low-bidding contractor actually gets paid for the time spent in preparing the estimate. The time spent on a bid that is not accepted must be considered as part of the overhead in running the contractor's firm.

Forms Used by Estimators

An estimator's task is in many ways similar to the tasks performed by bookkeepers—at least the record-keeping and estimate-preparation parts of his/her job. The use of a well-developed set of forms will aid the estimator in developing the estimate without forgetting any important facets of the project. In addition, the possibility of appreciable errors can be greatly minimized. There are several firms that produce forms of all types throughout the country. For the estimator involved in residential and small commercial projects, some forms that would be useful include

1. *Material quantity take off sheets,* which have columns for item unit dimensions, quantities of each item, and totals.

2. *General estimate sheets,* which have columns for total units, cost of each item, labor time involved, and labor costs.

note: Each of the above may be obtained without printed column headings so the estimator can use his/her own headings.

3. *General overhead sheets,* which list those items that need to be figured in for overhead items, such as main office rent and utilities; secretarial, estima-

MATERIAL COST RECORD

MEANSCO FORM F330

PROJECT _____ SHEET NO. _____

LOCATION _____

DATE	NUMBER	VENDOR	QTY.	UNIT PRICE	AMOUNT	QTY.	UNIT PRICE	AMOUNT	QTY.	UNIT PRICE	AMOUNT

CONDENSED ESTIMATE SUMMARY

MEANSCO FORM 115

PROJECT _____ TOTAL AREA _____ SHEET NO. _____
LOCATION _____ TOTAL VOLUME _____ ESTIMATE NO. _____
ARCHITECT _____ COST PER S.F. _____ DATE _____
OWNER _____ COST PER C.F. _____ NO. OF STORIES _____
QUANTITIES BY _____ PRICES BY _____ EXTENSIONS BY _____ CHECKED BY _____

NO.	DESCRIPTION	MATERIAL	LABOR	SUBCONTRACT	TOTAL	ADJUSTMENT
	SITE WORK					
	Excavation					

QUANTITY SHEET

MEANSCO FORM F180

PROJECT _____ SHEET NO. _____
LOCATION _____ SECTION _____ ESTIMATE NO. _____
ARCHITECT _____ OWNER _____ DATE _____
TAKE OFF BY _____ EXTENSIONS BY _____ CHECKED BY _____

DESCRIPTION	NO.	DIMENSIONS			UNIT	UNIT	UNIT	UNIT

LABOR COST RECORD

MEANSCO FORM 320

PROJECT _____ SHEET NO. _____
LOCATION _____

DATE	DESCRIPTION	AMOUNT	AMOUNT	AMOUNT	AMOUNT	AMOUNT

Figure 1-6. Typical estimating forms (courtesy of Robert S. Means Company, Inc., Kingston, Massachusetts 02364).

tor, draftworker and executive salaries; legal counsel; machine repair shop costs, equipment costs, and storage yard costs; and so forth.

4. Other forms that list the commonly used items in certain sizes of estimating projects, such as a form listing items involved in estimating residential construction (much like a general checklist).

These forms vary in size and complexity. They are generally available commercially. Some of the most common are published by Robert S. Means, Frank R. Walker, and National Blank Book.[5]

In addition, many construction firms have developed forms for their own use to fit more closely their own method of operation. Also, some have arranged with the suppliers of forms listed above to have forms custom-made to fit individual needs.

Since this book is intended to show you how to develop a material quantity take off list, the examples used will show answers (where appropriate) on segments of some of the forms listed above. To illustrate this, we will use forms supplied by one of the form suppliers. Figure 1-6 shows segments of some of the forms that will be used in the examples in later chapters.

[5] National Blank Book, Holyoke, Mass.

Chapter Two

Earthwork Operations

This chapter is included to illustrate that a minimal knowledge of earthwork operations is needed by most small construction firms. Although not much detail is required, this knowledge is important since some excavation work is necessary on all new projects and on many remodeling projects.

The authors will attempt to give some insight into the types of computations needed. In addition, some information on soil types, excavating equipment, and so forth is provided.

Most contractors in the house-building field will usually have an excavating sub-contractor evaluate the cost of earthwork on a project. However, the contractor should be familiar with the estimating methods used in order to be certain of getting the best price for his/her project. There are certain items of excavating that must be understood to estimate the probable cost of the building project. Among these are

Earthwork Computations

1. Calculating the volume of earth to be moved and how this volume might vary with the type of earth involved.

2. How to handle the estimated volume of earthwork.

3. The type of equipment needed to excavate and dispose of the earth involved.

Earth volume is calculated in a number of different ways, all of which involve determining the volume of a group of triangular or rectangular shapes. In all projects, it is first necessary to establish a *datum plane,* or reference elevation, from which all differences in height can be measured. On small projects it is most common to establish an arbitrary elevation as a datum plane and call it elevation 100.00 ft. Measurements are then made above and/or below the datum plane.

Example 2-1

Determine the volume of the excavation shown in Figure 2-1. To figure average depth of excavation, find the depth at each corner.

Point	Surface Elevation	−	Basement Elevation	=	Depth
A	103.00	−	95.00	=	8.00
B	105.75	−	95.00	=	10.75
C	103.00	−	95.00	=	8.00
D	101.50	−	95.00	=	6.50
				Total =	33.25

Average depth = (33.25) ÷ (4 readings) = 8.31 ft

Volume = average depth × length × width

= 8.31 × 40.0 × 25.0 = 8310 ft^3

Since earth volumes are generally computed in cubic yards, this volume must be divided by 27 ft^3 per cubic yard.

Volume = 8310 ÷ 27 ft^3/yd^3

Volume = 307.7 yd^3

Answer: Use 308 yd^3

note: The answer is given to the nearest $\frac{1}{2}$ yd^3. This is because the movement of earth cannot be done with any greater precision. Another point to bear in mind in this analysis is that this answer is the "in-place" volume of the earth involved.

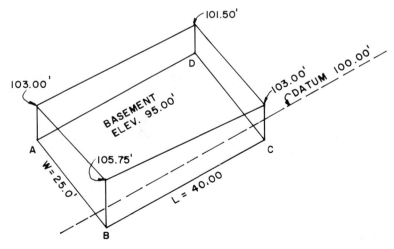

Figure 2-1. Sample excavation.

Table 2-1
Swell Factors in Excavation

Type of Earth	Percentage Swell
Sand and gravel	6 to 20
Loam and clay	20 to 25
Dense clay	25 to 40
Rock	30 to 50

The actual loose volume of earth to be moved from the excavation will appear to be greater than this because all earth *swells* upon being removed from its natural state. The percentage of swell varies with the type of earth involved in the excavation. Representative values of swell are shown in Table 2-1.

Example 2-2

If the excavation computed in Example 2-1 was in a clay–loam soil, what loose volume of earth must be moved by the excavator?

Solution: Clay–loam soil swells about 25% on being excavated. Therefore soil

$V = 1.25 \times$ volume-in-place

$= 1.25 \times 308$

Answer: V = 385 yd^3

Thus, the removal equipment must handle about 385 yd^3 instead of the "in-place" volume of 308 yd^3 previously calculated.

Earth Movement

Removal of excavated material can be an important part of the cost estimate on a project. It will also include the operation costs for a bulldozer or front-end loader—one of which will be used to spread the loosened material. If the earth excavated can be *wasted* by filling in low spots on the project, the additional cost can be quite low. If this is not the case, trucks for removal of excavated material must be provided and the cost of their operation must be included in the cost estimate.

Another item to be considered when costing the use of trucks is the possible need of an access road to bring materials and/or equipment to the project site. This item may require slag for the access road, which can later be used as a base for a permanent driveway.

A good access road into a project area will also improve the delivery of material and equipment. In addition, it will facilitate removal of debris and waste materials from the site.

Excavating and Related Equipment

For excavating, most residential builders/contractors will have available a backhoe and a front-end loader.

A small backhoe may be used to dig trenches as well as to excavate basements. If the backhoe attachment is mounted on the back of a tractor with a bulldozer blade at the front end, the unit can also be used as a grader, an excavator, and a loading unit. Thus, one piece of equipment can be used to serve three purposes. In certain cases, the front-end loader may also be used as a grading unit.

If you own the equipment, the cost of maintenance, eventual replacement, and operation must be included in determining the cost of a project. If you do not own the equipment, you must either rent one with its operator or subcontract the excavating work to another firm. In either case, some cost must be included in determining the project cost. It should be noted that excavating subcontractors have minimum charges for the use of equipment and operator. A contractor must pay for half a day, or some other similar minimum. It is therefore desirable to schedule operations to utilize the equipment fully while it is on the project site.

The contractor will normally take the following steps in performing excavation projects:

1. Clearing and grubbing. Many building sites have trees and underbrush that are in the way of the project. Removal of these items is known as *clearing and grubbing.* Some type of bulldozer is generally used for this purpose. The cost of this removal is figured on a "cost per acre" basis and should be included in the total estimate.

2. Excavation. This work can be done with a backhoe in most cases. Backhoes are available with buckets ranging in capacity from $\frac{3}{8}$ to $3\frac{1}{2}$ yd^3. The work that can be done by a wheel-mounted, $\frac{1}{2}$-yd^3 backhoe will be about 20 yd^3 for each hour of work (a more complete table of capacities and volume excavated per hour will be found in the appendixes of this book).

3. Loading and hauling. This is not always necessary on small projects since the excavated material can sometimes be spread on the site. If the excavated material must be hauled from the site, many types and sizes of trucks are available for lease on a daily, weekly, or monthly basis with or without drivers.

4. Waste. Any excavated material that cannot be used for fill and/or *backfilling* is classified as waste and must be removed from the site. Again, this is seldom a problem on small projects; however, you should keep in mind the possibility of costs for hauling this material.

Check the appendixes of this book for more information on these operations.

When the excavation work on a project involves the removal and transporting of rock, the problem becomes more complicated and more costly. The average builder/contractor will probably avoid this problem if at all possible. If you cannot, then subcontract this work to a specialty contractor—again including the subcontractor's costs in your estimate. If the rock is encountered in a totally unexpected location, you would probably be justified in asking for an extra cost added to your contract price.

Again, the variety of equipment available to the contractor varies considerably. Equipment can be obtained that is uniquely fitted for one type of operation. The contractor involved in residential or small commercial buildings will probably do best to obtain a piece of equipment that can do a variety of chores on a construction site.

Figure 2-2a shows a tractor that has a bulldozer blade at the front end. Figure 2-2b has a front-end loader at the front end and a backhoe unit at the rear. Obviously, many other combined or single units can be found. The appendixes in this book will illustrate the operating rates (productivity) of various types of equipment.

The versatility of any of this equipment is important to the contractor. With diligent searching, it is possible to obtain just the right capacity needed for the general projects undertaken by the contractor.

Once the foundation walls (discussed in Chapter 3) have been completed and are ready to receive the first-floor framing (discussed in Chapter 4), the builder can proceed with the subgrade work that remains and that must be done before backfilling around the building. Backfilling is the next earthwork operation. Again, since most construction is usually done in a definite sequence, the builder takes the following steps:

Additional Earthwork Operations

1. Waterproofs the exterior walls of basements and/or crawl spaces below the finished exterior grade.

2. Installs the foundation drain tiles if required. These drains are perforated tiles that are set on a granular (coarse sand) bed.

3. Covers the foundation drains with a gravel layer. This permits water to percolate into the drains and then into the storm sewer system.

4. Places downspout drain lines on top of the gravel layer (some projects may not require underground drain lines for downspouts).

5. Backfills around the structure and in areas that are slated to receive concrete slabs on grade, such as garages.

It is important to understand that backfill against a basement wall and/or a crawl-space wall cannot be started before the first-floor framing has been completely installed, including the subflooring. The relative relationships of these various construction items are clearly shown in Figure 2-3.

The sections that follow will discuss each of these construction steps. These steps should be clearly understood by the estimator to improve the accuracy and completeness of the estimate.

WATERPROOFING
Whenever habitable portions of a structure are built below the finished exterior grade of the building, there is always a chance of water seeping into the space. In

Figure 2-2a. Typical bulldozer unit (courtesy of Ford Tractor Operations, Troy, Michigan 48084).

Figure 2-2b. Combination unit with front-end loader and backhoe (courtesy of Ford Tractor Operations).

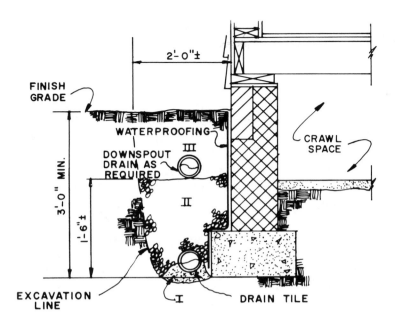

I = LAYER OF MEDIUM SAND TO ACT AS BED FOR FOUNDATION DRAIN TILE.

II = COARSE GRAVEL OR BROKEN STONE FOR EASY PASSAGE OF WATER.

III = EARTH BACK FILL (TOP 6" SHOULD BE TOPSOIL QUALITY) COMPACTED.

Figure 2-3.

order to prevent this the builder normally will put a protective coating on the foundation walls. This coating can consist of one or more of the following:

1. Bentonite (a type of clay) that can be obtained in panels or as a plaster that is troweled onto the outside face of the foundation walls.

2. Bituminous coatings, which are applied to the outside face of the foundation walls either with a brush or with a spray gun. These coatings can also be mixed with fillers and troweled on.

note: workers must use extreme caution when working with asbestos as a filler.

3. A protective board, asphalt coated, which is set into a mastic that has been applied to the outside face of the foundation walls.

Care must be taken when placing gravel or other backfill against a foundation wall that has been covered with the protective coatings listed. This care is necessary to prevent breaking the sealing effect of the coating. It is good practice to protect the waterproofing with *visqueen* or other protective covering to prevent damage during backfilling or other earthwork operations.

These waterproofing coatings must be unbroken, otherwise the water can seep behind the coating and negate its purpose. These coatings are sold under a variety of trade names. An estimator should learn the types that are commonly used by his/her firm.

INSTALLATION OF FOUNDATION DRAIN TILES

In building a residence with a *basement* and/or *crawl space* the general excavation will be about 2 ft 0 in. larger on each side of the foundation walls (as discussed previously). This space can be used to install the foundation drain tiles around the perimeter of the basement or crawl space. The main purpose of these tiles is to drain water from the soil and thus prevent the water from building up against the basement and/or crawl-space walls. The most common types of foundation drain tiles are perforated, unglazed clay tile pipe; unglazed clay tile pipe with unsealed joints; and perforated, polyvinyl chloride pipe.

The foundation drain tiles are generally sloped so water eventually flows into the storm sewers when possible. If the elevation of the storm sewers is higher than the foundation drain tiles, it may be necessary to install a *sump pump* to lift the water to this higher elevation. There also will be times when there will not be a storm sewer system available to collect the water from the foundation drain tiles. When this situation occurs, the water will be permitted to flow into a bed of granular (sand or gravel) material where the water can collect and gradually seep into the surrounding soils. Another method that is often used, when no storm sewers are available, is to locate a natural drainage ditch or waterway such as a creek, stream, river, or lake and let the water from the foundation drain tiles flow into this area.

As indicated in Figure 2-3, these tiles are placed outside of the foundation wall or footing at a level below the floor level of the inside usable space. In order for these tiles to function properly, they should be placed on a bed of sand and then covered by a layer of coarse gravel or broken stone. This gravel or stone creates a filter that permits the water in the surrounding soils to enter into the foundation drain tiles.

DOWNSPOUT DRAIN LINES

The downspout drain lines are placed directly above the filter of gravel or broken stone that has been placed over the foundation drain tiles. The gravel filter bed will be covered later under "Backfilling." The downspout drain tiles will be placed with sufficient slope to permit water to flow to the storm sewer. Remember, it is also necessary to provide a vertical drain-pipe section and T section or elbow at each downspout. This pipe is a glazed tile unit with a bell end on each segment. These segments fit together to create a sealed drain line. Some are provided with a self-sealing asphalt ring that seals the pipes when placed inside the belled end of the next segment. Others will need to be sealed by filling the bell ends with concrete mortar after the segments are fitted together.

If there is no basement or crawl space on the project being estimated, it will be necessary to excavate a trench for the downspout drain line before it can be installed. The amount of excavated material can be calculated as described earlier in this chapter.

BACKFILLING

After the foundation walls have been waterproofed, all drain tile work has been completed, and the walls have been braced by the first-floor framing (or other means), the backfilling operations can be completed. It was previously noted that the original excavation was constructed larger than building dimensions needed so that work on the foundation walls could be done more easily.

The next operation—backfilling—is done in three steps as follows:

1. Place a layer of sand (4 to 6 in. thick) at the bottom of the excavation (see Figure 2-3). On this bed layer, place the drain tiles required.

2. Over the drain tiles, place a layer (a minimum of 1 ft 0 in. thick) of gravel or broken stones. This will form a filter layer that will allow water to drain into the tiles (see Figure 2-3).

3. The final step will be to fill the remaining excavation outside the walls with earth backfill material. This material is placed, and compacted, until the top coincides with the final exterior ground level required.

Another backfill item will occur when the existing grade level is too low. In this case, layers of granular fill are used to raise the low grade to a level at the bottom of the slab-on-ground to be built over the position. Backfilling of low areas may be needed on the exterior of the residence to control the runoff of surface waters (rain or melting snow), so that the flow is away from the structure.

Summary

The estimator must be familiar with evaluating quantities of material and labor needed to accomplish the foregoing earthwork operations. The types of equipment needed and their productivity must be known as well. Again it is stressed that knowing the availability of equipment, the costs, and the productivity of the labor forces of one's own firm will be a distinct advantage to the estimator. Figure 2-4 illustrates some typical drain-tile types.

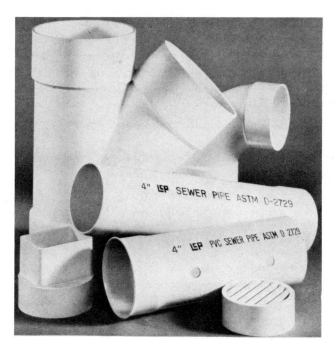

P.V.C. SEWER PIPE

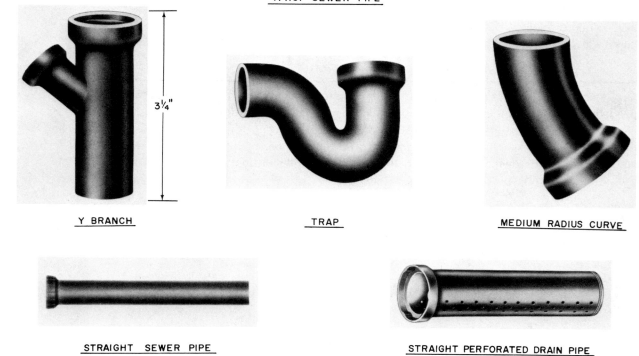

3¼"

Y BRANCH   TRAP   MEDIUM RADIUS CURVE

STRAIGHT   SEWER   PIPE   STRAIGHT PERFORATED DRAIN PIPE

VITRIFIED CLAY PIPE

Figure 2-4. Examples of drain tile (courtesy of the Logan Clay Products Company, Logan, Ohio 43138, and LCP Plastics, Inc., Carrollton, Ohio 44615).

Chapter Three

Foundation Work

All structures need foundations to transmit their loads to the ground. Most foundations are made with one or more of the following materials:

Plain or reinforced concrete.

Plain or reinforced concrete block.

Clay or concrete brick.

Because of the differences in these materials and in the construction methods, there are some differences in the methods used to estimate material quantities and costs.

Concrete Work

Concrete is a mixture of *portland cement, fine aggregate* (sand usually), coarse aggregate (broken stone, gravel, or slag), and water. As mixed, the concrete is a *plastic* mass; thus, it must be held by forms of some type while it solidifies and hardens. Concrete itself is weak in resisting tensile forces but very strong in resisting compressive forces. Because of this property, concrete must be designed using reinforcing steel to carry the tensile forces exerted on structural members. The following factors are among the most important and must be considered when estimating the materials and costs of foundation projects: formwork, reinforcing steel, and concrete. To understand each of these factors more clearly, they are discussed to some degree in the following sections.

FORMWORK

Note that the type, materials, and erection procedures are the province of the contractor. This is true unless special finishes are specified by the designer. The cost is generally calculated on the basis of the cost for each square foot of surface area involved. Forms can be constructed of

1. Lumber—frequently leaves board marks and/or surface grain marks on the finished surfaces. Most frequently used for walls that will be covered by finish materials or walls that are not exposed to view in the final structure.

2. Steel (metal)—excellent where forms are to be reused a number of times.

3. Plywood—large sheets and varieties of surfaces make this a popular material. Plastic-impregnated (coated) plywood gives a smooth finish to the project wall, thus reducing some *"finishing"* costs.

4. Plastic—generally *fiberglass*-reinforced forms that are highly reusable and can be furnished in a variety of surface textures.

Because all of these forms have a common purpose—to hold freshly mixed concrete in place until it hardens—the forms (and their supports such as shoring) must be designed to

1. Remain rigid in the desired shape.

2. Have the strength to support themselves, the plastic weight of the concrete and necessary *construction loads*.

note: Construction loads include the weight of equipment plus the weight of the concrete, the live load of vibrating equipment needed to consolidate or solidify the concrete mass to reduce the *porosity/permeability* of the concrete, and the weight of the workers needed to position the concrete.

3. Stay in place during the hardening stage of the plastic mass, so the concrete will remain in its designed position.

Forms for a typical wall are shown in Figure 3-1.

REINFORCING STEEL

Reinforcing steel is shown on the design drawings and is the responsibility of the design engineer. The contractor must follow the design instructions specifically. The steel in most projects is available in two forms:

1. Steel rods. Steel rods are specified by nominal size and length to be used. Typical sizes and weights of standard bars are shown in Table 3-1. Steel rods are estimated by determining the total weight of the specified materials as shown on the design drawings. Be sure to take off quantities of the sizes needed, since different sizes have different unit costs. Unit costs are listed as cost per pound or cost per ton. The supplier in your area will be able to give you unit costs based on size needed, bending required, and quantities needed. In addition to the cost of materials, the estimator must also include the labor cost of placing (positioning) the steel in the forms. Other factors to include will be the cost of accessories, such as form ties (see Figure 3-1) and other support media needed to hold the reinforcing rods in the required position while the plastic concrete is placed and hardens.

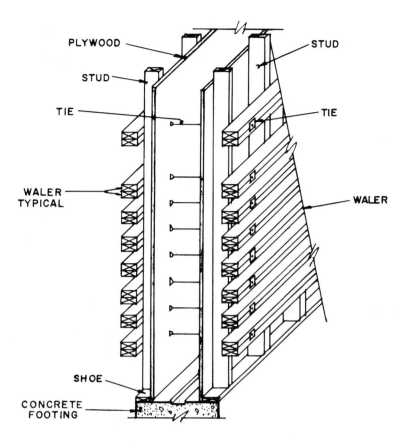

PLYWOOD

STUD

STUD

TIE

TIE

WALER
TYPICAL

WALER

SHOE

CONCRETE
FOOTING

WALL

Figure 3-1. Forms for a concrete wall.

2. Welded wire mesh (or fabric).[6] Costs of steel needed for a project can frequently be reduced by using welded wire mesh (wwm). This consists of steel in wire sizes rather than in steel rods. The wires are welded into square

Table 3-1
Reinforcing Bar Sizes and Weights

Bar Number	Diameter (in.)	Weight (lb/ft)
3	0.375	0.376
4	0.500	0.668
5	0.625	1.043
6	0.750	1.502
7	0.875	2.044
8	1.000	2.670
9	1.128	3.400

Source: Concrete Reinforcing Steel Institute.

[6] wwm design and detail is covered in the *Building Design Handbook* (McLean, Va.: Wire Reinforcement Institute, 1963).

or rectangular meshes that are supplied to the builder in flat sheets or rolls. The designer/engineer will specify the size (gauge) and the spacing of the wires in the two directions on the project drawings. The wwm is generally considered easier to place—thus less costly—whenever applicable. Table 3-2 lists the wire size (gauge), two-directional spacing, and the approximate weights of commonly used wwm. The estimator uses the project drawings and Table 3-2 to determine the weight of wwm needed on the project. As with reinforcing bars, the costs will be based primarily on the weight (costs are determined per pound or per ton).

All reinforcing steel is priced mostly on cost per pound and cost per ton. The magnitude of the cost per pound is affected by the following factors, among others:

1. The base cost of the steel rods (or wire), as furnished by the forming steel mill.

2. Size extras—the Nos. 5 and 6 bars are considered standards. All other sizes will have a size extra tacked onto the base cost.

3. Handling extras—designers/engineers will frequently require bars to be bent for design reasons. The fabricator shop (direct supplier of the steel) will

Table 3-2
Common Stock Styles of Welded Wire Fabric[a]

Style Designation		Steel Area (in.^{2}/ft width)		Weight (approximate lb/100 ft^2)
New Designation (By W-Number)	Old Designation (By Steel Wire Gauge)	Longitudinal	Transverse	
Rolls				
6×6–W1.4×W1.4	6×6–10×10	0.028	0.028	21
6×6–W2.0×W2.0	6×6–8 × 8[b]	0.040	0.040	29
6×6–W2.9×W2.9	6×6–6×6	0.058	0.058	42
6×6–W4.0×W4.0	6×6–4×4	0.080	0.080	58
4×4–W1.4×W1.4	4×4–10×10	0.042	0.042	31
4×4–W2.0×W2.0	4×4–8×8[b]	0.060	0.060	43
4×4–W2.9×W2.9	4×4–6×6	0.087	0.087	62
4×4–W4.0×W4.0	4×4–4×4	0.120	0.120	85
Sheets				
6×6–W2.9×W2.9	6×6–6×6	0.058	0.058	42
6×6–W4.0×W4.0	6×6–4×4	0.080	0.080	58
6×6–W5.5×W5.5	6×6–2×2[c]	0.110	0.110	80
4×4–W4.0×W4.0	4×4–4×4	0.120	0.120	85

[a] *Manufacturer's note:* Welded wire reinforcement must be positioned at the center of the depth of the slab, but not more than 2 in. below the top surface.
[b] Exact W-number size for 8 gauge is W2.1.
[c] Exact W-number size for 2 gauge is W5.4.
Source: Tech Facts (TF501) of the Wire Reinforcement Institute.

add a handling charge to the base cost. The cost may be added if the bars must be furnished in different lengths than the usual standard length of 20 ft 0 in.

4. If placement (erection) drawings are needed, the shop may also add an engineering charge to cover the cost of preparing these drawings.

Thus, ordering straight, standard-length bars will be the least expensive. They can then be cut to length and some minor bending can be done in the field. Be sure to include some labor costs for doing this work.

CONCRETE

Concrete is estimated on the basis of cubic yards of material needed, as detailed on the design drawings of the project. Costs are usually quoted as cost per cubic yard. Concrete can be furnished by mixing the required materials at the job site (field-mixed) or by purchasing it from a "ready-mix" concrete plant. The size of the job will determine which method is used. This is important since the cost of field-mixed and ready-mix are quite different and will have a substantial effect on the project cost. The estimator must be fully aware of this difference. In general (because of quantity needed), the ready-mix concrete is used mostly in residential construction. Such a use is actually most economical.

Concrete also entails other costs beyond the cost of placing the concrete in the proper form or location. Among these additional costs are

1. Curing of concrete. This refers to keeping the concrete moist until it has been properly hydrated. (*Hydrating* is a chemical reaction in which water is absorbed in the cement.) A good job of curing can greatly reduce the probability of cracking as the concrete hardens. Again, the cost is based on the cost for each square yard of surface being cured.

As was previously noted, concrete is a plastic mixture of materials including cement and water that can be formed into various shapes. The hardening of the concrete is the result of the hydrating. A certain percentage of water to cement is required. Since this hydration takes place over a period of several days, the concrete mass must not be permitted to dry out too rapidly. This is the reason for curing the concrete. Curing can be done by

(a) Periodic spraying or wetting down of the surface.

(b) Covering horizontal surfaces (slabs and steps) with straw, waterproof paper, or fabrics or spraying with water-impervious chemicals (silica glass).

(c) Protecting vertical surfaces, except the top, by the forms. Of course, concrete surfaces poured against the ground will not need protection.

2. Labor cost of stripping the forms (removal of the forms after the concrete has hardened enough to maintain its shape). The cost is based on square yards of surface to be stripped and should include the disposal of the forms. Braces and/or *shoring* must also be removed and eliminated.

Concrete Blocks   A *concrete block* is a masonry element made of a concrete mixture consisting of small-size coarse aggregate, fine aggregate, and cement. Using slag or expanded shale for the aggregates results in a light-weight block. These elements are frequently used for basement walls, some exterior or partition walls, and low foundation walls. Some typical concrete block sizes and shapes are shown in Figure 3-2.

PLAIN CONCRETE BLOCK WALLS

These elements are bonded together with a cement mortar. *Mortar* is made from a mixture of cement, hydrated lime, sand, and water. How these ingredients are

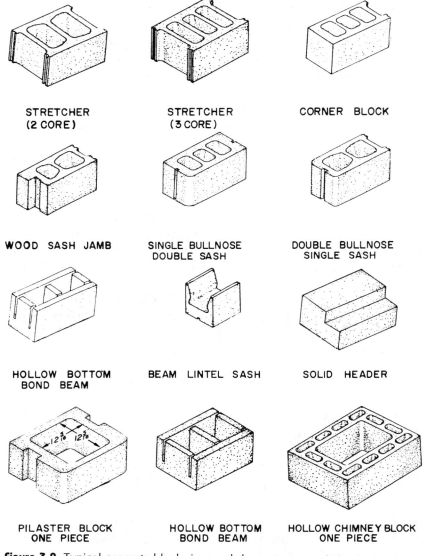

STRETCHER (2 CORE)   STRETCHER (3 CORE)   CORNER BLOCK

WOOD SASH JAMB   SINGLE BULLNOSE DOUBLE SASH   DOUBLE BULLNOSE SINGLE SASH

HOLLOW BOTTOM BOND BEAM   BEAM LINTEL SASH   SOLID HEADER

PILASTER BLOCK ONE PIECE   HOLLOW BOTTOM BOND BEAM   HOLLOW CHIMNEY BLOCK ONE PIECE

Figure 3-2. Typical concrete block sizes and shapes (courtesy of Cleveland Builders Supply Company, Cleveland, Ohio 44113).

mixed, and the ratio of each, will influence the strength of the bond in a wall.

The joints in concrete masonry walls vary in thickness, but the most common is about $\frac{3}{8}$ in. This gives face dimensions of 8 × 16 in. on the stretcher units for an area of 0.89 ft² for each block (or 1.00/0.89 = 1.12 blocks = $1\frac{1}{8}$ blocks for every square foot of wall surface). To find the number of blocks needed in a wall, use the following steps: determine the square feet of wall to be built, and multiply the result by $1\frac{1}{8}$.

Example 3-1

A contractor is to build a concrete block wall that is 24 ft 0 in. long and 9 ft 4 in. high. Use standard 8 × 16 blocks and $\frac{3}{8}$-in. joints and determine the number of blocks needed (neglect waste for now).

> **Solution:** Wall area is 24.0 ft × 9.33 ft, or A = 224 ft². Number of standard blocks is 1.12 × A, or
>
> $N = 1.12 \times 224$

Answer: N = 251 blocks needed

REINFORCED CONCRETE BLOCK WALLS

When basement or foundation walls have unusually heavy earth loads pushing against them, the concrete block wall may need to be reinforced with steel. This reinforcing can be either vertical, horizontal, or both.

To reinforce the wall vertically, reinforcing rods are placed into the cores of the block at the required spacing. You would then fill the cores with a strong, high-slump concrete mix or grout.

There are several ways of reinforcing the wall horizontally. The most common method is to make one complete course of block into a reinforced concrete beam called a *bond beam* at a specified level in the wall. This can be done with lintel blocks (see Figure 3-2) or with regular blocks having the upper three fourths of the block webs cut and broken out. The concrete can be contained in block cores by using metal lath in the joint below the bond beam (the width needed is about 1 in. less than the width of the wall, whereas the length can be obtained from the plan of the project—total square feet will be needed), or filling the cores of the block below with paper, styrofoam, or mortar. In some localities, manufacturers have blocks formed with slots in the webs into which the reinforcing can be placed.

Bricks used in construction can be of the following types:

Brick Walls: Concrete and Burned-Clay Elements

1. Clay brick that is made by mixing, molding, and burning clays. These bricks come in many shapes and finishes.

2. Concrete brick that is molded from a concrete mixture but in the size and shape of standard bricks, rather than in the form of a hollow concrete block.

The brick can be used as an exterior or interior decorative facing to walls in residential construction. The brick can be backed up with a concrete block wall or by a wood or steel stud-framed wall. In any case, the brick must be attached to the backup in a positive manner.

The joints in brick walls will vary in thickness, as in concrete masonry; however, the most commonly used thicknesses are about $\frac{3}{8}$ in. for horizontal joints. In modular construction, when working with standard common brick, the horizontal dimension from center line to center line of mortar joint is 8 in., and the vertical dimension from the center line of one mortar joint to the center line of a mortar joint three joints above is also 8 in. When using standard common brick, three bricks cover 64 in.^{2} (8 × 8 in.) or 0.44 ft^2 (64 in.^{2} divided by 144 in.^{2}/ft^2). With this in mind, the face area of one brick and one mortar joint can be obtained by dividing by three, or 0.44 divided by 3 = 0.147 ft^2 per brick (or 1.00 divided by 0.147 = 6.80 bricks = $6\frac{3}{4}$ bricks for every square foot of wall surface).

To find the number of bricks needed in a wall, use the following steps: determine the square feet of wall to be built, and multiply the result by $6\frac{3}{4}$.

Example 3-2

How many standard brick units would be needed to cover the wall of Example 3-1? Do not make allowance for waste.

Solution: From Example 3-1, the wall area was determined to be 224 ft^2. From the equation above,

$$N = 6.80 \times \text{area}$$

$$= 6.80 \times 224$$

$$\text{or } N = 1523.2$$

Answer: Use 1523 bricks

The standard common brick we will use is $3\frac{5}{8}$ in. × $2\frac{1}{4}$ in. × $7\frac{5}{8}$ in., as was used in the above calculation. However, face brick varies greatly in size. Some of the types available include

Norman	$3\frac{5}{8}$ in. × $2\frac{1}{4}$ in. × $11\frac{5}{8}$ in.
Roman	$3\frac{5}{8}$ in. × $1\frac{5}{8}$ in. × $11\frac{5}{8}$ in.
Baby Norman	$3\frac{5}{8}$ in. × $1\frac{5}{8}$ in. × $7\frac{5}{8}$ in.

To determine the number of bricks required in a wall using one of the other variations of brick sizes, it is necessary to follow the procedures outlined previously. Brick or block can be estimated in the following methods:

1. By determining the number of units or elements needed. Use procedures as shown in Examples 3-1 and 3-2. When this method is used, it is necessary to determine the quantities of mortar needed to build the wall.

2. By multiplying the wall height by the perimeter of the center line of the wall. Many costing items will list costs for completely erected walls on this basis.

Units used in brick construction show four different exposures. The names associated with these exposures are

Stretcher	Long edge horizontal, side exposed
Header	End view exposed, long end horizontal
Soldier	Long edge vertical, side exposed
Rowlock	End view exposed, long end vertical

See Figure 3-3 for example of the foregoing brick exposures.

The appearance of a brick wall depends upon the pattern the bricklayer uses (called for by the architect/designer) in setting up the wall. The pattern is known as the *pattern bond*. The term *pattern bond* is used to indicate the various patterns exposed in the brick wall or facing. The most commonly used pattern bonds are shown in Figure 3-4.

Brick attached to the face of a wall (masonry or framed) is known as a *veneer*. The brick veneer (facing) used in most residential projects is shown in the following figures. Figure 3-5 shows the construction with a wood-framed backup wall. Notice especially the corrugated metal ties used to anchor the veneer to the backup. Corrugated ties are spaced (normally) at 2 ft 0 in. on center (oc) in each direction with ties being put into the horizontal joints of the masonry. The quantity needed will then be the wall area divided by four. Figure 3-6 shows a typical wall section and related details.

Figure 3-5 illustrates how the wood floor and wall framing fits onto the foundation wall. In order to tie this framing to the foundation, it is necessary for the estimator to include anchor bolts in his/her estimate. The normal requirements include

1. Using $\frac{1}{2}$-in.-diameter bolts that extend 15 in. into the core of the hollow block foundation wall. The core of the block containing the anchor bolt must be grouted with a concrete mixture.

2. Spacing anchor bolts not more than 8 ft apart. One anchor bolt shall be placed not more than 12 in. from each end of the wall sill plate.

Bolts will also be needed at the top of masonry piers used at the foundation level.

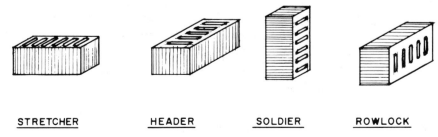

| STRETCHER | HEADER | SOLDIER | ROWLOCK |

Figure 3-3. Examples of brick exposure.

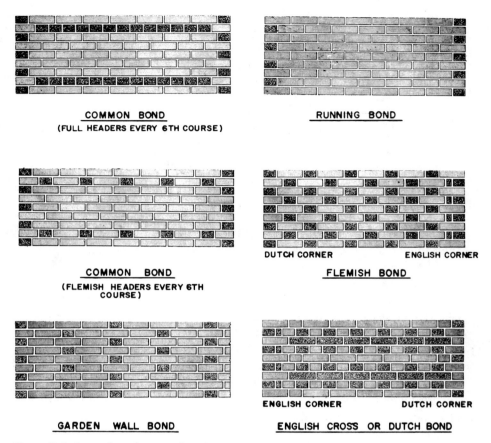

COMMON BOND
(FULL HEADERS EVERY 6TH COURSE)

RUNNING BOND

COMMON BOND
(FLEMISH HEADERS EVERY 6TH COURSE)

DUTCH CORNER   ENGLISH CORNER

FLEMISH BOND

GARDEN WALL BOND

ENGLISH CORNER   DUTCH CORNER

ENGLISH CROSS OR DUTCH BOND

Figure 3-4. Examples of pattern bonds (courtesy of Cleveland Builders Supply Company).

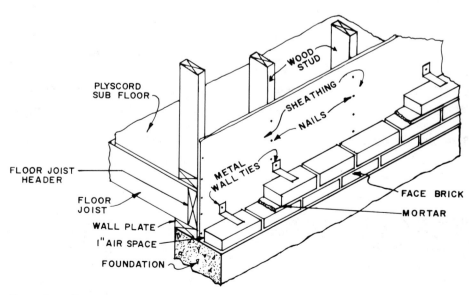

Figure 3-5. Illustration of brick veneer showing wood frame back-up details.

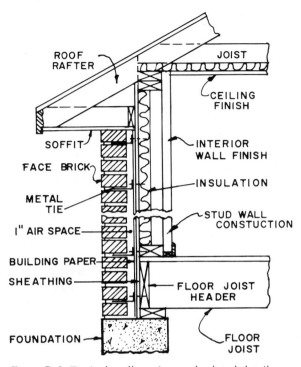

ROOF RAFTER
JOIST
CEILING FINISH
SOFFIT
INTERIOR WALL FINISH
FACE BRICK
INSULATION
METAL TIE
STUD WALL CONSTUCTION
1" AIR SPACE
BUILDING PAPER
SHEATHING
FLOOR JOIST HEADER
FOUNDATION
FLOOR JOIST

Figure 3-6. Typical wall section and related details.

Masonry Piers

There are several places in the construction of residential structures where the use of masonry piers is the natural solution to a building project. Chief among these are in the use of foundation piers—including piers in basement construction—and porch or *portiere* columns. Most of these use brick-size masonry elements, either of clay or of concrete. This normally means a minimum pier size of 8 × 12 in. (nominal). If the piers are relatively long units (height greater than 10 times the smallest lateral dimension), their strength must be increased by the addition of vertical reinforcing bars.

When hollow masonry concrete blocks are used for the building of piers, the minimum size is nominally 8 × 16 in. These structures can be reinforced with reinforcing rods set into the cores. The cores are then filled with concrete. If the cores of the blocks are not filled with concrete, the height should not exceed four times the least dimension of the pier.

Example 3-2
An 8 × 12-in. pier 5 ft 4 in. high is to be built of standard common clay brick units. How many bricks will be needed?

Solution: Each brick course consists of three units. Three courses will occupy 8 in. of pier height.

$$\text{Number of courses} = \frac{5\text{ ft 4 in.}}{\frac{8}{3}} = \frac{64 \times 3}{8} = 24$$

$$\text{Number of bricks} = \text{number of courses} \times \text{bricks/course}$$

$$= 24 \times 3$$

$$N = 72$$

Answer: 72 bricks are needed

Steel Posts   There are a variety of steel components that can be used to support floor girders—either wood beams or steel beams. These can be placed into the following two categories:

> **1. Steel pipe columns.** These are steel pipes that range from about $2\frac{1}{2}$ in. in diameter to 5 or 6 in. in diameter. They are carefully cut to the proper length and then have a steel plate shop-welded to each end. The cap (or top) plate is welded or bolted to the floor girder, whereas the base plate is bolted onto a concrete foundation. These columns have no adjustment, so accurate length fabrication is very important.
>
> **2. Adjustable jack posts.** These are steel pipes with a heavy, threaded rod at one end. The rod can be turned in and out to adjust the length of the jack post as needed. Again, top and bottom plates are required.

The latter type is most generally used for repair of sagging floor systems. These steel units are frequently used because they take up less floor space than wood posts or masonry piers.

Wooden Posts   Another alternate support structure can be columns and posts of wood. These can be of the following two types:

> **1. Solid wood posts.** The most usual sizes would be 6 × 6-in. or 8 × 8-in. (nominal) timbers. The sizing and estimating of wood will be covered thoroughly in Chapter 4.
>
> **2. Built-up posts.** An example would be two 2 × 6-in. boards spiked together.

Although these items may be relatively inexpensive, remember that their load-carrying capacity is less than either steel or masonry. Thus, more units will be required. This may not be favorable in the design layout proposed by the designer/engineer.

Post Note   Since posts are put in to eliminate sections of load-bearing walls, they usually carry substantial loads. This load should not be transferred directly into the ground or onto the basement floor slab. Therefore, check to make sure that there is some type of footing or foundation to transfer these loads into the supporting ground.

These transfer elements might be rectangular or square footing pads, or thickened sections of the floor slab. See Chapter 2 for more information on this material.

Chapter Four

House Framing

After the foundation work has been completed, the framing of floors, walls, partitions, ceilings, and roof is the next order of business in the construction of a residence. Since this is the major portion of any house construction, it should be next in the estimating procedure.

This area of work involves many new terms, each of which will be defined as it comes up in the book. In addition, enough illustrations will be included to clarify the definitions. Since construction goes in a definite sequence, the components will be covered in the following order:

Part I: Floors

Part II: Walls and Partitions

Part III: Roofs and Ceilings

Part I

Floors

Floor framing is obviously related to the foundation of the structure. Basically, the floor frame consists of the following components:

Floor-Supporting Structures

1. Bearing posts. These are posts that support the main structural floor members. They transfer the loads from the floors and walls to the foundation structure. They may be wood or steel, and in some cases brick or block piers.

2. Floor girders. These are main support members that are supported by the bearing posts and that, in turn, carry the joists of the floor frame. They may be steel or a combination of wood and steel.

3. Floor joists. These are the direct load-bearing members of the floor frame. In most residences these will be wood beams, such as 2 × 6, 2 × 8, 2 × 10, or 2 × 12 nominal* lumber. They are spaced as required to support the superimposed loads.

4. Bridging. This consists of wood or metal pieces that brace floor joists so they do not twist under load.

5. Subfloor. This is the wood-based material or plywood covering the floor joists on which underlayment or final flooring is carried. This material transmits the floor loads to the joists.

6. Underlayment. This is the material placed on top of rough subflooring to provide a level surface on which the finished floor covering is applied.

Note that in some cases (especially for second-floor frames) the bearing posts indicated in item 1 above can be replaced by a bearing partition. Each of these components will be handled separately in discussing the estimate.

BEARING POSTS AS SUPPORTS

Wood-bearing posts may be one solid piece of timber such as nominal 4 × 4 or 6 × 6. Quite often, they are made of two or more pieces of lumber nailed together. The post is sized by the designer on the basis of the load to be carried and the height of the post. Another factor that often governs the post dimensions will be the width of the floor girder that the post carries. The bearing posts would be listed on an estimate by listing the nominal dimensions plus the length required.

The other types of posts will be covered in those parts of this book pertaining to the material in question.

note: Masonry piers and steel posts were covered in Chapter 3.

The material for bearing partitions is taken off as in the section of this book on wall framing.

FLOOR GIRDERS: SOLID OR BUILT-UP MEMBERS

Floor girders may be single timber members, but usually consist of two or more members joined together as in Figure 4-1.

Another wood-girder type that is common in larger structures is the *flitch-plated beam*. This is a beam made up of a combination of wood members and a steel plate. The flitch plate is used to give the beam the strength it needs without adding excessive width to the beam (see Figure 4-2).

In addition, some designers will specify the use of glue-laminated girders or plywood-boxed girders.

1. The glue-laminated girders are fabricated of board lumber that is glued together under high pressure to form a single beam. These girders are most frequently used as rafters in "cathedral"-type ceilings in larger homes. The sizes vary in depth by ¾- or 1½-in. increments depending on whether 1× or 2× lumber was

_____
* See Table 4-1 for actual dimensions of "nominal"-sized wood members.

Table 4-1
Standard Dressed (S4S)ᵃ Lumber Sizes

Nominal Size $b \times h$ (in.)	Standard Dressed Size (S4S) $b \times h$ (in.)	Nominal Size $b \times h$ (in.)	Standard Dressed Size (S4S) $b \times h$ (in.)
1 × 3	$\frac{3}{4} \times 2\frac{1}{2}$	3 × 4	$2\frac{1}{2} \times 3\frac{1}{2}$
1 × 4	$\frac{3}{4} \times 3\frac{1}{2}$	3 × 6	$2\frac{1}{2} \times 5\frac{1}{2}$
1 × 6	$\frac{3}{4} \times 5\frac{1}{2}$	3 × 8	$2\frac{1}{2} \times 7\frac{1}{2}$
1 × 8	$\frac{3}{4} \times 7\frac{1}{2}$	3 × 10	$2\frac{1}{2} \times 9\frac{1}{2}$
2 × 3	$1\frac{1}{2} \times 2\frac{1}{2}$	4 × 4	$3\frac{1}{2} \times 3\frac{1}{2}$
2 × 4	$1\frac{1}{2} \times 3\frac{1}{2}$	4 × 6	$3\frac{1}{2} \times 5\frac{1}{2}$
2 × 6	$1\frac{1}{2} \times 5\frac{1}{2}$	4 × 8	$3\frac{1}{2} \times 7\frac{1}{2}$
2 × 8	$1\frac{1}{2} \times 7\frac{1}{2}$	4 × 10	$3\frac{1}{2} \times 9\frac{1}{2}$
2 × 10	$1\frac{1}{2} \times 9\frac{1}{2}$	6 × 6	$5\frac{1}{2} \times 5\frac{1}{2}$
2 × 12	$1\frac{1}{2} \times 11\frac{1}{2}$	6 × 8	$5\frac{1}{2} \times 7\frac{1}{2}$
2 × 14	$1\frac{1}{2} \times 13\frac{1}{2}$	6 × 10	$5\frac{1}{2} \times 9\frac{1}{2}$
		6 × 12	$5\frac{1}{2} \times 11\frac{1}{2}$

ᵃ S4S means that the wood member has been "surfaced" (planed to a smooth finish) on all four sides.

used in the construction. The width varies depending on the width of planks used. For example, a girder made by gluing twelve 1 × 4 boards would have a finished dimension of $3\frac{1}{4} \times 9$ in. The estimate sheet would list the girder's finished size and length, since these girders are sold by the individual units.

2. Plywood-boxed girders can be put together in a shop or at the job site. They consist of a frame of dimension lumber in the form of a truss. The frame is then covered with plywood sheathing to complete the girder. These units are generally used to span large openings such as garage-door openings.

If a wood beam were used to replace this flitch plate, the wood beam would have to be about 17 times* the thickness of the plate.

$$17 \times \tfrac{1}{4} = \tfrac{17}{4} = 4\tfrac{1}{4} \text{ in.}$$

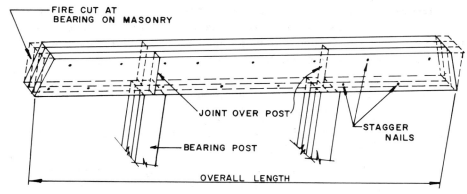

Figure 4-1. Built-up girder and bearing posts.

* This figure is obtained by dividing the modulus of elasticity of steel (about 29,500,000 psi) by the modulus of elasticity of wood (average value of about 1,760,000 psi). Further discussion of this factor is beyond the scope of this text.

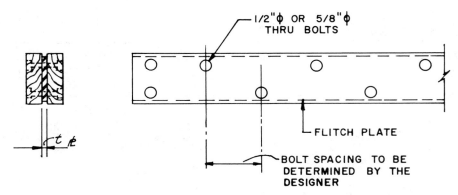

Figure 4-2. Typical flitch-plated beam or girder.

In other words, a $\frac{1}{4}$-in. steel plate could be used to replace $4\frac{1}{4}$ in. of the total width of a wood beam. As an illustration, the above flitch-plated beam (see Figure 4-2) would be approximately $7\frac{1}{4}$ in. wide if only wood were used.

Example 4-1
A flitch-plated beam is made up of two wood beams 2 × 12 in. nominal plus a steel plate 11 × $\frac{5}{16}$ in. thick. What size wood beam (solid) would have the same strength?

> **Solution:** Wood (B') to replace steel is 17 × plate thickness, or
>
> $B' = 17 \times \frac{5}{16} = 5.313$ in. (approximately $5\frac{1}{2}$)
>
> Add B' to two thicknesses of 2 × 12, or
>
> Full width = $(2 \times 1\frac{1}{2}) + 5\frac{1}{2} = 8\frac{1}{2}$ in.

Answer: Use $8\frac{1}{2}$ × $11\frac{1}{2}$ in. actual size beam

In some cases—especially to avoid using large wood beams or even flitch-plated beams on large spans—the main floor girder can be a steel-rolled section. A steel beam could also be used for its higher resistance to deflection—or "bouncing" movements. There are numerous shapes of steel members available to contractors. The more commonly used ones are

1. H- or I-shaped members, which are most commonly used as major structural beams over sizable span lengths.

2. C- or channel-shaped members, which are frequently used in pairs—back-to-back to form again an I-shaped member.

3. Steel angles, which are L-shaped members usually used as lintels to carry masonry across openings (door or window openings).

Table 4-2 gives the major design and detailing dimensions (or factors) needed to use steel members. Structural and/or miscellaneous steel is costed at so many dollars per pound or per ton. This price generally includes the cost of fabricating

Table 4-2
Dimensions of Selected Steel Shapes

Figure	Standard Designation	Dimensions (in.)		Weight (No./ft)	Surface Area[a] (ft²/ft)
		Width	Height		
Wide flange					
	W 12 × 26	6.490	12.22	26.00	4.12
	W 10 × 15	4.000	9.99	15.00	2.96
	W 8 × 15	4.015	8.11	15.00	2.65
Channel					
	C 10 × 15.3	2.600	10.00	15.30	2.49
	C 8 × 11.5	2.260	8.00	11.50	2.05
Angle					
	L 6 × 4 × 1/2[b]	4.000	6.00	16.20	1.66
	L 4 × 3 × 3/8[b]	3.000	4.00	8.50	1.17

Source: Manual of Steel Construction of the American Institute of Steel Construction.
[a] Adapted from 1982 Estimating Guide of the Painting and Decorating Contractors of America.
[b] The third figure in the designation refers to the thickness of the angle in inches.

and delivering the steel members. Fabrication would include cutting to length and attaching steel connection angles or plates. Remember again that the steel must be lifted into position. This could involve constructing a gin-pole type of hoist or the renting of a small, mobile crane to do the task.

A *gin-pole* is a pulley on a V-shaped frame. A hoisting rope runs over the pulley and is used to lift pieces of lumber or steel that are too heavy to be handled easily by two workers. Again, this involves an additional cost factor for the estimator.

FLOOR JOISTS

Floor joists are an important part of an estimate. The usual spacing of floor joists is 16 in. on center (oc). This can be written as $\frac{16}{12}$ ft oc. When you divide by $\frac{16}{12}$, it is the same as multiplying by $\frac{3}{4}$. This makes for simple calculating of the number of pieces required. The number of joists needed can be obtained by multiplying the length of floor to be covered by $\frac{3}{4}$ and adding one (see Example 4-2).

Example 4-2
Determine how many joists will be needed on a structure 12 ft 0 in. long. Use 16-in. spacing.

Solution: N = number of joists = $(\frac{3}{4} \times 12.0) + 1$

Answer: N = 10 joists (see Figure 4-3)

If a partition is positioned parallel to the joist system, the joist closest to the partition should be doubled by adding an additional joist to the system. This will

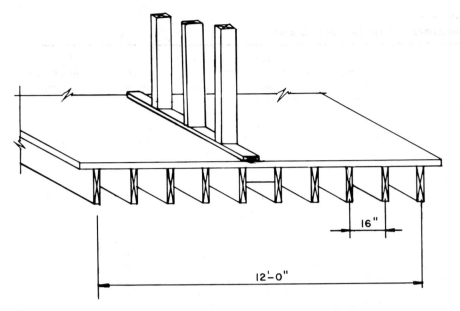

Figure 4-3.

also be necessary if an opening is to be framed into the floor frame. Doubled joists should not be more than 8 in. apart.

In addition to the main floor joists, other material will be needed to complete the floor frame. These additional components are an important part of the floor frame. They are called header joists or box sills, rim joists, trimmer joists, and tail joists.

See Figure 4-4 for an illustration of all main components of a floor frame. Figure 4-5 illustrates how doubled joists are blocked to have both joists working

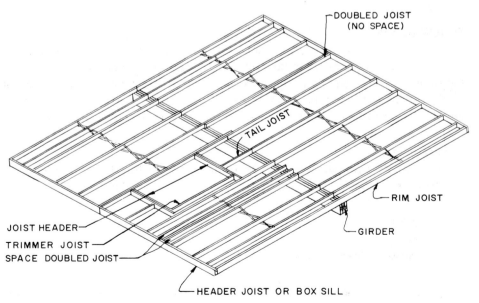

Figure 4-4. Main components of a floor frame.

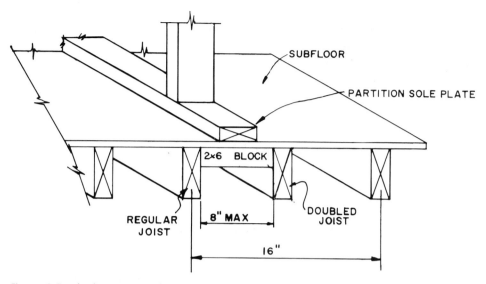

Figure 4-5. Blocking required for double joists to act as a single unit.

together to carry the partition load. The blocking shown can generally be made from scrap pieces of joists or wall studs.

An important factor to observe in the floor frame is the method of joining floor joists over girders or bearing partitions. Figure 4-6 shows joists tied together in a butt joint over the girder or partition. The joists can also lap each other over the girder or partition.

Two other methods that can be used are

1. Metal joist hangers as shown in Figure 4-7.

2. Wood ledgers on the girder to support the joists (see Figure 4-8).

Note how these different support styles affect the length of the floor joists. In

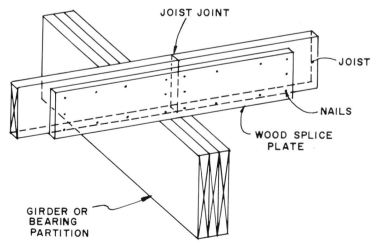

Figure 4-6. Butt joist over a support.

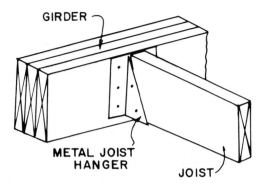

Figure 4-7.

addition, certain other items must be added to the estimate as the method of joist support changes. Included are

1. Wood splice plates, in which a piece of $\frac{5}{8}$- or $\frac{3}{4}$-in. plywood could be used as splice plates in place of the 2× lumber.

2. Wood *ledgers*.

3. Metal lumber, such as joist hangers.

BRIDGING

Bridging of various styles can be used to brace joists together and to have the floor act as a unit. The more commonly used types are shown in Figure 4-9.

It is sometimes necessary to use a combination of these bridging types in one structure. For example, if the space between joists is to be used for running *HVAC ducts,* the herringbone or solid bridging would need to be replaced by strap bridging to allow for easy pass-through of the ductwork. (HVAC is the abbreviation for heating–ventilating–air-conditioning.)

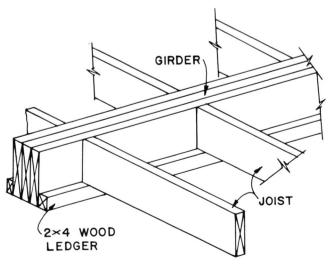

Figure 4-8.

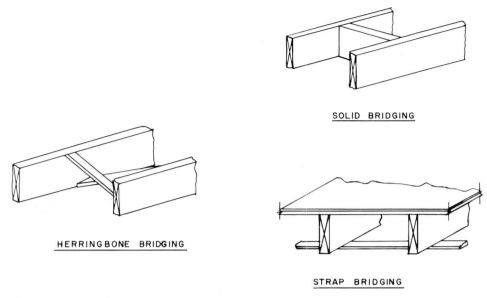

SOLID BRIDGING

HERRINGBONE BRIDGING

STRAP BRIDGING

Figure 4-9. Examples of types of bridging.

SUBFLOORING

Subflooring can be of *plywood* or common boards. The individual (common) boards should be laid at an angle of 45° with the joists. The plywood may have a thickness of $\frac{1}{2}$ or $\frac{5}{8}$ in. and should be laid with the long dimensions perpendicular to the joists. Butt joints in the plywood should be staggered in successive courses (see Figure 4-10).

Become thoroughly familiar with the manufacturer's standard designations for grades of plywood. All plywood used in floor construction should be exterior

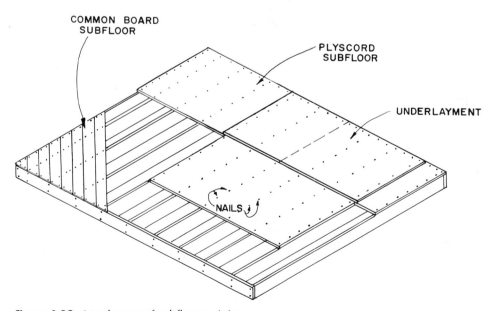

COMMON BOARD
SUBFLOOR

PLYSCORD
SUBFLOOR

UNDERLAYMENT

NAILS

Figure 4-10. Attachment of subfloor to joist.

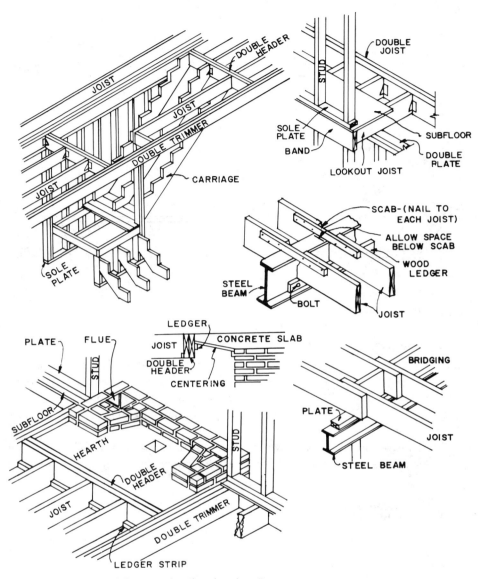

Figure 4-11. Standard framing details related to floor joist.

grade to avoid delamination of the wood in case it accidentally becomes saturated with water.

Some standard framing details related to floor joists are shown in Figure 4-11. Local customs vary, so check carefully on local building codes before beginning a house project.

Summary on Floor Framing

In estimating materials for floor framing, a number of shortcuts can be used. Some that can be easily remembered are

1. The number of joists at 16 in. oc will equal ¾ of the run (or length of the building) plus one. In addition, add one extra joist at each end of the building

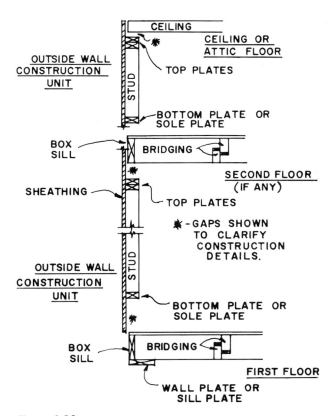

Figure 4-12.

under outside walls, plus one extra joist under each partition running parallel to the joists, and one extra joist at each side of an opening (such as a stair opening or trap door).

2. Add extra joist material for box sills and for 2 × 6 or 2 × 8 wall plates or sill plates (see Figure 4-12).

3. Linear footage of 1 × 3 bridging required will be three times the length of the run.

4. In figuring the amount of subflooring needed, be sure to allow for waste as follows:

    (a) 1 × 8 diagonal boards—add 20% waste.
    (b) 4 × 8-ft sheets plywood sheathing—add 5% waste.

5. For "quick pricing," get the total board footage by multiplying the first floor area by the following factors.* Deduct 0.05 from each factor if there is no center wall or girder.

    (a) Use 1.60 for 2 × 8 joists, box sills, wall plates, and bridging.
    (b) Use 1.95 for 2 × 10 joists, box sills, wall plates, and bridging.

6. For the framing of a second floor, figure as above but omit the 2 × 8 plates (see Figure 4-12).

* Board feet required equals actual framed floor area multiplied by the factor noted.

In estimating lumber for construction, you will encounter the term *foot board measure* (fbm). The ordering of lumber is based on the nominal size of lumber called for on the drawing. We have indicated that the actual size of lumber used differs from the nominal size. The foot board measure of a piece of lumber is actually the size of the rough cut board from which the finish board is shaped. By definition, one fbm is nominally 1 in. thick × 1 ft wide × 1 ft long (or an end area of 12 in.^{2}). The following examples will illustrate how the fbm is determined.

Example 4-1
Determine the fbm of a nominal 2 × 8 board.

Solution: From Table 4-1, the actual dimensions are $1\frac{1}{2} \times 7\frac{1}{2}$ in. One 2 × 8 board has a nominal end area of 2 × 8 or 16 in.^{2}

$$fbm = (16 \text{ in.}^2/board) \div (12 \text{ in.}^2/fbm)$$

Answer: = 1.33 fbm/ft of length

Example 4-2
Determine the fbm of a nominal 4 × 6 post.

Solution: From Table 4-1, the actual dimensions are $3\frac{1}{2} \times 5\frac{1}{2}$ in. One 4 × 6 post has a nominal end area of 4 × 6 or 18 in.^{2}

$$fbm = (18 \text{ in.}^2/board) \div (12 \text{ in.}^2/fbm)$$

Answer: = 1.50 fbm/ft of length

Part II

Walls and Partitions

Wall framing is another important aspect of house construction. Exterior walls are used as major structural supporting elements and also serve to resist lateral forces such as wind. They protect the inhabitants from the weather as well. Interior partitions serve to separate functional areas of the home. In addition, these partitions are frequently structural load-bearing elements.

This part of this chapter will outline the methods by which the materials needed for walls and partitions can be determined. The exterior walls and interior partitions will be covered separately.

Exterior Walls   Exterior walls can be constructed by at least two different methods. The two major methods are designated as *platform-frame* construction and *balloon-frame* construction. The differences (and similarities) will be discussed next.

Platform-frame construction, as shown in Figure 4-13, consists of a one-story wall structure topped with a "platform frame" that forms the second floor or ceiling of the building. This method is relatively simple because the construction can consist of the following steps:

1. Build first floor—may be framed over basement, over a crawl space, or on a slab of ground.

2. Build one wall flat on the floor—wall can be completely framed and sheathed (thus ensuring that it has been built "square") before Step 3.

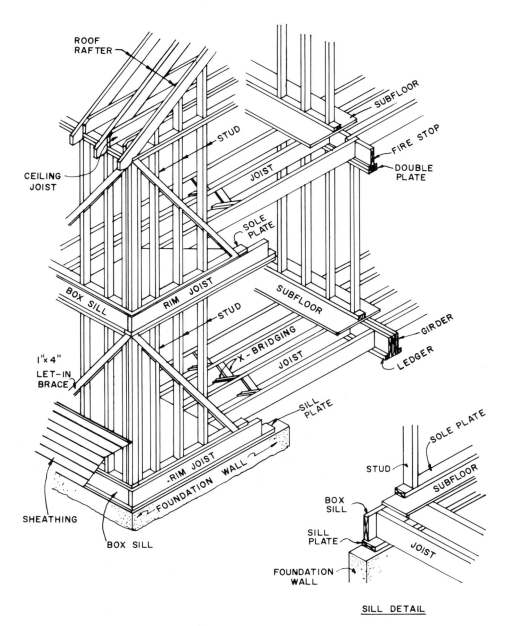

Figure 4-13. Western or platform-frame construction.

3. Tilt wall into position, then plumb and brace the wall in the proper position.

4. Repeat Steps 2 and 3 with the remaining load-bearing walls and partitions.

5. Build second-floor frame (if any) in its proper position.

6. Repeat steps 2, 3, and 4 for second-floor walls (if any).

7. Top second-floor walls with the ceiling and roof frames.

This type of framing is also known as *western framing*. It is used commonly in many sections of the country. The insert in Figure 4-13 shows the details of the sill construction for this type of wall framing.

Balloon-frame construction is shown in Figure 4-14. This construction uses

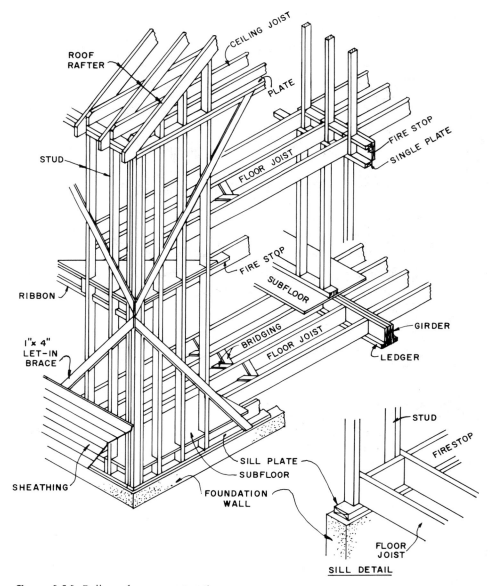

Figure 4-14. Balloon-frame construction.

full-height wall studs with the second-floor framing being supported by *ribbons* set into the wall studs. Generally, this type of construction requires more temporary bracing than is needed for platform frames. Again, the insert in Figure 4-14 shows the simplicity of this type of wall construction.

In determining the materials needed in a wall, it is possible to use a layout of each wall or some shortcut. Since some waste will be encountered, the more exact layout might be more meticulous than needed. Instead, a shortcut method might be more efficient and realistic. Some of the estimating shortcuts that can be used effectively include:

Estimating Procedures

1. For studs at 16 in. oc, estimate one stud per linear foot of wall plus two extra studs for each corner exceeding four corners.

2. Add one extra stud for each opening, and add one extra stud per junction point where interior partitions meet exterior walls.

3. For plates, estimate three times the linear footage of the walls.

4. Estimate two pieces 1 in. × 4 in. × 10 ft long per corner for bracing exterior wall frames—these braces are not needed if plywood sheathing is used.

5. All openings require *headers* to support the wall framing above them. The headers are illustrated in Figure 4-15, and the sizes of headers needed are tabulated in Table 4-3.

The extra studs obtained by using estimating shortcut 1 will be used to furnish the following items shown in Figure 4-15: trimmers, rough sills, and backup studs where interior partitions meet exterior walls. (This junction is shown in Figure 4-16.)

Note the placement of the backup studs in Figure 4-16. About 1 in. of the studs (minimum) projects outside the interior partition. This space permits the anchoring of the edge of the inside wall-finish material.

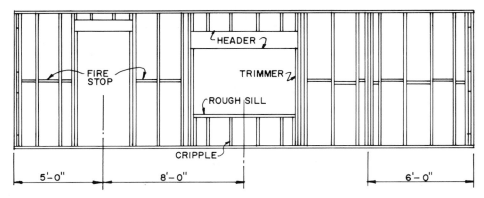

Figure 4-15. Typical wall framing for openings.

**Table 4-3
Headers Required for Wall Openings**

Opening Type	Maximum Width of Opening	Number of Pieces	Nominal Size (in.)	Length (ft)
Windows	3 ft 0 in.	2	2 × 6	4
	5 ft 0 in.	2	2 × 6	6
	7 ft 0 in.	2	2 × 8	8
	9 ft 0 in.	2	2 × 10	10
	11 ft 0 in.	2	2 × 12	12
	13 ft 0 in.	2	2 × 12	14
Doors	3 ft 6 in.	2	2 × 6	4, 5
	5 ft 0 in.	2	2 × 6	6
	7 ft 0 in.	2	2 × 8	8
	9 ft 0 in.	2	1 × 10	10
	11 ft 0 in.	2	2 × 12	12
	16 ft 0 in.	2	Two 2 × 12 + 11 × $\frac{1}{4}$ flitch plate	17

Additional Framing Needed

In many homes and small buildings, the roof construction is sloped. This gives rise to *gable* construction at the ends of the building. The gable needs a series of varying length studs. The variation depends upon the slope of the roof. These slopes vary depending on the designers. Some of the more common slopes are 4 vertical to 12 horizontal, 5 vertical to 12 horizontal, and 6 vertical to 12 horizontal. This subject will be covered thoroughly in Part III.

To determine the length of studs required for a gable, sum up the distances of each stud from the end (eave). Multiply this sum by two (for the two sides needed) and again by the ratio of the roof slope. Add in the length of the center-line stud. Example 4-3 will illustrate this procedure:

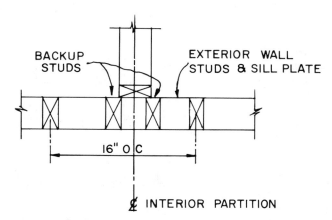

Figure 4-16. Interior partition, exterior stud-wall junction.

Example 4-3

A house gable is 26 ft 0 in. long and has a roof slope of 5 vertical to 12 horizontal (see Figure 4-17). What is the total length of studs needed? How many 8-ft-long studs would be needed? The first stud (of measurable length) is 2 ft 4 in. from end.

Solution: Total length $= \frac{5}{12}(2$ ft 4 in.$) + (3$ ft 8 in.$) + (5$ ft 0 in.$) + (6$ ft 4 in.$) + (7$ ft 8 in.$) + (9$ ft 0 in.$) + (10$ ft 4 in.$) + (11$ ft 8 in.$) \times 2 + \frac{5}{12} \times (13$ ft 0 in.$)$

$= \frac{5}{12}(56$ ft 0 in. $\times 2 + (13$ ft 0 in.$)$

Answer: Total length = 52 ft 1 in.

Number of 8-ft 0-in. studs = total length ÷ 8.0

$= 6.51$

Answer: Use seven 8-ft 0-in. studs

There are many types of materials used to cover the wall frame in a residential building. Some of the more commonly used materials are

Sheathing (Covering) the Wall

1. Sheathing lumber placed horizontally or at a 45° diagonal slope. Common sizes are 1 × 8, 1 × 10, or 1 × 12.

2. Asphalt-impregnated fiberboard in 4 × 8-ft or 4 12-ft sheets, usually $\frac{5}{8}$ or $\frac{3}{4}$ in. in thickness.

3. Exterior construction grade plywood sheets in 4 × 8-ft size normally. Plywood thicknesses are usually $\frac{5}{8}$ or $\frac{3}{4}$ in.

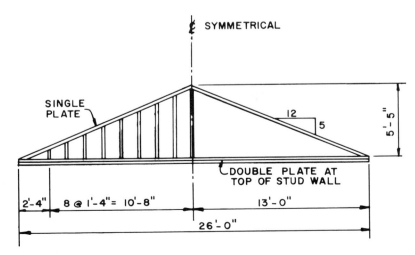

Figure 4-17.

Some details of each of these types are covered in the sections that follow. Check drawings carefully since new types of sheathing are constantly being developed. One of the more promising types is a foil-faced foam sheathing board.

Sheathing boards may be tongue-and-grooved, shiplapped, or square-edged. See Figure 4-18 for a view of these forms. Note that joints in the boards should occur over wall studs. Sheathing boards should be covered with felt building paper under the final finish material on the wall.

Fiberboard should be homogeneous, high-density structural-insulation board conforming to Insulation Board Institute (IBI) Specification No. 2 and ASTM 0227.* This board should be applied with its long dimension vertical.

Plywood sheathing should be of the proper exterior construction grade. Thickness of the plywood is a function of the stud spacing.

Both diagonal-placed sheathing lumber and plywood sheathing will brace the wall. Using either type will eliminate the need for diagonal bracing built into the frame as shown in Figures 4-13 and 4-14.

Example 4-4

Referring to Figure 4-15 and to the shortcut methods outlined in the section on Estimating Procedures, determine the number of wall studs needed for the wall shown. Studs are set at 16 in. oc.

Solution: Shortcuts 1 and 2: Wall length = 26 ft 0 in. with two openings and one junction

Studs needed = 26 × 1 + 2 openings × 1 + 1 junction × 1

Answer: = 29 studs total

Example 4-5

If the door opening is 3 ft 4 in. wide and the window opening is 5 ft 0 in. wide, determine the size of the header needed for each opening.

Solution: Door opening = 3 ft 4 in.

Answer: From Table 4-2, use two 2 × 6 × 3 ft 7 in. long

Window opening = 5 ft 0 in.

Answer: From Table 4-2, use two 2 × 6 × 5 ft 3 in. long

Example 4-6

For the wall shown in Figure 4-15 determine the number of 4 × 8-ft sheets of sheathing materials that would be needed.

Solution: From the right—wall space = (5 ft 0 in.) − ½ door width

= (5 ft 0 in.) − (1 ft 8 in.)

= 3 ft 4 in.

= 1 sheet

---

* ASTM refers to the American Society for Testing Materials—a group that has standardized tests for evaluating all types of material.

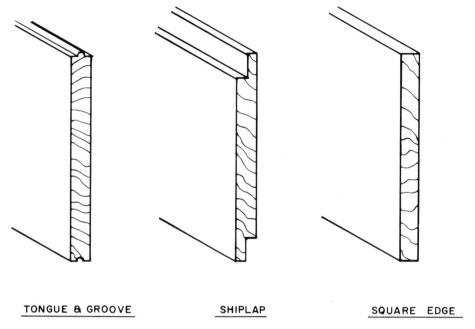

TONGUE & GROOVE   SHIPLAP   SQUARE EDGE

Figure 4-18. Example of typical sheathing boards.

Between door and window—wall space = (8 ft 0 in. − ½ door − ½ window

      = (8 ft 0 in.) − (1 ft 8 in.) − (2 ft 6 in.)

      = 3 ft 10 in.

      = 1 sheet

From window to right side—wall space = (26 ft 0 in.) − distance from left to center line of window − half window

      = (26 ft 0 in.) − (13 ft 0 in.) − (2 ft 6 in.)

      = 10 ft 6 in.

      = 3 sheets

Total number required = 1 + 1 + 3

Answer: 5 sheets 4 × 8-ft sheathing

note: Excess material will be used in the spaces above the door and window openings, plus in the space below the window sill.

Part III

Roofs and Ceilings

The construction discussed thus far must now have the top covered. To do this, the subjects of ceiling framing and roof framing must be added.

There are, of course, many varieties of roof/ceiling framings that are specified by the designer. The type of covering to be used is related to the area of the country in which the structure is to be located. For example, sloped roofs are commonly used where precipitation (in the form of rain or snow) is a common occurrence. In the South and West, roofs having flat tops are very common.

In this part of the chapter, the variety of shapes and construction will be covered in enough detail to help the estimator take off material quantities.

Ceilings   The next area to be studied involves the framing of the ceiling joists. This framing can be accomplished by two methods:

1. Separate ceiling joists that rest on exterior walls and interior-bearing walls. The number and lengths of joists needed would be similar to the floor joists. The method of take off on this type will follow the methods discussed in Part I of this text. It should be noted that in this construction, the joists may need to act also as tie-bars for the sloped members of the roof.

2. The ceiling can be attached to the bottom chord of trusses used to form the sloped roof of a building. This alternative is discussed in succeeding sections.

Roof Framing   Roof framing varies in types in the following ways: rafter construction with sheathing, sloping roof beams with roof decking, and roof trusses with sheathing. There are many different shapes used to frame the roof of any building project. A few common shapes used in residential buildings are shown in Figure 4-19. Any single project can use various combinations as shown in Figure 4-20.

The shapes in Figure 4-19 show that the roofs commonly used frequently are sloped. The contractor/builder/estimator must understand how to lay out and cut the rafters needed for the support of so-called ''stick'' roofs.

RAFTER AND SHEATHING

All of the roof types shown in Figure 4-19 are supported by rafters attached to the ceiling framing (this was covered in a previous section). There are a number of rafter types used in roof construction. Figure 4-21 illustrates the location of the rafter forms used in construction of roofs.

The term $\frac{1}{4}$ *pitch* is used to describe the slope of a roof. This is illustrated in Figure 4-22. The out-to-out dimension of a building is known as the *span*. The total *run* is the horizontal distance from the ridge of the roof to the outside of the

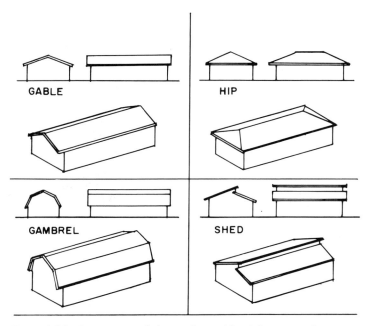

Figure 4-19. Common roof shapes for residential construction.

wall line. The term *unit run* is applied to a 12-in. portion of the rafter's run, whereas the *unit span* is the sum of the 12-in. runs of a pair of common rafters (or 24 in.). This is shown in Figure 4-23.

Also shown in Figure 4-23 is the *rise,* or the total vertical dimension of the roof rafter. The distance that the roof rises in the 12 in. of the unit run is known as the *unit rise*. The slope of the roof is usually given by its *pitch,* which is the unit rise divided by the unit span. The slope itself is listed as the unit rise : unit run. For example, the ¼ pitch previously cited has a slope of 6 : 12.

Example 4-7
Given unit rise = 6 in., what is the pitch of the roof?

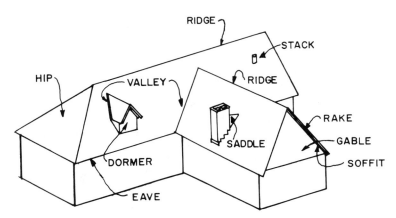

Figure 4-20.

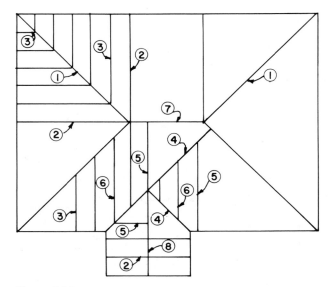

1. HIP RAFTERS
2. COMMON RAFTERS
3. HIP JACKS
4. VALLEY RAFTERS
5. VALLEY JACKS
6. CRIPPLE JACKS
7. MAJOR RIDGE
8. MINOR RIDGE

Figure 4-21.

Solution: Pitch = (unit rise)/(unit span, or 24 in.)

$$= \frac{6}{24}$$

Answer: $\frac{1}{4}$

Example 4-8

A roof spans a distance of 26 ft 0 in. out-to-out of walls. The roof has a 1-ft 4-in. overhang on each side. The slope of the roof is 5 vertical to 12 horizontal. Determine the actual rafter length.

Solution: From trigonometry, the slope length of a triangle having 5- and 12-in. legs is equal to the square root of the sum of the squares of the two legs, or

$$L^2 = 5^2 + 12^2 = 169$$

$$L = 13 \text{ in.}$$

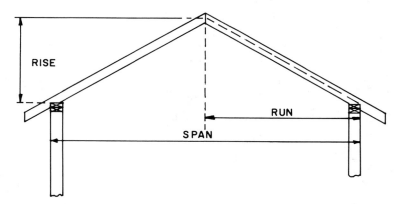

RISE

RUN

SPAN

Figure 4-22.

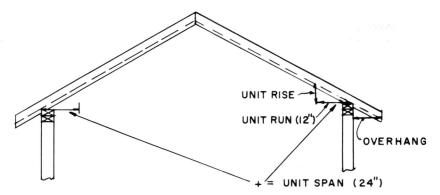

Figure 4-23.

Thus, the rafter has 1 in. added to 12 in. of horizontal run. The total horizontal distance from ridge to overhang is

$$H = \frac{\text{span}}{2} + (1 \text{ ft } 4 \text{ in.}) = \frac{(26 \text{ ft } 0 \text{ in.})}{2} + (1 \text{ ft } 4 \text{ in.})$$

$$= 14 \text{ ft } 4 \text{ in.}$$

Line: $L = \frac{13}{12}(H) = \frac{13}{12}(14 \text{ ft } 4 \text{ in.})$

$$= 15 \text{ ft } 6.3 \text{ in.}$$

To this length must be added a distance for the slope at each end of the rafter to get a plumb cut at the ends. With a 6-in. rafter, add

$\frac{5}{12} \times \frac{5}{5} \times 2$ or 4.6 in. to the line L

Thus, the overall length is (15 ft 6.3 in.) + (4.6 in.), or 15 ft 10.9 in.

Answer: Cut rafter from 16-ft 0-in. length of 2 × 6

The sheathing used on rafter-system roofs can be board lumber or plywood. In order to use the more common thicknesses of these materials, the spacing of the rafters must be controlled. Most building departments specify 16-in. spacing (maximum) for the rafters. In some instances, however, 24-in. spacing is permitted with thicker sheathing. Table 4-4 gives the relationship between plywood thickness and rafter spacing. In today's building market, the preferable sheathing is the plywood because of the speed of erection and the increased rigidity imparted to the roof.

Other terms related to rafter construction that should be known include the so-called *birdsmouth,* or notch, cut into a rafter so it will rest securely on a wall. This notch is shown in Figure 4-24.

The part of a rafter outside the *plumb cut* is known as the *overhang.* Note that the use of the plumb cut at both ends of a rafter means that the *actual length* of a rafter is different from the *line length.* Figure 4-25 gives an illustration of the differences between these two terms.

There are many other roof-framing items that must be added in a typical estimate. Some of these are shown in Figure 4-26. The *collar beam* shown is usually placed at alternate rafters or at every third rafter.

Table 4-4
Plywood Roof Sheathing[a]

| Plywood Thickness (in.) | Maximum Rafter or Joist Spacing (in. oc)[b] | | | |
| | Asphalt Shingles and Wood Shingles and Shakes | | Asbestos–Cement Shingles | |
	Edges Blocked[c]	Edges Unblocked	Edges Blocked[c]	Edges Unblocked
$\frac{5}{16}, \frac{3}{8}$	16	—	—	—
$\frac{5}{16}, \frac{3}{8}$	20	—	—	—
$\frac{3}{8}, \frac{1}{2}$	24	24	16	—
$\frac{5}{8}$	30	24	24	16
$\frac{1}{2}, \frac{5}{8}$	32	24	24	16
$\frac{3}{4}$	36	30	32	24
$\frac{5}{8}, \frac{3}{4}, \frac{7}{8}$	42	32	32	24
$\frac{3}{4}, \frac{7}{8}$	48	32	42	28

[a] Plywood continuous over two or more spans, grain of face plys across supports; structural 1 and 11, standard and C-C exterior construction grades only.
[b] For $\frac{1}{2}$-in. plywood or less, use 6d common or 5d threaded nails; for 1-in. plywood or less use 8d common or 7d threaded nails.
[c] Unsupported edges of sheathing should be blocked using wood blocking, tongue-and-grooved edges (5 ply, $\frac{1}{2}$ in. or thicker) or special corrosion resistant metal H clips. Use two clips for spans 48 in. or greater, one clip for lesser spans.

RAFTERS AND ROOF DECK

Interesting effects can be obtained by a designer using heavier rafters at wide spacing with heavy wood planking as the roof covering. This wood planking is generally cut with a tongue-and-grooved cross section. The plank is formed from 2×8-in. or 4×8-in. wood planks. The final thicknesses are about $1\frac{5}{8}$ and $3\frac{1}{4}$ in. A typical cross section is shown in Figure 4-27.

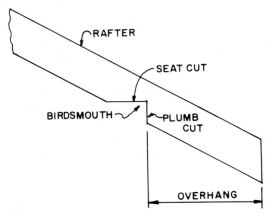

Figure 4-24. Rafter notch.

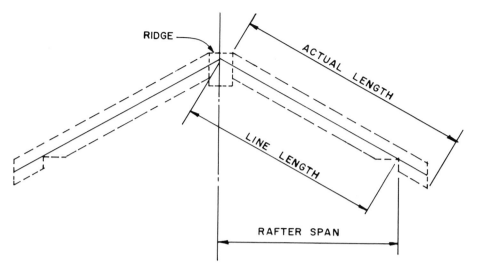

Figure 4-25.

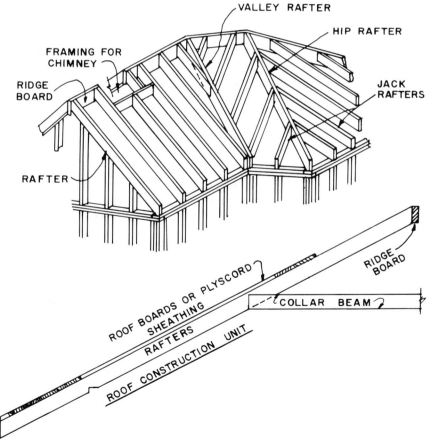

Figure 4-26.

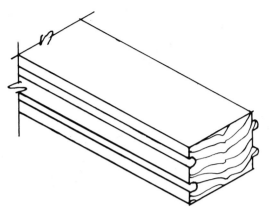

Figure 4-27.

The rafters are typically 4, 6, or 8 ft from center to center. This type of construction is used in residential construction to form cathedral ceilings in living rooms or family rooms. The architect/engineer of the project will determine the size of the sloping beams. These computations are beyond the scope of this book.

ROOF TRUSSES

The roof trusses mentioned at the beginning of this section provide an economical method of framing both the roof and the ceiling of small structures. They are economical because they can be easily prefabricated by local building material suppliers and delivered to the job site ready for erection. In the appendixes of this text you will find typical spans and details for some common types of wood trusses. The members of the more common trusses for residential construction are made up of individual pieces cut from 2 × 4 or 2 × 6 stock. These pieces are tied together in the form of a series of triangles. Junction points are connected by wood or metal gusset plates or by metal gang-nail plates. When properly joined together, the truss acts as a unit to span the entire width of the building.

Figure 4-28 shows a typical building with roof trusses and indicates how they span the full width of the structure. Note that the interior wall is a non-load-bearing structural unit and could thus be built after installing the roof trusses and the roof sheathing.

Compare the roof trusses shown in Figure 4-28 with the ceiling joist-and-rafter-type roof system of Figure 4-29. You should note the central load-bearing wall in Figure 4-29. This wall must be built before the ceiling joists and roof rafters can be erected. Usually the ceiling joist-and-rafter uses 16-in. spacing of the structural members. The truss system most frequently used is based on a 24-in. spacing of trusses.

Example 4-9
A house is 46 ft 0 in. long. The wall construction includes gable construction at each end, so the end truss can be placed 2 ft 0 in. from the ends. How many trusses need to be purchased?

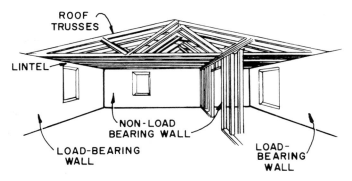

Figure 4-28.

> **Solution:** Number of trusses = [(length of house) − 2(2 ft 0 in.)] ÷
> 2 + 1 truss
>
> = [46 ft 0 in.) − (4 ft 0 in.)] ÷ 2 + 1
>
> = 21 + 1

Answer: N = 22 trusses required

As mentioned previously in this chapter, roof framing is covered with lumber boards, roof planks, or plywood sheets. In determining the amount of covering to be used, it is necessary to determine the actual slope length times the overall length of the roof. Table 4-4 will aid in making these calculations. The actual roof area will be equal to the ground (or flat) area of the roof multiplied by the factor in Column 3 of Table 4-5 that applies to the pitch of the roof.

Roof Sheathing

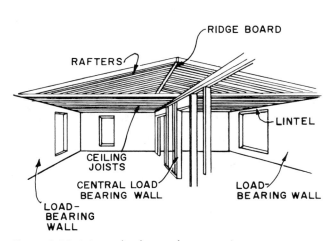

Figure 4-29. Joist and rafter roof construction.

Table 4-5
Roof Pitch and Waste Factors

1	2	3	4	5	6	7
		Factor to Use for Actual Roof and Insulation Areas	Plan Roof Factors Including Waste (use only for roofing material)[a]		Cut-up Roof Factors Including Waste (use only for roofing material)[a]	
Rise in Inches per Foot Run	Equivalent Pitch					
			Roof Types			
			Gable	Hip	Gable	Hip
3	$\frac{1}{8}$	1.03	1.12	1.16	1.17	1.23
4	$\frac{1}{6}$	1.06	1.15	1.19	1.21	1.26
5	$\frac{5}{24}$	1.09	1.18	1.22	1.23	1.34
6	$\frac{1}{4}$	1.12	1.21	1.24	1.25	1.34
7	$\frac{7}{24}$	1.16	1.25	1.29	1.20	1.37
9	$\frac{3}{8}$	1.25	1.34	1.38	1.39	1.46
12	$\frac{1}{12}$	1.42	1.51	1.56	1.57	1.64

Source: Drake Construction Co., Cleveland, Ohio.

[a] Does not include materials for accessories such as starter course, hip and ridge materials, valley materials, flashings. For actual roof area multiply ground or flat area of roof by proper factor from Column 3 and add proper percentage for cutting and waste. Do not forget overhangs.

Example 4-10

A house is 26 ft 0 in. $\times$ 46 ft 0 in. in plan area. The roof has a $\frac{1}{4}$ pitch and overhangs the walls by (1 ft 4 in.) on all four sides. Find the roof area.

> **Solution:** Plan area = [(26 ft 0 in.) + 2(1 ft 4 in.)] $\times$ [(46 ft 0 in.) + 2(1 ft 4 in.)]
>
> = 1367.2 ft^2

For $\frac{1}{4}$ pitch, factor from Column 3 is 1.12

Thus, the total roof area is 1.12 $\times$ plan area

Roof area = 1.12 $\times$ 1367.2

Answer: A = 1531.3 ft^2

Example 4-11

If the roof of Example 4-7 is sheathed in plywood, how many 4 $\times$ 8-ft sheets would be needed?

> **Solution:** One half of A, or 765 ft^2, is on each side
>
> Theoretical $N = A \div$ (32 ft^2/sheet)
>
> = 765 $\div$ 32

Answer: N = 23.9 per side or a total of 48 sheets

It should be noted that in actual construction, dimensions will not always work out to full sheets of plywood or lumber dimensions. Thus, waste factors must usually be added to calculated dimensions. In plywood, it is usual to add 5% to calculated values. In Example 4-11, adding 5% to the number of sheets needed would require adding two more sheets of plywood to the order.

Chapter Five

Roofing and Exterior Finish Materials

Previous chapters have covered the basic framing, including the foundations, floors, walls, partitions, ceilings, and roof framing. The next areas to be discussed are the roofing and exterior finishes. These items are next in the estimating program, since it is extremely important to enclose the building as soon as possible to make it weatherproof. These items will be covered in the following sequence:

1. Roofing.
2. Cornices and gutter boards (also called *fascia boards*).
3. Gutters and downspouts.
4. Windows.
5. Exterior doors.
6. Louvers.
7. Exterior wall finishes.

Roofing

The first item to be discussed will be roof coverings. Completion of the roof covering will offer workers protection while working on interior items. This is important in most areas of the country. There are many materials that can be used for this purpose. The list that follows covers only some of the materials that can be used—those most generally used in residential construction. The most commonly used are

1. Roof shingles. These can be made of
   (a) Wood shakes.

(**b**) Asphalt.

(**c**) Asbestos.

2. Slate shingles.

3. Built-up roofing construction.

4. Clay tile in various shapes.

Examples of some of these are shown in Figure 5-1.

Of these four categories, the ones listed under the first category are by far the most frequently used on homes. A little more detail on these may be helpful to the estimator.

1. Wood shakes are usually made of red cedar, cypress, or redwood in various lengths. The minimum roof slope for using wood shakes is 4 : 12. Less than one half of the shingle is exposed, for example, the 18-in. shake has $8\frac{1}{2}$ in. exposed. Thus, to obtain the number of squares of wood shakes needed, the estimator must multiply the actual area by $18 \div 8\frac{1}{2}$, or 2.12.

2. Asphalt (or composition) shingles are 12 × 36 in. and come in one-, two-, or three-tab styles. Again only about one half of the shingle (the tab portion) is exposed. The shingles must be laid over a layer of *roofing felt* and nailed to solid wood sheathing with hot-dipped, zinc-coated steel nails. The minimum slope is again 4 : 12.

3. The asbestos shingles are made of an asbestos fiber and portland cement mixture compressed into the desired shape under pressure. These are much stiffer, more fire resistant, and more expensive than asphalt shingles.

The slate shingles and clay-tile roof coverings are relatively more expensive than the roof shingles discussed previously. If these are specified on a given project, the estimator should study the construction procedures involved before

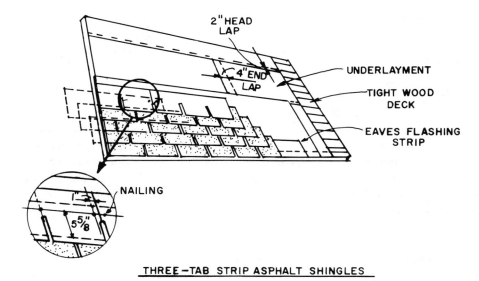

THREE—TAB STRIP ASPHALT SHINGLES

Figure 5-1. Examples of roof coverings.

attempting to make a take off. The built-up roof noted in the list of commonly used materials above is used in flat, or nearly flat, roofs. This type is constructed of layers of building felt imbedded in asphalt and frequently covered with stone chips or gravel to protect its waterproofing quality.

All of the materials previously listed, with the exception of built-up roofing, require the application of a layer of roofing felt over the roof sheathing before applying the finished roofing material. Roofing felt, which may also be called *building paper,* is basically a tar or asphalt-impregnated paper or rag base and is sold in rolls of 108, 216, and 432 ft². These rolls will provide coverage of 100, 200, and 400 ft², respectively. There is a reduction in coverage because when roofing felt is installed, there is a 2-in. overlap for each width applied. This material is sold in either 15 or 30 lb per *square roll.* Note that one square equals 100 ft², thus the rolls indicated above would be listed as containing one, two, or four squares.

Fifteen-pound felt is generally used; however, if unusual conditions such as delay in shipping of finished roofing materials should occur, it is advisable to use 30-lb felt for better temporary protection.

To estimate the quantities of materials needed for the roofing of a project, the roof area must be determined. In general, the roof area is found by first measuring the length of the roof. Next, the length of the rafters (total) is determined. These measurements were clarified in Chapter 4. The roof area is then obtained by multiplying the roof length by the total rafter length.

There are adjustments that should be made to the total area required for roofing. Some estimators make no deductions for roof openings that are less than 4 ft². Some deduct half of the area of openings with dimensions between 4 and 8 ft², and deduct the full area for openings with dimensions larger than 8 ft². Other estimators ignore roof openings entirely and do not make deductions for them.

In addition, remember that the estimator will again be required to increase the material quantities to account for waste and ridge material. This can be done by increasing the net roof area by 10% for simple gable roofs, 15% for simple hip roofs, and 20% for roofs with valleys and dormers.

Example 5-1

A gable roof is 42 ft 0 in. in overall length and has a total width of 24 ft 0 in. The roof pitch is $\frac{1}{4}$. What is the total number of roofing squares needed to cover this roof?

Solution: From Table 4-5, the roof factor for determining the total length of the rafters is 1.12 for a roof having a pitch of $\frac{1}{4}$. Thus, the roof area equals

Area = length × width × roof factor

$$= 42.0 \times 24.0 \times 1.12$$

$$A = 1129 \text{ ft}^2$$

Since 1 square = 100 ft², the area expressed in squares is

$$A = 1129 \div 100$$

$$= 11.3 \text{ squares}$$

To account for waste, the roof area should be increased by 10% for gables.

$A = (1129 \times 1.10)$

$= 1242 \text{ ft}^2$

Number of squares $= 1242 \div (100 \text{ ft}^2/\text{square})$

$= 12.42 \text{ squares}$

Answer: Order 13 squares

Cornice and Gutter (Fascia) Boards

In residential construction, the fascia or trim boards at the perimeter of the roof lines are usually called *cornice* and *gutter boards*. The cornice board is placed at the roof line along the rake (or slope) of a gable roof. The gutter board is placed at the bottom of a sloping roof and, as its name suggests, is frequently used for attachment of the gutters. These members usually are 1 × 6 members, and the most common material is redwood.

Both of these items are purchased by the board foot measure. To estimate the quantities required it is necessary to review the project drawings and determine the length of each. Remember, even though these items are part of the exterior finish, they are carpentry items and will be installed by the carpenter. They should be installed at the time the roof sheathing is applied.

Example 5-2

For the roof of Example 5-1, determine the amount of redwood lumber needed for the cornice and gutter boards.

Solution: Length of gutter boards $= 2 \times 42.0$

$= 84.0 \text{ ft}$

Length of cornice boards $= 2 \times 24.0 \times 1.12$

$= 54.0 \text{ ft}$

Total length needed $= 84.0 + 54.0$

$= 138.0 \text{ ft}$

1.0 ft of 1 × 6 = 0.5 board ft

Quantity needed in board feet is

Quantity $= 138.0 \text{ ft} \times (0.5 \text{ fbm/ft})$

Answer: Quantity = 69 fbm

Gutters and Downspouts

Most residential construction requires gutters at the bottom of the roof slopes along the gutter boards, and *downspouts* at the low ends of the gutter slope. The

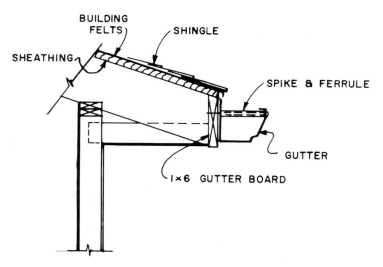

BUILDING FELTS   SHINGLE

SHEATHING

SPIKE & FERRULE

GUTTER

1×6 GUTTER BOARD

Figure 5-2.

downspouts either will be connected to underground downspout drain lines or will have an elbow at the bottom that permits the water to splash out onto the ground or onto *splash blocks.* Gutters and downspouts usually are either galvanized steel or aluminum. Both are also now available in rigid plastic. This may be a more economical solution in those areas of the country where plastics are common products.

To estimate quantities of materials for downspouts and gutters, determine the total linear footage of gutters shown on project drawings and count the number of downspouts. The length of downspouts is determined by measuring the height of the structure from grade to underside of the gutters. In addition to the gutters and downspouts, a number of miscellaneous items will be needed to complete the installation. Among these are

1. *Downspout brackets*—needed to hold the downspouts against the wall of the structure.

2. *Wire baskets*—one at each downspout to keep debris and leaves from clogging the downspout.

3. *Spikes and ferrules*—to support the gutter.

4. *Gutter accessories* including gutter corners, gutter connectors, and gutter end caps.

The interrelationship of these components is shown in Figure 5-2.

There are many varieties and styles of windows available throughout the country. **Windows** Those that are most commonly used in residential construction include

1. *Fixed sash*—no opening available.

2. *Single* or *double hung*—single-hung windows have the lower sash operable vertically; double-hung windows permit both sashes to open vertically.

3. *Horizontal-sliding units* have one or more sashes that can be opened by sliding horizontally.

4. *Awning windows* have sashes hinged at the top—the sash opens outward.

5. *Casing units,* or *casement windows,* have ventilating sashes hinged at the side and open outward.

These windows are available in many sizes and combinations. In addition, they are available in aluminum or steel, as well as in wood and plastic-clad wood. The steel units are used more frequently in commercial structures than in residences. There are many so-called "standard" sizes and combinations. Use of these standards generally means a more economical project.

The horizontal-sliding and sliding plus fixed sash are very common in residential construction. For this reason, Figures 5-3 and 5-4 have been inserted. To

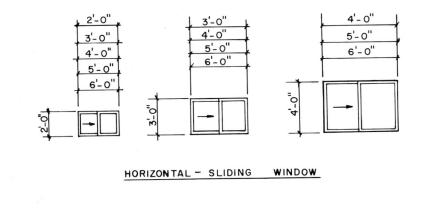

HORIZONTAL — SLIDING   WINDOW

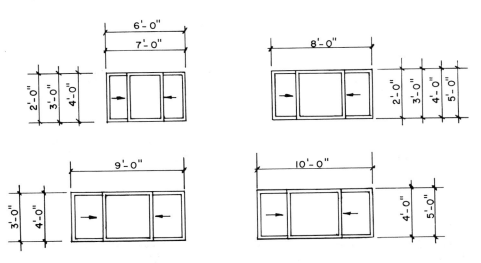

COMBINATION   WINDOW
(HOR. SLIDING — FIXED)

Figure 5-3.

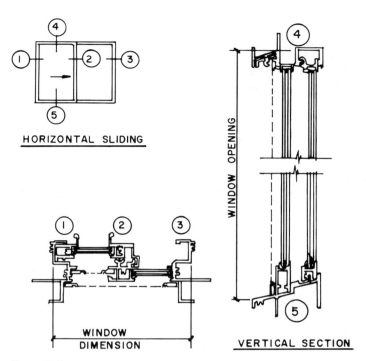

HORIZONTAL SLIDING

WINDOW OPENING

WINDOW DIMENSION

VERTICAL SECTION

Figure 5-4.

illustrate the "standard" sizes available we have included Figure 5-3. Typical construction details are shown in Figure 5-4.

Estimating of windows consists of determining the number of each size needed in the project. Since project drawings include elevations of each wall of the structure, counting all windows is usually easy to do.

Exterior Doors

Exterior doors vary in thickness from $1\frac{3}{8}$ to $2\frac{1}{4}$ in. with the $1\frac{3}{4}$-in. thickness being the most common. The height will vary from 6 ft 0 in. to 8 ft 0 in. with the 6-ft 8-in. height being the most common. The width varies from 2 ft 6 in. to 3 ft 6 in. for single doors. Figure 5-5 indicates some common styles of wood doors available to the builder.

These doors are *prehung* in frames and are ready to install into the rough openings we left for them in our work in Chapter 4. The parts of the frames for exterior doors are illustrated in Figure 5-6. The door must have certain hardware to operate properly. The type of hardware will vary with the type of door used. Hardware will be discussed in Chapter 8.

Figure 5-5.

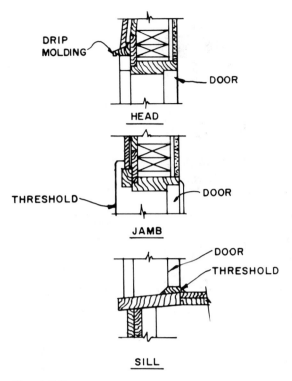

Figure 5-6.

Many of these same styles of doors are available in hollow steel doors and frames. The hollow steel units have a cellular paper or some form of plastic (styrofoam) core, which increases the insulating qualities of the door. Some of the construction details for steel doors are shown in Figure 5-7. Again, attempting to use standard sizes will improve the economy of the project being undertaken.

Garage doors generally are available in two basic styles—an upward-acting sectional wood door and a solid panel overhead door. Either style is available with many variations of trim and with or without windows. These doors may be manually operated, or they can be equipped with automatic electric operators. Figure 5-8 shows some of the styles available for sectional doors and some of the standard installation details for sectional doors. Figure 5-9 indicates some styles available and standard installation details for solid panel overhead doors.

When estimating materials for the exterior doors, follow a procedure similar to the one for estimating windows. Doors are purchased in the same manner as windows—by the unit. Again, count or take off each unit, then put a small check mark next to the dimension or unit number on the elevation to verify that this unit has been accounted for. Door hardware is covered as a separate item in a later chapter.

Louvers   *Louvers* are installed in houses to provide some natural ventilation. They are available with fixed or adjustable blades, or any combination. Stock louvers are

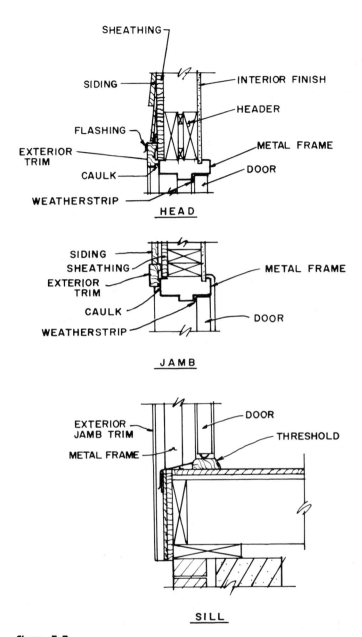

Figure 5-7.

usually rectangular or triangular in shape. They come in various sizes and different materials. The more common materials are wood and aluminum. Louvers are purchased as a unit based on size, shape, and material. Again, it is recommended that the estimator place a small check mark next to each unit on the elevations as the louver is counted or taken off.

Louvers generally open into unoccupied areas of the structure, such as attic spaces, soffit areas, and crawl spaces. Here again, study of types, sizes, and styles available in a given area will help the estimator in taking off the louvers on a project.

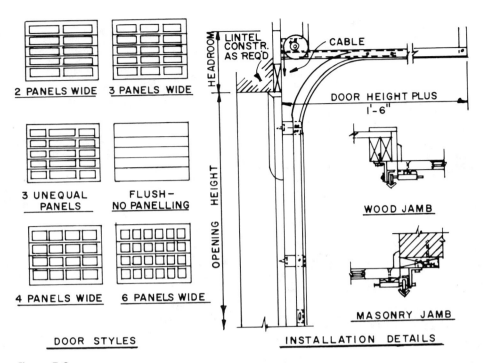

Figure 5-8.

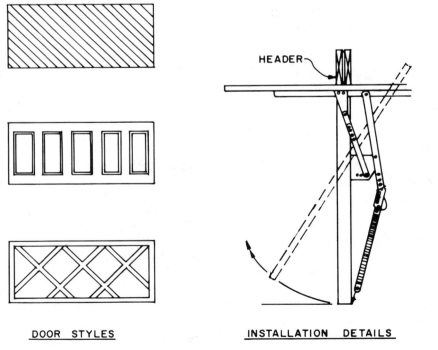

Figure 5-9.

The types of materials used vary widely based upon the architectural appearances in various parts of the country. Among the most commonly seen are **Exterior Wall Finishes**

1. Stucco. This term generally refers to the plaster applied to the exterior of a structure. It can be applied in either two- or three-coat applications. The individual coats are described as follows:

(a) Two-coat operation consists of a *base coat,* which is plastered onto a wire-mesh reinforcing net that is attached to the structural wall, and a *stucco finish.* This second coat is frequently textured in appearance and sometimes tinted to give a uniform color to the finish.

(b) Three-coat operation begins with a *scratch coat* that is plastered onto the wire mesh. This is followed by a *brown coat* used to build up the thickness of the plaster. Then comes the *stucco finish,* which finishes off the surface of the wall.

Stucco is made up as a *mortar* consisting of a properly proportioned mixture of

(a) **Cement.** *Portland cement* with *masonry cement* or *lime* (quicklime or *hydrated lime*)—used to cement the stucco into a unit.

(b) **Aggregate.** Sands or expanded clay products such as *vermiculite.*

(c) **Water.** Use clean, potable water.

Stucco is generally taken off, for estimating purposes, in square yards of surface to be covered.

2. Lap siding. This material is also known as *bevelled siding* or *clapboard siding.* The lap siding is shaped as shown in Figure 5-10 (the same general shape is used whether the siding is made of wood, aluminum, or plastic-coated steel). In wood (most frequently cedar), the siding is shaped from nominal 1 × 6-in. lumber up to 1 × 12-in. lumber. The actual width of the siding is $\frac{1}{2}$ in. less than the nominal, and the pieces of siding lap about 2 in. over each other. Therefore, the exposed face of the siding ranges from about $3\frac{1}{2}$ to $9\frac{1}{2}$ in. It is thus necessary for the estimator to increase the amount of wood ordered to cover this situation. The same shape is also made from medium-density exterior grade plywood.

Some very popular types of lap siding in today's market are made of aluminum, vinyl (plastic), or steel sheets. These are formed to the shapes of wood lap siding. Their popularity comes from their relative maintenance-free characteristics. These sidings usually are painted, anodized, or otherwise have their final finished color built into them.

3. Vertical tongue-and-grooved boards. These are a popular type of residential siding. The boards are formed with a V joint as shown in Figure 5-11. They can be made of cedar, redwood, pine, or hemlock boards. These units are formed from 1 × 6-in. to 1 × 12-in. planks (the actual size being less by $\pm\frac{1}{2}$ in. as previously noted). The architect may choose to use uniform-width planks on a project or go with random-width units. Occasionally, the wider planks have groves formed in the exterior face.

4. Plywood sheets. These are strips with batten boards applied at the joints. Figure 5-12 shows this style of siding. Plywood sheets are also available with

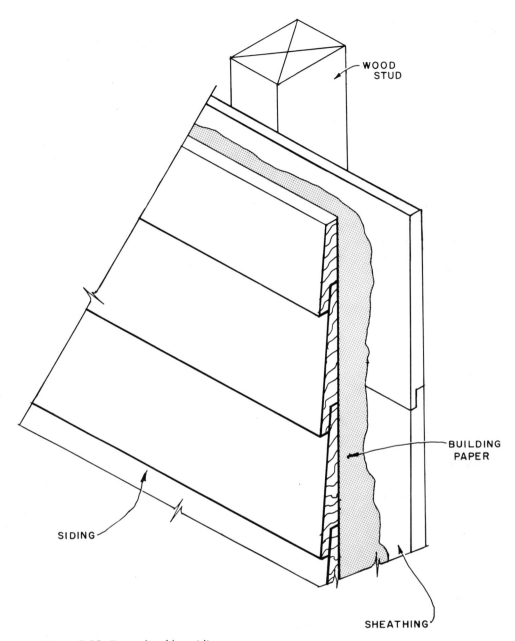

Figure 5-10. Example of lap siding.

square channel grooves that are 4 or 8 in. on center, usually referred to as "Early American pattern." Plywood is available in either smooth- or rough-sawn textures and is usually made of fir, cedar, or redwood. The plywood sheets with vertical batten boards are illustrated in Figure 5-12. Note that only exterior-grade plywood can be used in this type of application.

5. Brick veneers. This type of exterior facing consists of a single *wythe* of face brick attached to the structural wall of the project. This wall can consist of

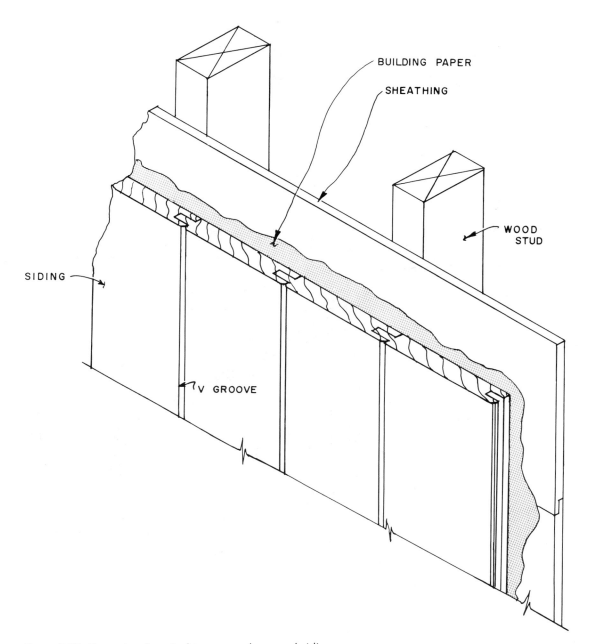

BUILDING PAPER

SHEATHING

WOOD STUD

SIDING

V GROOVE

Figure 5-11. Example of vertical tongue-and-grooved siding.

(a) Wood-framed stud wall with exterior wood of fiberboard sheathing. A waterproof membrane of building felt is required over the wood sheathing.

(b) Concrete block backup wall.

The method of tying the brick veneer to the structural wall is similar to the method of attachment to the foundation wall illustrated in Chapter 3.

There are many types of bricks with differing textures and colors that are available to suit any architectural design. The estimator will need to be able to determine the actual area to be covered by the veneer in order to determine

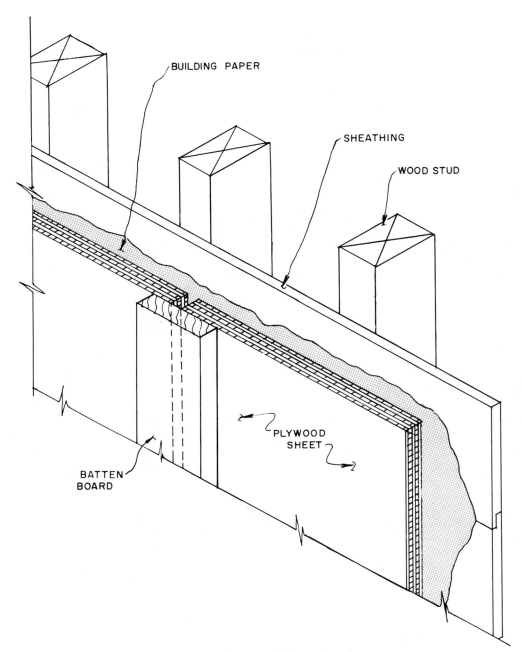

BUILDING PAPER

SHEATHING

WOOD STUD

PLYWOOD SHEET

BATTEN BOARD

Figure 5-12. Example of plywood sheets with batten boards.

the quantities to be used. The various items that must be determined include

    (a) Number of bricks needed. The standard brick size is $7\frac{5}{8} \times 3\frac{5}{8} \times 2\frac{1}{4}$ in. Three courses of brick will cover an 8×8-in. face area (using $\frac{3}{8}$-in. joints). So 1 ft^2 of wall to be covered will require $6\frac{3}{4}$ standard bricks. Bricks are purchased at a certain cost per 1000 (M) bricks.

    (b) Cement mortar will be needed to cement the brick veneer into a single unit. The amount of mortar needed will vary with the joint thickness. Based on the use of $\frac{3}{8}$-in. joints, we need about 9 ft³ of mortar for every 1000 bricks in the veneer.

(c) An allowance for the metal ties used to anchor the facing to the structural wall. These ties are most frequently corrugated strips of galvanized sheet metal that are nailed to the sheathing and imbedded into the mortar joints.

6. Field stone veneers. This type of finish is handled in much the same fashion as the brick veneers. It is economical if a source of supply is close to the project. Some factors for the estimator to consider are

(a) Stonework is estimated by the square foot of wall surface or by the cubic foot of stone needed. Ordinary stones 4 to 12 in. in diameter are used normally. The larger sizes would need to be split to form a wall facing.

(b) It will take about 1 ft³ of mortar to set about 4 ft³ of stone. This is due to the unevenness and the irregularity of the size of the stone.

7. Cut stone veneers. These are similar to the foregoing except that the stones are cut to fairly uniform thickness before being delivered to the job site. This makes this type more usable as a veneer. The usual thickness for veneer use is 4 in., and the height will usually vary from 1 to 15 in. Again, the amount of mortar needed will vary greatly with stone size, bed thickness, and so forth. A good rule of thumb is that 4 to 5 ft³ of mortar will be needed to lay 100 ft³ of cut stone.

As can be seen, the architect has many choices that can be used to achieve the desired finished product. Most of these finish materials are virtually maintenance free. Stucco finish may or may not require painting. Any type of wood siding will definitely require staining or painting at regular intervals. In addition, any wood trim, such as windows, doors, soffits, and fascia boards will require staining or painting regardless of the type of wall finish used. Painting will be covered in Chapter 7.

In order to estimate the quantity of exterior finish materials needed on a project, it is necessary to determine the total area to be covered. The following step-by-step procedure can be used:

1. Determine the gross area involved by taking the total length of the wall(s) involved and multiplying by the height of the wall.

2. Determine the total area of wall openings. This can be done by one of two methods:

(a) Summing up the actual areas of the involved wall openings.

(b) Using an average figure of 10 ft² for each opening (unless the opening is unusually large—like a garage door, for example). You would then multiply this by the number of openings.

The second method is simpler and is usually sufficiently accurate for estimating purposes.

3. The required area will be the gross area found in Step 1 minus the sum of the openings found in Step 2.

Chapter Six

Insulation and Interior Finishes

Having completed the discussion on excavation, foundations, house framing, waterproofing, drainage, backfilling, roofing, and exterior finishes, the contractor is ready to begin the interior finish work. The interior work sets the tone of the home—down-to-earth, functional, plush and elegant, and so forth.

The factors to be considered can be listed in the following general categories:

1. Insulation and related factors.

2. Interior finishes including
    (a) Interior walls and ceilings.
    (b) Millwork and other specialty items.
    (c) Finished floorings.

A substantial portion of the total cost of the home is involved in these items. It is interesting to note that in some areas, builders are signing contracts in which homeowners are permitted to do one or more of these items by themselves, thus reducing the total cost of the home project to the homeowner.

The present interest in and problems of energy conservation have caused builders to become increasingly involved with the subject of insulating all buildings to minimize energy (heating and cooling) losses. The amount of insulation required for each type of building depends, in great measure, on federal, state, or local government regulations and codes. In addition, the utility companies that provide the supply of energy being used will have their own requirements that must be observed by the builder. Whether the energy comes from natural gas, oil, or

Insulation and Related Factors

electricity, the supplies can become critical at any time. The conservation of energy must be considered a high priority factor in the erection of many types of buildings—including residences.

The amount of insulation required in a particular situation is based both on the type of material being used and on the thickness of the insulating mass. The thermal resistance of a given insulating material is directly proportional to the material's resistance to *heat flow*. This resistance is listed as the "R" value of the material. The "R" value is thus a measure of the insulating capabilities of the material. As the "R" value increases, so do the insulating capabilities. Many materials have insulating properties—wood, masonry, and even air. Two materials widely used to insulate buildings are styrofoam and fiberglass.

Styrofoam comes in rigid panels and is used with foundation walls and floor slabs. The fiberglass comes in *blanket rolls* or in *batts*. Figure 6-1 shows how the required level of insulation varies throughout the United States. The insulation values needed for ceilings, walls, and floors over unheated crawl spaces are indicated in the table included in Figure 6-1.

Fiberglass is the most common type of insulation used in residential construction, and also comes in blankets or batts. Both kinds are packaged in a compacted form to save on shipping space. The larger values required in some areas of the country can be obtained by applying one or more layers of the standard thicknesses as shown in Table 6-1. To obtain an *R*-38 value, for example, install two layers of 6½ in. (*R*-19) to get a total value thickness of 13 in. of fiberglass. The area covered by one roll of insulation will vary with the thickness. For example, each roll of 6½-in. insulation will cover 22.5 ft². In contrast, a roll of 3½-in. material will cover 45 ft².

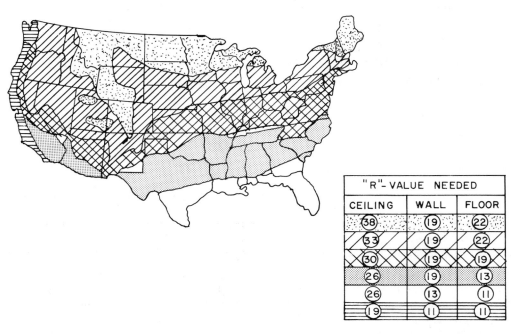

"R"- VALUE NEEDED		
CEILING	WALL	FLOOR
38	19	22
33	19	22
30	19	19
26	19	13
26	13	11
19	11	11

Figure 6-1.

**Table 6-1
Standard Thicknesses of
Fiberglass Insulation**

R Value	Thickness (in.)
R-30	8
R-22	7
R-19	$6\frac{1}{2}$
R-13	$3\frac{1}{2}$
R-11	$3\frac{1}{2}$

Example 6-1

The floor and roof of a small home each cover 1380 ft² of area.

(a) How many rolls of $6\frac{1}{2}$-in. insulation are needed to give the roof an R-38 value?

Solution: The values in Table 6-1 note that a $6\frac{1}{2}$-in. thick insulating mat gives an R-19 value. Therefore, the roof will need a double layer of $6\frac{1}{2}$-in. insulation (or 13-in. thickness).

$$\text{Number of rolls} = \frac{\text{feet}^2 \text{ of area}}{\text{feet}^2 \text{ per roll}} \times \text{number of layers}$$

$$= \frac{1380 \times 2}{22.5}$$

$$= 122.66$$

Answer: Use 123 rolls of $6\frac{1}{2}$-in. insulation

(b) What insulation is needed to give the floor an R-22 value?

Solution: Again, Table 6-1 shows that two layers of $3\frac{1}{2}$-in. insulation are needed for the required R value. Thus,

$$\text{Number of rolls} = \frac{\text{floor area}}{\text{Ft}^2 \text{ per roll}} \times \text{number of layers}$$

$$= \frac{1380}{45} \times 2$$

$$= 61.33$$

Answer: Use 61 rolls of $3\frac{1}{2}$-in. insulation

INTERIOR WALLS AND CEILINGS　　　**Interior Finishes**

As previously noted, the construction of a residence must follow a definite sequence to achieve the desired results. Thus, the builder cannot begin the interior finish work until certain items dealing with mechanical and electrical work are in place. Among the items are

1. Rough-in plumbing—concealed lines for water supply, sewers, and so forth, which are installed to the point where fixtures are to be attached. These lines should be installed (and tested) before they are covered by the interior finish.

2. Heating and air-conditioning ducts, which must be installed up to surface grills.

3. Electrical wiring, junction boxes, outlet boxes, and so forth, which are to be installed.

These items will be discussed in more detail in Chapters 9 and 10.

To begin to understand the estimating of finishes, it is necessary to review some of the more common types of finishes that are used on walls and ceilings. Among these are the following.

Lathing and Plaster

There are several steps required prior to and during the lathing operation before any plaster can be applied. First, a *ground strip* must be installed. This is a $\frac{3}{4} \times \frac{3}{4}$-in. wood strip applied to the walls and partitions around doors, windows, and at the floor. These serve as a guide for plastering to a given thickness. The ground strip is installed by the carpenter.

After the ground strip has been installed, it is necessary to reinforce all inside corners of walls and ceilings. One trademarked strip is called Cornerite, which is an expanded metal lath bent at a 90° angle. The legs are either 2 or 3 in. wide. The units come in standard lengths of 4 ft 0 in. and 8 ft 0 in.

Next, the sections of rocklath are applied. This material consists of a core of gypsum plaster with a paper covering on both faces. The standard units are 16 × 48 in. and are $\frac{3}{8}$ or $\frac{1}{2}$ in. in thickness. The $\frac{3}{8}$-in.-thick units are most commonly used in residential construction. Rocklath is bundled six units to a bundle if $\frac{3}{8}$ in. thick—otherwise, bundles contain four units of $\frac{1}{2}$-in.-thick pieces.

Rocklath is estimated (as are most wall and ceiling finishes) in square yards of surface to be covered. One unit of $\frac{3}{8}$-in.-thick rocklath will cover $5\frac{1}{3}$ ft^2, so six units per bundle will cover about 32 ft^2. Thus, about 3.6 yd^2 of wall surface will be covered by one bundle of units ($\frac{3}{8}$ in. thick).

Next, outside corner beads are installed at every outside corner of walls and at openings that do not receive wood trim. The bead is a strip of formed galvanized metal (sometimes combined with a strip of metal lath) placed on the corners before plastering to reinforce each corner and to provide a harder, more durable edge. The standard length of these strips is 8 ft 0 in. The items just discussed are shown in Figure 6-2.

The plaster comes next and is usually applied in two coats. The first coat (often referred to as the rough coat, brown coat, or scratch coat) is usually $\frac{3}{8}$ in. thick and consists of a gypsum and perlite mix. This mixture is usually purchased in 80-lb bags, and each bag will cover approximately $7\frac{1}{2}$ yd^2. Remember, wall surfaces are taken off in square yards of surface to be covered.

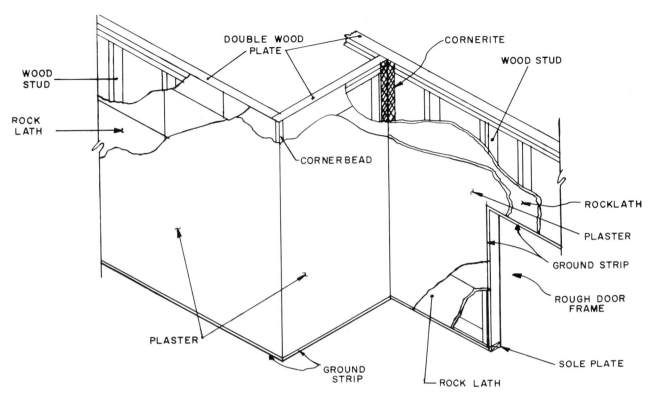

Figure 6-2.

The second, or finish, coat will vary slightly throughout the country. The basic finish coat will consist of a mixture of hydrated lime, a form of plaster of paris known as *gauging plaster,* and water. There are two types of lime: standard hydrated lime (quicklime), which must be soaked overnight, and double hydrated lime, which does not need to be soaked. The normal mix ratios are one part gauging plaster to five parts lime. This coat is applied in a $\frac{1}{16}$-in. thickness. For estimating purposes, normally expect to use 50 lb of gauging plaster and 250 lb of lime for every 100 yd^2 of surface area.

Drywall

Drywall construction uses gypsum plaster sheets with paper facing. The paper on the face is specially prepared to take the final decorating finish. This finish can be paint, wallpaper, or other wall coverings. These sheets have very shallow recesses formed along their longitudinal edges. When properly installed, these recesses are used for bedding a perforated paper tape in joint cement. The lather (installer of the drywall) will finish the joint cement so it is flush to the surface of the facing paper. This way, the joint will become invisible when decorating is completed. Drywall usually comes in $\frac{1}{4}$-, $\frac{3}{8}$-, $\frac{1}{2}$-, and $\frac{5}{8}$-in. thicknesses and 4 × 8-, 9-, 10-, or 12-ft surface dimensions. See Figure 6-3 for construction details on walls with drywall.

There is very little preparatory work required before applying drywall. Drywall sheets are applied directly to wood studs with as few joints as possible. The sheets are attached with 12$\frac{1}{2}$ gauge unfinished bright steel nails. The nails are

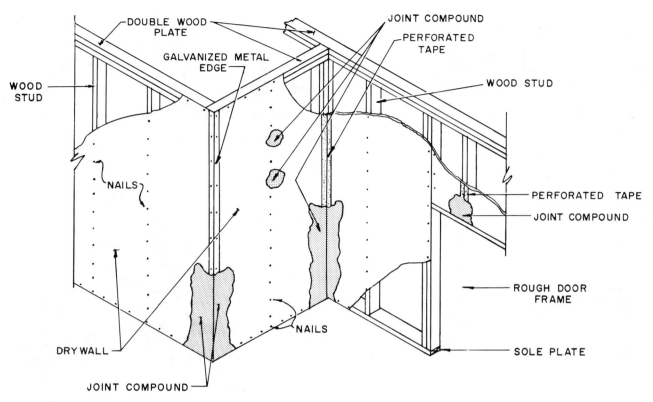

Figure 6-3.

placed ⅜ in. from the edge of the sheets and at each intermediate stud or ceiling joist. They should be spaced 7 in. apart on ceilings and 8 in. apart on walls. These nails should be driven slightly below the surface of the drywall to form a "dimple" or depression.

   note: Drywall surfaces are estimated in square feet.

After all the drywall has been nailed in place, all exterior corners are reinforced and protected with a formed galvanized metal edge. This is then nailed into place. These edges generally come in 8-ft 0-in. lengths.

   Now the lather is ready to tape the joints between the sheets of drywall and all interior corners of walls and wall/ceiling intersections. This tape is a perforated paper strip that is embedded into a premixed joint compound to reinforce the joints and provide a smooth surface. For estimating purposes most estimators will expect one roll of tape to cover approximately 700 ft² of drywall surface. The same joint compound used to embed the tape is also used to fill the dimples created at each nail and to provide a smooth surface at the exterior corners where the metal corner beads were installed. The joint compound is purchased in pre-mixed form and comes in 1- or 5-gal containers.

   Applying joint tape and compound is a two-step procedure. In the first step a layer of joint compound is spread over each of the joints and then the tape is pressed into the compound and worked in securely. In the second step, done after the first application of compound has dried thoroughly, a coating of joint compound is applied over the tape. The edges are smoothed out as much as possible with a trowel. During this application, the lather will fill in all of the dimples created when the wall sheets were nailed in place. After the second application of joint compound has dried thoroughly, the edges of every area that received the compound must be sanded to provide a smooth, flush surface. For estimating purposes a gallon of joint compound will cover approximately 300 ft² for the first coat and approximately 100 ft² for the second, or finish, coat.

It should be noted that there are places where special drywall must be used. Some areas that need special attention are

1. The wall between a residence and an adjoining garage, which needs fire-rated material. The drywall used here (usually $\frac{5}{8}$ in. thick) is applied on the garage side of the wall. If living quarters are above the garage, the fire-rated drywall should be used for the garage ceiling as well.

2. Kitchen and bathroom walls, which need drywall that is water resistant.

In some areas, the drywall has a foil facing on the outside to aid in the control of water vapor passing through the wall.

MILLWORK AND OTHER SPECIALTY ITEMS
Once the walls and ceilings have been lathed and finished, the next step in the construction process is to finish the wood trim and other detail interior finish work. This finish material is known as *millwork*. Millwork consists of

1. Interior doors.

2. Wood *casing* (trim) around windows and doors.

3. Wood base at the floor line of walls and partitions.

4. Closet shelves, clothes rods, and so forth.

In addition, some specialty items must be considered. Some of these items are

1. Bathroom vanities.

2. Kitchen cabinets.

3. Kitchen counters.

These items are all necessary in the completion of a residence and should be carefully entered in any cost estimate. See Figure 6-4 for some details of these.

Again, the foregoing items can vary drastically in cost. The estimator must be aware of all those items as they may greatly affect the cost of a particular project. We will now look at these items in a little more detail.

1. Interior doors are generally $1\frac{3}{8}$ or $1\frac{3}{4}$ in. thick, with the $1\frac{3}{8}$-in. size being the most common. Most interior doors are 6 ft 8 in. in height (the range is 6 ft 0 in. to 7 ft 0 in.). The width of the doors will vary from 1 ft 6 in. (small closets), to 2 ft 0 in. (bathrooms) and on up to 3 ft 4 in. for single doors. Most interior residential doors are of a hollow-core, flush-type door. Actually, many of the styles shown in Figure 5-5 are used in interior doors as well.

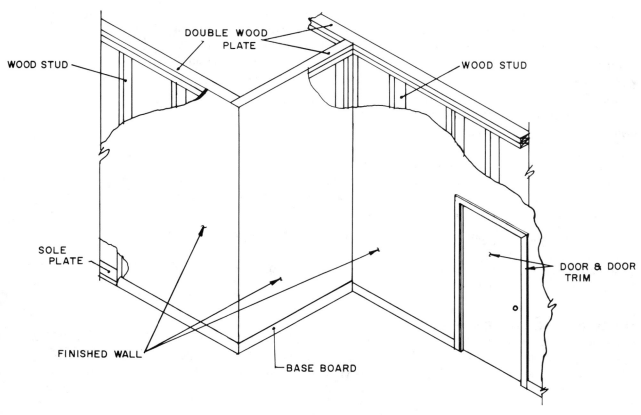

WOOD STUD

DOUBLE WOOD
PLATE

WOOD STUD

SOLE
PLATE

DOOR & DOOR
TRIM

FINISHED WALL

BASE BOARD

Figure 6-4.

As was the case for exterior doors (Chapter 5), interior doors are usually prehung in frames and are installed in the rough openings left for them in the wall-framing procedures discussed in Chapter 4 (Part II). The parts of the interior door frames are shown in Figure 6-5. Observe carefully the door schedule on project drawings. These interior doors can be

    (a) Single units in frames.
    (b) Bifolding doors in drywall-enclosed openings.
    (c) Louvered doors on closets.
    (d) Metal.
    (e) Sliding types, occasionally.

2. Wood casing is used to trim around openings, such as doors and windows. Note that the wood trim around interior doors is usually furnished with door frames discussed earlier. Some of the shapes of strip moldings used as trim are illustrated under "Wood Moldings" in the appendixes of this book.

3. Wood base at the floor line of walls and partitions is also shown in the appendixes. This material is furnished in stock lengths. The total length of each style of base molding is needed in preparing an estimate. Remember that all interior work is to be finished in some manner—stained, painted, and so forth.

4. Closet shelving and/or rods are to be furnished as shown on the drawings of the project. Each unit must be counted and included in the completed estimate.

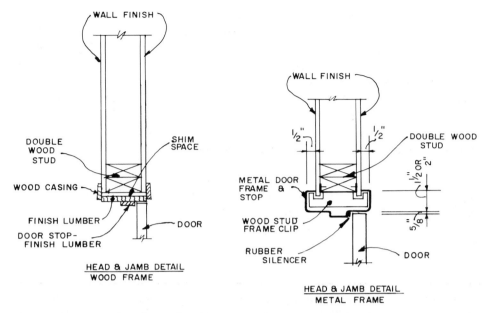

Figure 6-5. Interior door frame details.

5. Vanities and other bathroom items can reflect the luxuriousness of the project. Again, many styles are available—from simple wood-finish units to the opulence of marble.

6. Kitchen cabinets and counters are another area where the homeowner may make his/her wishes of paramount importance. The variety is very large and can be costly. Again, each unit should be listed on the estimate.

FINISHED FLOORING

As was the case with wall coverings or finishes, there are many types of floor coverings available to the owner and builder. The more commonly used materials for residential construction are carpeting, resilient flooring, wood flooring, and ceramic tile.

1. Carpeting and resilient flooring are in many ways decorative. Thus they will be covered in Chapter 7. The subflooring under these must be covered with underlayment to provide a smooth finish. *Underlayment* sheets are usually made of particle board $\frac{3}{8}$ in. thick. They are usually 4 ft 0 in. × 4 ft 0 in. The underlayment is nailed to the subflooring—making certain that the joints in the underlayment are staggered with the joints in the subflooring.

2. Wood flooring is frequently used in residential construction because of its distinctive natural appearance, excellent wearing qualities, moderate cost, underfoot comfort, and ease of installation and maintenance. Wood flooring can be used in all rooms above grade, with the possible exception of kitchens and bathrooms. Recently, with the advent of improved methods of protection from dampness, many builders have begun using wood flooring in rooms below grade as well.

Hardwood strip flooring has been and continues to be the most popular type used in residential construction. Strip flooring usually comes in 2¼-in.-wide strips, although it can be purchased in narrower or wider widths. Currently, homeowners are placing a greater demand on builders to provide plank flooring and parquet flooring. Plank floors are intended to simulate, or resemble, the floors of early colonial America. Plank floors are installed in random lengths and in widths varying from 3½ to 8 in. Strip and plank flooring are usually milled from nominal 1-in.-thick lumber. This gives a finished product that is $\frac{25}{32}$ in. thick. The other types again are more decorative—they are covered in Chapter 7.

3. Ceramic tile is often used in kitchens and bathrooms. The underlayment needed must be water resistant, and in some cases will need sheet-metal bases to prevent deterioration of the subflooring below.

Summary   The foregoing discussion shows the wide range of materials and methods of construction with which the estimator must be familiar. We can emphasize the estimating take off procedures in the following manner:

1. Insulation is taken off in square feet of surface area to be covered. The insulating value of materials varies directly with the thickness (mass) of the material being used.

2. Finishing of walls and ceilings can be separated into
(a) Rocklath base with applied plaster finishes, which are taken off in square yards of surface area to be covered. Plaster finishes can be applied in two or three layers. The number of layers will affect the labor costs in applying these finishes.
(b) Drywall construction, which is generally taken off in square feet of surface area being covered. If the decorative finish of this material (see Chapter 1) is paint, wallpaper, or fabric covering, the drywall must have joints and nail dimples finished flush with taping and joint compound. This builds up labor costs again. If the drywall is to be covered with paneling, the joint finishing will not be required.

3. Millwork is taken off by the linear feet of a given molding shape required. Be sure to allow for mitering of corners in determining the lengths needed.

4. Floor finishes are taken off in square feet of surface area to be covered. The estimator must be certain to coordinate all parts of the estimate—the floor framing, the structural subflooring, the floor finish, and the floor covering (if any) should be coordinated carefully.

The subjects covered in Chapter 6 are expanded on in Chapter 7. Together, these two chapters are the focus of attention by the homeowner. The builder must thus be careful to clear these areas with the homeowner to avoid making costly mistakes.

Chapter Seven

Decorating

Now that our building is watertight, all of the interior ceilings and walls have been finished, doors have been hung, and cabinets have been installed, we are ready to discuss decorating. Decorating and hardware, which will be discussed in Chapter 8, are usually the last items of work to be done prior to occupancy of the building.

In estimating materials, be sure to include the costs of drop cloths and other plastic covering to protect adjacent finished surfaces during these decorating procedures. Decorating can usually be separated into the following categories:

1. Exterior painting and staining.

2. Interior painting and varnishing.

3. Interior wall coverings.

4. Floor coverings.

Exterior Painting and Staining

There are some basic materials that should be considered for residential construction. These are wood, masonry, galvanized steel, aluminum, and plastic materials. There are certain standards that apply to decorating each of the materials listed above. These standards are as follows:

1. **Smooth wood siding, plywood, and trim.** You would need two coats of primer and one coat of finish paint. **note:** Textured plywood should be finished only with pigmented stains.

2. **Rough wood siding, shakes, and shingles.** You would need one coat each of primer and finish paint. Some manufacturers recommend thinning the finish paint and using it as the primer.

3. **Masonry or stucco.** You would need two coats of finish paint, but no

primer. With stucco, some contractors prefer to tint the finish coat of stucco with the final color. This eliminates the need to paint the surface.

4. Galvanized steel. You would need one primer coat and one finish coat. Again, substantial work (and time) can be saved by using prefinished steel siding material. A variety of colors and surface textures are available.

5. Aluminum siding. This is very popular in new home construction as well as in remodeling work. The finish is relatively maintenance free. It is also available in a series of different colors and textures.

6. Plastic siding. This is fairly new to the housing market. It seems to have very good credentials toward becoming a very popular surfacing material.

Local painting subcontractors may vary these practices based on their own experience. It would be wise to check with the painting subcontractor before making the material take off for a project.

When preparing a material take off for the exterior painting it is always a good idea to have a checklist of items that may require painting. The following is an example of such a checklist:

1. Wall surfaces. Calculate total area (square feet).

2. Windows. Count total number.

3. Doors. Count total number; list overhead doors separately and convert their measurements to square footage values.

4. Soffits. Calculate total area (square feet).

5. Gutters and downspouts. Calculate total length (linear feet).

6. Wood trim. Calculate total area (square feet).

7. Shutters. Count total number.

Keep in mind that when using more than one color, a separate take off must be made for each color.

After completing the calculations required in the checklist, the next step is to determine the quantities of paint to purchase. There are many guides available to help you. These guides have tables indicating the amount of coverage a gallon of paint will provide. One such guide is prepared and published by Painting and Decorating Contractors of America.[7]

Interior Painting and Varnishing

Interior painting and varnishing will include walls, ceilings, wood trim, doors, windows, window stops and stools, shelving, unfinished cabinets, and wood and concrete floors. Most painters prefer to follow a definite sequence to protect the work that has already been completed. The normal sequence is as follows:

Step 1: Wood trim. If the trim is to be painted, first apply an undercoat or primer. This should be allowed to dry completely. Then, apply a second coat, which

[7] *Estimating Guide 1982* (Falls Church, Va.: Painting and Decorating Contractors of America, 1982).

is usually a one-to-one ratio of undercoat and finish coat mixed together. If the trim is to be stained or left its natural color, first apply the stain (if required), followed by one coat of sealer, such as shellac. The finish coat, which would consist of one coat of paint or two coats of varnish, would not be applied until after all the walls and ceilings have been completed.

Step 2: Ceilings. Most painters will apply two coats of paint to either plaster or drywall ceilings—a primer coat and a finish coat. (With latex paints, the primer and finish coat will be of the same material).

Step 3: Walls. Walls are painted in the same manner as ceilings.

Step 4: Sanding. After the walls and ceilings have been painted, the wood trim must be sanded lightly as preparation for the finish coat of paint or varnish.

Step 5: Trim. The next step is to apply the finish coat(s) to the wood trim. For painted wood finishes, apply one coat of the finish enamel. Enamel is used because of its resistance to wear. If the project calls for stained or natural wood finish, one coat of gloss varnish can be applied. After the gloss varnish has dried completely, the surface must be sanded very lightly. After sanding, the final coat (which is a satin varnish) can be applied.

Step 6: Floors. The final step is to finish the floors of the project. Wood floors are either painted or varnished. Varnished floors are first rough sanded, then stained if required. After the stain has dried, apply one coat of sealer, such as shellac. Once the shellac has dried completely, the floor should be smoothed out with steel wool. Two coats of varnish are then applied. It is often advisable to use steel wool on the first coat of varnish. If the floors are to be painted, rough sand them first, then apply one coat of primer. After the primer has dried completely, apply two coats of the finish paint, allowing each coat to dry thoroughly.

Remember that there are many prefinished hardwood floors available. This will be discussed in detail later in this chapter.

Concrete floors, such as in garages or basements, should first be cleaned with water to eliminate all dust. Allow at least one day for them to dry. Then apply two coats of enamel, allowing each coat to dry completely. Remember to provide good ventilation when painting or varnishing and to allow for sufficient drying time.

When preparing a material take off for interior painting, it is a good idea to establish a checklist as was done for exterior finishes. The following is an example of such a checklist:

1. Wood trim.
   (a) Doors. Count total number and convert to square footage.

   note: count louvered doors separately.

   (b) Windows. Count total number.
   (c) Molding. Calculate linear footage.
   (d) Shelving. Calculate square footage (two sides).

2. Ceilings. Calculate square footage (usually for each room).

Table 7-1
Surface Areas of Rooms with 8-ft Ceilings[a]

Wall Dimensions	3	4	5	6	7	8	9	10	11	12	13	14	15	16	17	18	19	20	21	22	23	24	25
3	105	124	143	162	181	200	219	238	257	276	295	314	333	352	371	390	409	428	447	466	485	504	523
4	124	144	164	184	204	224	244	264	284	304	324	344	364	384	404	424	444	464	484	504	524	544	564
5	143	164	185	206	227	248	269	290	311	332	353	374	395	416	437	458	479	500	521	542	563	584	605
6	162	184	206	228	250	272	294	316	338	360	382	404	426	448	470	492	514	536	558	580	602	624	646
7	181	204	227	250	273	296	319	342	365	388	411	434	457	480	503	526	549	572	595	618	641	664	687
8	200	224	248	272	296	320	344	368	392	416	440	464	488	512	536	560	584	608	632	656	680	704	728
9	219	244	269	294	319	344	369	394	419	444	469	494	519	544	569	594	619	644	669	694	719	744	769
10	238	264	290	316	342	368	394	420	446	472	498	524	550	576	602	628	654	680	706	732	758	784	810
11	257	284	311	338	365	392	419	446	473	500	527	554	581	608	635	662	689	716	743	770	797	824	851
12	276	304	332	360	388	416	444	472	500	528	556	584	612	640	668	696	724	752	780	808	836	864	892
13	295	324	353	382	411	440	469	498	527	556	585	614	643	672	701	730	759	788	817	846	875	904	933
14	314	344	374	404	434	464	494	524	554	584	614	644	674	704	734	764	794	824	854	884	914	944	974
15	333	364	395	426	457	488	519	550	581	612	643	674	705	736	767	798	829	860	891	922	953	984	1015
16	352	384	416	448	480	512	544	576	608	640	672	704	736	768	800	832	864	896	928	960	992	1024	1056
17	371	404	437	470	503	536	569	602	635	668	701	734	767	800	833	866	899	932	965	998	1031	1064	1097
18	390	424	458	492	526	560	594	628	662	696	730	764	798	832	866	900	934	968	1002	1036	1070	1104	1138
19	409	444	479	514	549	584	619	654	689	724	759	794	829	864	899	934	969	1004	1039	1074	1109	1144	1179
20	428	464	500	536	572	608	644	680	716	752	788	824	860	896	932	968	1004	1040	1076	1112	1148	1184	1220

Source: *Estimating Guide 1982* of Painting and Decorating Contractors of America.
[a] Figures include side walls and ceilings in square feet.

3. Walls. Calculate square or linear footage based on a common ceiling height (usually for each room).

4. Hardwood floors. Calculate square footage.

5. Concrete floors. Calculate square footage.

Tables 7-1 and 7-2 show typical charts for determining areas of rooms with 8- and $8\frac{1}{2}$-ft ceilings. Similar charts are available for 7-, $7\frac{1}{2}$-, 9-, $9\frac{1}{2}$-, 10-, 11-, and 12-ft ceiling heights. The tables give the total wall area plus the ceiling area.

Example 7-1
Given a room 12 ft wide by 24 ft long, determine the total wall plus ceiling area. Ceiling height is 8 ft.

Solution: Using Table 7-1, find 12 ft at the left side. Next, follow across that row to the number below the 24-ft dimension.

Answer: Area = 864 ft²

As was the case for exterior painting, there are many guides available to us for determining the quantities of paint required for each item to be painted.

Interior Wall Coverings   In addition to painted surfaces for interior wall finishes, there are a number of other materials available to the owner and builder. Some of the more common

Table 7-2
Surface Areas of Rooms with 8½-Ft Ceilings[a]

Wall Dimensions	3	4	5	6	7	8	9	10	11	12	13	14	15	16	17	18	19	20	21	22	23	24	25
3	111	131	151	171	191	211	231	251	271	291	311	331	351	371	391	411	431	451	471	491	511	531	551
4	131	152	173	194	215	236	257	278	299	320	341	362	383	404	425	446	467	488	509	530	551	572	593
5	151	173	195	217	239	261	283	305	327	349	371	393	415	437	459	481	503	525	547	569	591	613	635
6	171	194	217	240	263	286	309	332	355	378	401	424	447	470	493	516	539	562	585	608	631	654	677
7	191	215	239	263	287	311	335	359	383	407	431	455	479	503	527	551	575	599	623	647	671	695	719
8	211	236	261	286	311	336	361	386	411	436	461	486	511	536	561	586	611	636	661	686	711	736	761
9	231	257	238	309	335	361	387	413	439	465	491	517	543	569	595	621	647	673	699	725	751	777	803
10	251	278	305	332	359	386	413	440	467	494	521	548	575	602	629	656	683	710	737	764	791	818	845
11	271	299	327	355	383	411	439	467	495	523	551	579	607	635	663	691	719	747	775	803	831	859	887
12	291	320	349	378	407	436	465	494	523	552	581	610	639	668	697	726	755	784	813	842	871	900	929
13	311	341	371	401	431	461	491	521	551	581	611	641	671	701	731	761	791	821	851	881	911	941	971
14	331	362	393	424	455	486	517	548	579	610	641	672	703	734	765	796	827	858	889	920	951	982	1013
15	351	383	415	447	479	511	543	575	607	639	671	703	735	767	799	831	863	895	927	959	991	1023	1055
16	371	404	437	470	503	536	569	602	635	668	701	734	767	800	833	866	899	932	965	998	1031	1064	1097
17	391	425	459	493	527	561	595	629	663	697	731	765	799	833	867	901	935	969	1003	1037	1071	1105	1139
18	411	446	481	516	551	586	621	656	691	726	761	796	831	866	901	936	971	1006	1041	1076	1111	1146	1181
19	431	467	503	539	575	611	647	683	719	755	791	827	863	899	935	971	1007	1043	1079	1115	1151	1187	1223
20	451	488	525	562	599	636	673	710	747	784	821	858	895	932	969	1006	1043	1080	1117	1154	1191	1228	1265

Source: Estimating Guide 1982 of Painting and Decorating Contractors of America.
[a] Figures include side walls and ceilings in square feet.

materials used are wallpaper and vinyl wall coverings, prefinished wood paneling, and ceramic tile.

1. Wallpaper is a wall covering consisting of a paper-like material, usually decorated in colors, which is pasted or otherwise applied to the walls or ceilings of rooms. Fabric-backed wall coverings are similar to wallpaper except that they are generally much heavier and much more durable. When applying a vinyl covering, you must make sure to use the proper adhesives. Vinyl wall coverings and their adhesives must contain mildew inhibitors. Both papers and vinyls can be purchased in prepasted materials.

When estimating the material requirements for wallpaper or vinyl fabric, it is necessary to determine the square footage of walls, and ceilings if necessary, or linear footage of wall for common ceilings. This area is to be calculated for each room or group of rooms destined to receive the same material.

After calculating the square footage, divide that number by 30 to determine the number of single rolls of paper or vinyl required. A single roll of paper or vinyl usually comes in 27-in. widths and will cover 36 ft^2; therefore, dividing the area by 30 automatically allows 6 ft^2 of waste per roll. This will account for leftover ends, small cutouts, and normal pattern match. Remember, some papers with an unusual match pattern will require greater allowance for waste. Table 7-3 shows a handy chart that can be used to determine the number of single rolls required for various size rooms.

After determining the number of single rolls required, deduct one single roll of wall material for every two average-size doors or windows, or for every 36 ft^2 of opening. When measuring for yard goods with no match such as wide vinyls, measure the area as above, take out for openings, and add 10% for waste.

When preparing the material take off, be sure to include such items as num-

Table 7-3
Paperhanging Walls and Ceilings

Size of Room	Single Rolls of Side Wall Height of Ceiling			Yards of Border	Rolls of Ceiling
	8 ft	9 ft	10 ft		
4 × 8	6	7	8	9	2
4 × 10	7	8	9	11	2
4 × 12	8	9	10	12	2
6 × 10	8	9	10	12	2
6 × 12	9	10	11	13	3
8 × 12	10	11	13	15	4
8 × 14	11	12	14	16	4
10 × 14	12	14	15	18	5
10 × 16	13	15	16	19	6
12 × 16	14	16	17	20	7
12 × 18	15	17	19	22	8
14 × 18	16	18	20	23	8
14 × 22	18	20	22	26	10
15 × 16	15	17	19	23	8
15 × 18	16	18	20	24	9
15 × 20	17	20	22	25	10
15 × 23	19	21	23	28	11
16 × 18	17	19	21	25	10
16 × 20	18	20	22	26	10
16 × 22	19	21	23	28	11
16 × 24	20	22	25	29	12
16 × 26	21	23	26	31	13
17 × 22	19	22	24	28	12
17 × 25	21	23	26	31	13
17 × 28	22	25	28	32	15
17 × 32	24	27	30	35	17
17 × 35	26	29	32	37	18
18 × 22	20	22	25	29	12
18 × 25	21	24	27	31	14
18 × 28	23	26	28	33	16
20 × 26	23	28	28	33	17
20 × 28	24	27	30	34	18
20 × 34	27	30	33	39	21

Source: Estimating Guide 1982 of Painting and Decorating Contractors of America.

ber of yards of border material and wheat paste for paper and vinyl adhesives. Normally, 5 lb of wheat paste will apply approximately 65 single rolls of paper. One gallon of vinyl adhesive will apply up to 10 yd, or 130 ft^2, of heavy-weight vinyl. For estimating, this equals approximately four single rolls.

Example 7-2
(a) How many single rolls of wallpaper will be needed for the walls of the room of Example 7-1?
(b) If the indicated room has a 6-ft × 6-ft 8-in. sliding door, a window 5 ft

wide × 3 ft 8 in. high and an archway 6 ft × 6 ft 8 in., how many rolls of paper can be deducted?

(a) Solution: Area from Example 7-1 = 864 ft² (includes ceiling)
Subtract area of ceiling (12 × 24) −288

576 ft² (area of walls alone)

One single roll covers 30 ft²

Number of rolls = 576 ÷ 30 = 19.2

Answer: Use 19 single rolls

(b) Solution: Areas to be deducted

Sliding Door: 6 × 6.67 = 40.0 ft²
Archway: 6 × 6.67 = 40.0 ft²
Window: 5 × 3.67 = 18.4 ft²
Total = 98.4 ft²

Rolls to be deducted = 98.4 ÷ 36

= 2.7 rolls

Answer: Deduct 2 rolls so that total number required = 17 rolls

2. Prefinished wood paneling is usually manufactured from hardwood species. Some of the softwood species, such as California redwood, knotty pine, and western red cedar, are also used for interior paneling. These softwoods are usually not prefinished. Other manufacturers assemble softwood veneers into paneling plywood with surface textures such as embossing, striations, or relief grain. Some manufacturers produce softwood or hardwood panels with printed overlays simulating hardwood grains.

These prefinished wood panels are usually $\frac{1}{4}$ in. thick and are available in 4 × 8-ft sheets. Special sizes such as 4 × 7 ft or 4 × 10 ft are usually available by special order. Paneling should be applied over a drywall surface. If paneling is used, it is not necessary to tape the drywall joints or to fill nail dimples, nor is it necessary to provide exterior corner bead. Paneling is usually applied with an adhesive (applied from tubes) and then nailed with colored finish nails.

When preparing the material take off for paneling, calculate the total square footage required and convert this area into number of sheets. Also determine the total number of linear feet of outside corners to purchase. In addition, in cases where the paneling is not applied the full height of the wall, determine the amount of edging (or top cap) required. At times, wood casing and base and ceiling moldings are available in matching prefinished material. If these are listed, do not forget to deduct them from the previous moldings list in which they were listed as unfinished.

Example 7-3
Looking again at the room in Example 7-1, determine the number of sheets of wood paneling needed.

Solution: On a square foot basis, each sheet covers 4 × 8 ft, or 32 ft²

Wall area (Example 7-2) = 576 ft²

Number of sheets = 576 ÷ 32

Answer: = 18.0 sheets

You can verify by using the room perimeter.

Room perimeter = 2 × 12 ft + 2 × 24 ft

= 72 linear ft

Number of sheets = 72 ÷ 4 ft/sheet

Answer: = 18.0 sheets

note: The door and archway would require deducting at least one panel each to reduce the total required to 16 sheets.

3. Ceramic tile is made from nonmetallic minerals fired at high temperatures and manufactured in modular sizes (individual tiles) that make the installation easier. These glazed wall tiles are typically $4\frac{1}{4}$-in. units and are $\frac{5}{16}$ in. thick. However, they are available in other sizes as well. The tile is manufactured in plain and scored surfaces, in bright, matte, and crystalline finishes, and in hand-decorated and sculptured designs.

Tile is generally applied over drywall or plaster finishes. Remember, when used over tubs and on shower walls the drywall must be of a waterproof type. As with paneling, it is not necessary to tape drywall joints, fill nail dimples, or add corner bead behind tile walls. The tiles are secured to the wall with a waterproof adhesive. Edges of every tile installation, such as tops of wainscoats and vertical edges at corners, should be finished with a bullnose tile. After the tiles have all been installed, and the adhesive has thoroughly dried, the joints (see Table 7-4) between each tile must be grouted with mortar or silicone grout.

Special cove base tiles are also available, although they are not usually used in residential construction. Special tile pieces such as soap dishes, paper holders, towel bar posts, and other accessories for bathroom uses are also available.

The material take off for ceramic tile will require the determination of square footage for standard tile pieces. Also increase the area approximately 10% to account for waste. It will also be necessary to determine the linear footage of bullnose tile for unfinished edges. If special sections such as soap dishes are required, they should be listed on the estimate sheets. Do not forget to include adhesive and grout.

Floor Coverings

As was the case with wall coverings or finishes, there are many types of floor coverings available to the owner and builder. The more commonly used materials for residential construction are carpeting, resilient flooring, wood flooring, and ceramic tile.

**Table 7-4
Recommended Joint Widths for
Ceramic Tile**

Tile Description	Joint Width (in.)
Mosaic tile[a]	
$2\frac{3}{16}$ in.^{2} or smaller	$\frac{1}{32}$ to $\frac{1}{8}$
Paver and special tile	
$2\frac{3}{16}$ to $4\frac{1}{4}$ in.^{2}	$\frac{1}{16}$ to $\frac{1}{4}$
6 in.^{2} and larger	$\frac{1}{4}$ to $\frac{1}{2}$
Quarry tile	
3 to 6 in.^{2}	$\frac{1}{8}$ to $\frac{3}{8}$
6 in.^{2} and larger	$\frac{1}{4}$ to $\frac{1}{2}$
Glazed tile	
3 in.^{2} and larger	$\frac{1}{8}$ to $\frac{1}{2}$

[a] Mosaic tile is usually mounted on 12 × 12-in. sheets, so joint widths are predetermined by manufacturer.

1. Carpeting can be selected and specified according to how it is made and of what it is made. The term broadloom refers to the typical carpet product that is over 6 ft wide. Most carpets, except the rubber-backed loomed type, are available in widths of 9, 12, 15, and sometimes 18 ft. The most common and generally used width is 12 ft 0 in. The length of each roll varies with each manufacturer. Loomed carpet generally is made in $4\frac{1}{2}$-ft widths with a $\frac{3}{16}$-in. attached rubber cushioning.

Modern carpet can be classified according to its construction as tufted, woven, or knitted. Carpet may also be selected according to the pile fibers of which the yarns are made, which include wool, nylon, acrylics, polyester, and polypropylene.

As a general rule carpeting should not be used in service areas, such as utility, laundry, or furnace rooms. However, you will undoubtedly find the occasion where carpeting may be required in the kitchen. Kitchen carpeting, when desired, will normally be a glued-down, flat-surfaced carpet that is easily cleaned. Today's homes frequently show carpeting in bathrooms as well.

All carpeting should be installed over cushioning or padding to increase resilience and durability. Sometimes cushioning is bonded to the carpet (loomed carpet). Separate cushionings are made of cellular rubber, jute and hair, or hair felt. One thing to remember is never to use rubber cushioning over radiant-heated floors.

Carpeting is usually purchased by the square yard. Before beginning a material take off there are a number of things that must be considered. First, determine the type of floor that is to receive the carpeting. This has a great deal to do with the choice of cushioning and the type of carpeting to be used. Second, determine the amount of use the carpeting will receive.

Areas subject to high wear (great amounts of foot traffic) should be provided with a carpet that has a high resistance to wear. Family rooms and hallways are prime examples of high-wear areas. Finally, caution should be used when estimating for the materials in order to provide as few seams as possible and also to make every attempt to place the seams in areas where the least traffic will occur. It is not always possible to eliminate all seams in traffic areas but the contractor should try to minimize the number as much as possible.

When preparing the material take off, determine where the seams will be placed and then determine the number of square yards of carpeting required (remember, 1 yd² contains 9 ft²). Generally, some waste will occur when ordering materials this way.

Remember to include the cushioning when estimating materials. Determine the linear footage of tack strip required to hold the edges of carpet in place along walls as well. Finished edge strips at areas when the carpeting stops, such as doorways, will also be needed.

2. Resilient flooring is a class of flooring products distinguished by resilience and dense, nonabsorbent surfaces. A variety of decorative colors, patterns, and textures are available in sheet or tile form.

Resilient flooring is manufactured in different thicknesses and from a variety of ingredients. Tile sizes range from 9 in.² to 36 in.² with the 12 × 12 in. being the most popular. Sheet forms are generally made in 6-in. widths. Matching resilient accessories such as wall base, thresholds, stair treads, and feature strips are available.

Resilient flooring is classified according to ingredients, such as asphalt, vinyl, vinyl asbestos, rubber, cork, and linoleum. Those most commonly used in residential construction are vinyl–asbestos tiles and sheet vinyl.

Rubber or vinyl wall bases are available in 2½-, 4-, and 6-in. heights in several types. The most common types are

1. Straight type, which is a simple vertical strip with a rounded top.

2. Set on cove type, which sits on floor tile and has a curved cove bottom with a rounded top.

3. Butt cove type, which has a curved bottom that butts up against the floor tile.

Vinyl base is available in 50-ft coils or in 4-ft lengths. Rubber base normally is available in 4-ft lengths only. Exterior and interior corners of rubber base are usually premolded. Vinyl base is more flexible; therefore, corners are usually field bent. Finished edge end stops are available in vinyl and rubber.

Vinyl and rubber stair treads are readily available and come in lengths ranging from 3 to 12 ft. Thresholds are also available in vinyl or rubber and come in 2¾- or 5⅛-in. widths, ½ in. high. Standard lengths are 3 or 4 ft.

When preparing estimates for resilient flooring, it is necessary to calculate the total square footage required. Remember, sheet goods are purchased by number of square feet, but tile is purchased by the carton (one carton of 12 × 12-in. tile will cover 45 ft²). The estimate will also need to include base materials, thresholds, and stair treads or nosings. In addition, remember to include adhesive for applying resilient flooring.

3. Wood flooring can be found in several forms. This text has already discussed wood strip flooring in Chapter 6. Several other forms serve as decoration as well as flooring. This section will discuss the subject further.

Parquet flooring is available in many styles such as blocks or strips of uniform length. Parquet flooring usually comes in blocks of 6 × 6 in., 9 × 9 in., or 12 × 12 in. and is usually ½ in. thick. This type of flooring is generally used where a formal appearance is requested. Figure 7-1 shows the three styles already discussed.

All hardwood flooring, strip plank, and block are readily available in a prefinished product ready for use immediately after installation. The terms hardwood and softwood do not necessarily signify the degree of hardness of the wood. Actually, some softwoods are much harder than some of the hardwoods. The

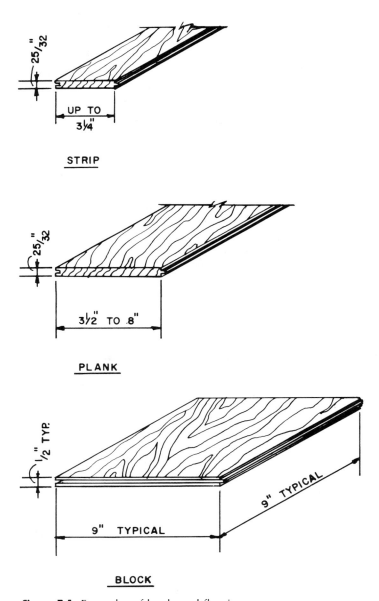

STRIP

PLANK

BLOCK

Figure 7.1. Examples of hardwood flooring.

distinction is that hardwoods come from trees having broad leaves, whereas softwoods are obtained from trees that bear needles and cones. Approximately 12 types of wood are commonly used for flooring. Of these types, hardwoods account for 80% of the residential flooring. The reason for the popularity of hardwoods is basically greater wear resistance and their appearance.

The most commonly used hardwood is oak, which accounts for better than 90% of the hardwood flooring made. Other hardwoods commonly used are maple, beech, birch, and pecan. The most often used softwood is southern pine, which exceeds 50% of the softwood flooring made. The second most popular is Douglas fir, with approximately eight other species being used in less than 10% of all softwood flooring. With this background, this text will limit its coverage to hardwood flooring.

Hardwood flooring is manufactured to a standard pattern (see Figure 7-2), producing flooring that is side matched and end matched. Standard tongue-and-grooved strip flooring is generally installed over wood subfloors, or possibly over wood sleepers, and is attached by blind (concealed) nailing at the intersection of the tongue and shoulder. Figure 7-3 indicates the method of nailing. The flooring strips are of random length, and the proportion of short pieces depends on the grade. Uniform short lengths of tongue-and-grooved flooring, known as single-slat flooring, also can be installed with a pasty-like adhesive (mastic).

Traditionally, hardwood flooring is packaged and sold in bundles containing pieces of more or less the same length, 6 in. longer or shorter than the nominal length.

Flooring boards wider than $3\frac{1}{4}$ in. are referred to as planks. Sometimes, random plank installations include both plank and strip-sized boards. Plank floors are installed in end-to-end random pattern with end joints staggered and are secured with nails or screws. Contemporary plank flooring is installed with wood screws in the face of each plank, and the screws are covered with wood plugs to give the

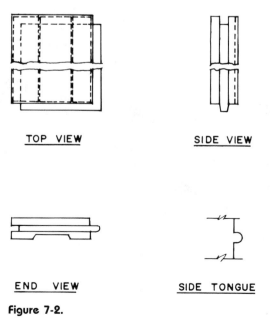

TOP VIEW   SIDE VIEW

END   VIEW   SIDE TONGUE

Figure 7-2.

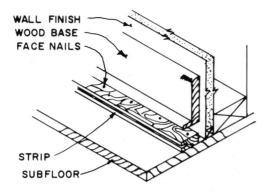

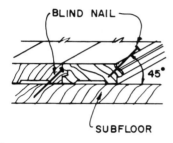

Figure 7-3.

appearance of the peg installation of colonial America. Narrower, strip-sized boards are usually secured by blind nailing.

Plank flooring is available in end- and side-matched boards in the same thickness as strip flooring. Because the cross-grain dimension in plank flooring is greater than in strip flooring, it is affected more by humidity. Plank edges are often eased, or beveled, to accentuate joints and avoid unsightly loose joints.

Parquet floors consist of individual strips of wood (single slats) or larger units (blocks) that are installed in a definite geometric pattern. The blocks are manufactured either by laminating several hardwood veneers or by tying several solid hardwood strips into a standard-sized unit to ease installation. Unlike strip and plank floors, parquet flooring is generally installed with a mastic. Oak is by far the most commonly used species for pattern floors. However, other species are used as well—quite often a mixture of hardwood species is positioned at random in a single block.

Block flooring is manufactured in several basic types, such as solid-unit block, laminated plywood block, and slat block (also referred to as mosaic parquet hardwood slat). Solid-unit block uses short lengths of strip flooring joined together edgewise to form square units. In laminated block, three or more plies of veneer are bonded with adhesive. Slat block uses narrow slats of wood that have been preassembled into larger units to assist in the installation. Figure 7-4 indicates some of the various patterns of block flooring that are available to the builder.

When preparing the material estimate for hardwood flooring, it is necessary to determine the areas (square footage) involved for each type of flooring. Strip

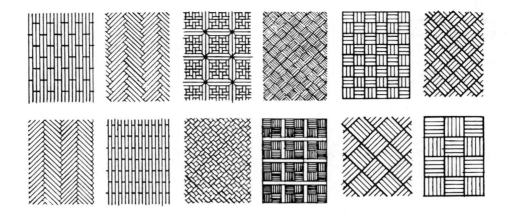

POPULAR SINGLE-SLAT   TYPICAL SLAT BLOCK   TYPICAL UNIT-BLOCK
PATTERNS ACHIEVED WITH   PATTERNS. PICKETS FORMING   PATTERNS ; HEAVY LINES
UNIFORM- LENGTH PRECUT   BORDERS MAY BE PART OF   SHOW INDIVIDUAL BLOCKS,
WOOD STRIPS.   BLOCK OR SEPARATE.   LAID IN SQUARE OR DIAGONAL
                                                         PATTERNS.

Figure 7-4.

flooring is purchased by the board foot; therefore, the area must be converted to board feet based upon the material size being used. In addition, strip flooring creates a great deal of waste because of the end-match conditions. Because of this waste consideration, add 35 to 40% to the area calculations before calculating the number of board feet. Plank flooring and parquet or block flooring are generally purchased by the square foot. Each of these types will result in very little waste; therefore, add 5 to 10% to the area calculations when determining the amount of material required. Because of manufacturers' various sizing methods, it is recommended that the estimator note on the take off sheets that the quantity listed is either actual coverage or includes a specific percentage of waste.

   4. Ceramic tiles that are used on floors can generally be separated into three categories—ceramic mosaic tile, which usually comes in 1 × 1-in. units; paver tile, which is similar to mosaic tile but comes in sizes 4 × 4 in. or larger; and quarry tile, which is typically a 6 × 6-in. unglazed clay unit. In addition, there are rustic tiles on the market that are handmade ceramic tiles. These tiles are very common in the California area and are gaining popularity throughout the country. The common sizes for these rustic tiles are 6 × 6 in., 8 × 8 in., and 10 × 10 in. with thicknesses from $\frac{1}{2}$ to $\frac{3}{4}$ in.

   Mosaic tiles are generally produced from porcelain or natural clay. They are available in either a glazed or a matte finish. The individual tiles are generally face or back mounted to form larger units for ease in handling and installation. These larger units are usually 12 in.² Mosaic tiles are normally $\frac{1}{4}$ in. thick.

   Quarry tile is an unglazed tile with a surface area of 9 in.² or more and with a thickness of $\frac{1}{2}$ to $\frac{3}{4}$ in. Typical tile sizes are 3 × 6 in., 6 × 6 in., 4 × 8 in., 6 × 9 in., and 9 × 9 in. Paver tile is similar in appearance to quarry tile. It is similar in composition to mosaic tile but is usually $\frac{1}{2}$ in. thick and much larger, 6 in.² or more. Typical tile sizes are 4 × 4 in., 4 × 6 in., 6 × 6 in., and 4 × 8 in.

In residential construction most tile work will be installed over wood sub-floors or directly to concrete floors. Wood subfloors are subject to greater deflection (bending), expansion, and contraction than concrete floors. With this in mind, it is important for the tile installation to be either completely isolated from the subfloor or bonded to the subfloor with a tile-setting material that can resist movement without breaking the bond. Most residential work will utilize a bonded method of installation. A typical bonded thin-set installation uses epoxy mortar or epoxy adhesives. However, most of the tile work will be restricted to small areas such as bathrooms; therefore, also consider the use of organic adhesives.

After installing the tile in the adhesive and maintaining the proper joints as indicated in Table 7-3, grout the joints between the tiles. Grouting should be delayed for at least 16 hr. Grout should be cleaned off the face of the tile as soon as possible to prevent it from hardening.

There are some special considerations to remember when installing tile floors. If thick tile (or setting beds) is used, it may be necessary to provide a transition edge at adjacent floor area to compensate for changes in elevation. This can be accomplished at doors with a threshold of marble, slate, or even hard-wood. To install tile in a shower receptor, it will be necessary to install a water-proof membrane or pan under the tile, and the tile must be sloped $\frac{1}{4}$ in. per foot to the drain.

When preparing the material take off for floor tile, determine the square footage required for each type of tile. Add approximately 10% to the area for waste. Special items such as thresholds must be included. Finally, do not forget the adhesive and grout.

Chapter Eight

Hardware

In the preceding chapters, a step-by-step discussion of the various phases of house construction has been followed. Each chapter has dealt with the individual portions of residential construction, beginning with clearing the site and continuing through interior decorating in Chapter 7. The hardware requirements for residential construction are the next element to be covered. Hardware can best be described as metal products used in construction. It can be further categorized as rough hardware or finish hardware.

Rough hardware usually includes those items that are meant to be concealed when the final finish work has been completed. Some of the common items that are generally considered as a part of rough hardware are

1. Anchor bolts, washers, and nuts.

2. Joist hangers (beam hangers)—see Figure 8-1.

3. Metal bridging—see Figure 8-2.

4. Truss splice plates, flitch plates, and tie-down plates (to resist wind up-lift)—see Figures 8-3 and 8-4.

5. Nails and wood screws.

6. Miscellaneous metal framing accessories, such as post bases and cap connectors—see Figures 8-5 and 8-6.

7. Package receivers and mail chutes.

8. Ventilating louvers and roof vents.

9. Pocket frames and track for recessed sliding doors.

Finish hardware, or architectural hardware, has a definite finished appearance as well as a function. It is usually associated with doors, windows, and cabinetry and may be considered part of the decorative treatment of a room or building. The more common items normally associated with finish hardware are listed in the following manner:

1. Exterior and interior door hardware, including
(a) Hinges—sometimes referred to as butts.
(b) Locksets and latchsets.
(c) Sliding door track and pulls.
(d) Folding door track and pulls.
(e) Screen and storm doors.
(f) Special trim items.

2. Window hardware, including
(a) Operating devices—vary with the type of window used.
(b) Trim items.

3. Miscellaneous hardware, including
(a) Cabinets.
(b) Drawers.
(c) Closet hardware.

Rough Hardware

In most residential construction the quantities of rough hardware items will be limited. Some of the items that are listed in the introduction to this chapter may not even be used in most homes. Others, such as nails, will always be used. We will now look at each type of item.

ANCHOR BOLTS

Anchor bolts were first discussed in Chapter 3 along with the foundation material take off. The discussion at that time was limited to the installation of anchor bolts in foundation walls or footings for the purpose of securing the sill plates for stud-wall construction. There are homes built with masonry walls, rather than stud walls, and wood roof construction. In a case such as this, the contractor must provide anchor bolts at the top of the masonry wall.

These bolts secure a wall plate, which is used to support the roof rafters or trusses. When estimating anchor-bolt materials, it is necessary to count the number of bolts required and determine the length of each (usually this length will be given on the drawings). Do not forget to provide nuts and washers for each bolt.

JOIST HANGERS

In Chapter 4, floor joists and the methods of supporting them were discussed. Figure 4-7 includes a diagram that indicates a metal joist hanger. Figure 8-1 shows some of the different styles of joist hangers available. Joist hangers are usually made from 16- or 18-gauge galvanized steel. If the drawings and specifications for the home you plan to build call for joist hangers, or if their inclusion is by your own choice, they will ordinarily be used only at an interior supporting girder. Whenever possible, the joist should sit on top of a bearing wall or girder. How-

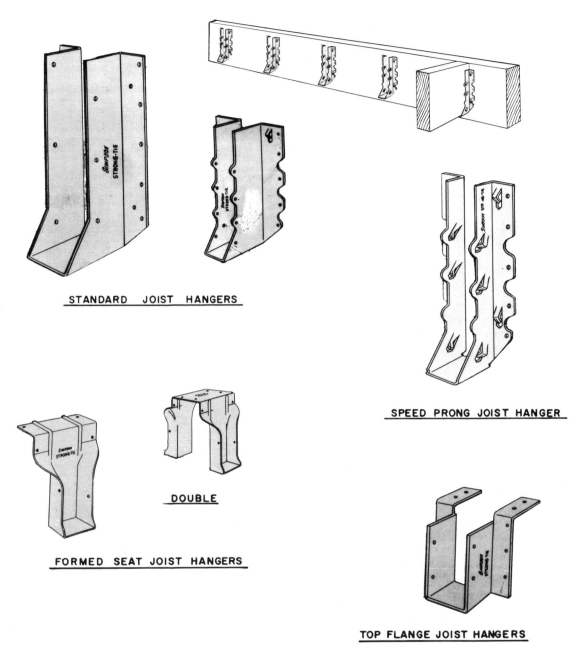

STANDARD   JOIST   HANGERS

SPEED PRONG JOIST HANGER

DOUBLE

FORMED SEAT JOIST HANGERS

TOP FLANGE JOIST HANGERS

Figure 8-1. Examples of joist hangers (courtesy of Simpson Company, San Leandro, California 94577).

ever, if you need joist hangers at girders, the simplest way of estimating materials is to review your joist take off and provide one joist hanger for each joist end supported by the girder.

METAL BRIDGING

Bridging was also discussed in Chapter 4. Figure 4-9 indicates three types of bridging. Metal bridging can be used whenever herringbone or strap bridging is

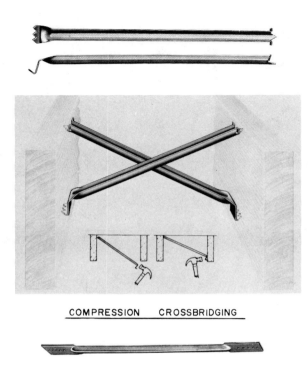

COMPRESSION   CROSSBRIDGING

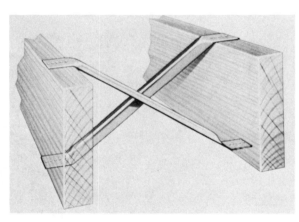

JOIST   BRIDGING

Figure 8-2. Examples of metal bridging (courtesy of Cleveland Steel Specialty Company, Cleveland, Ohio 44137).

called for. In estimating materials for metal bridging, keep in mind that two pieces are needed for each joist space with herringbone bridging and one piece is needed for each joist space with strap bridging.

To determine the total number of pieces needed, calculate the total number of joist spaces and the number of rows of bridging. The total number of pieces required will be the number of rows multiplied by the number of spaces. This figure is then multiplied by the number of pieces per space. Figure 8-2 indicates two methods of installing herringbone bridging.

TRUSS SPLICE PLATES, FLITCH PLATES, AND TIE-DOWN PLATES

Truss splice plates, flitch plates, and tie-down plates are items that will not always be a part of residential construction. Truss splice plates are the pieces of metal used to hold together the individual wood members of a truss. (Some manufacturers may use plywood.) They are usually made up by punching a piece of sheet metal to form a series of projecting, pointed edges that are pressed into the sides of the wood members. They may also be flat sheet metal with holes to receive nails. Figure 8-3 shows typical splice plates and the way a truss is held together. Trusses are generally purchased as prefabricated units. Therefore, the project material take off would not include individual splice plates. However, if for some reason the contractor wants to build trusses for a project, splice plates for every joint will be needed.

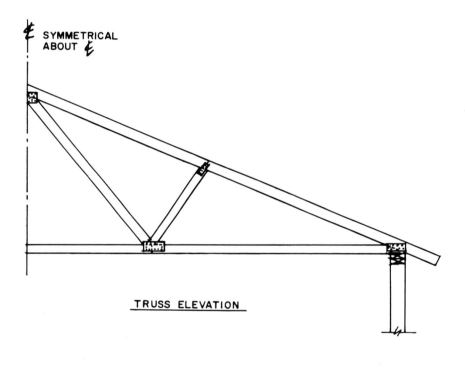

TRUSS ELEVATION

SPLICE PLATES

Figure 8-3.

The use of flitch plates was discussed in Chapter 4. Remember that a flitch-plated beam is made up of a combination of wood members and one or more steel plates. One thing to be aware of when estimating materials for flitch-plated beams is the need for bolts to hold the wood and steel together to make the member act as one unit.

Metal tie-down plates are designed to provide wind and seismic ties for trusses and rafters. They are also used for general tie purposes such as when one wood member crosses another. They are usually made from 18-gauge metal and are bent to standard shapes (see Figure 8-4).[8] Each shape is designed for a different capacity to resist uplift.

NAILS AND WOOD SCREWS

Nails and wood screws, particularly nails, are two items of rough hardware that will be required for every home being built. There is no set rule of thumb for determining the quantities required. As experience is gained in building and estimating, the estimator will most likely obtain a "feel" for the quantities required.

There are endless varieties and styles of nails available. Each phase of house construction will require specific nails that are intended for a definite use. For example, the contractor will not use the same type, or size, nails to secure roof shingles as he/she would use to secure the sheathing on the stud walls. Any good estimator should have an adequate knowledge of nails, screws, and any other type of fastener. He/she should continually be keeping up-to-date with the current methods for securing members of structures together.

There are three basic types of nails—common, finishing, and casing. Nails are purchased by weight, and are referred to by size and style, such as 4d common nails. Table 8-1 gives an example of various size nails and the approximate number of nails per pound. There are similar tables available for other types of nails. There are also tables available that indicate the type of nail to use for different types of work with a rough estimate of quantities.

The term "16d common" nail is referred to verbally as a "16 penny" common nail. This term probably originates from the term "pennyweight."

Rough framing usually requires 16d common and smaller nails. Common nails are the heaviest in shank and have a flat head. Box nails are thinner and also have a flat head. They are usually used for nailing boards and plywood. Finishing nails are thinner and have finer heads. They are usually used for finishing work because the small heads allow for countersinking. Casing nails have heavier shanks with a rounded head. They are used for boards and flooring.

There are also ring-shank nails, which are used to install plywood floors. The rings grab the wood so that there is no slippage, which may cause squeaking. Drywall nails are also ring shanked.

Most nails are smooth finished, but others have electrogalvanized finishes for exterior, nonrusting use and resin-coated finishes for holding power.

---

[8] Timber connectors shown in Figures 8-4, 8-5, and 8-6 are fully detailed in the *Catalog on Timber Connector Items* (Simpson Company, San Leandro, Calif.).

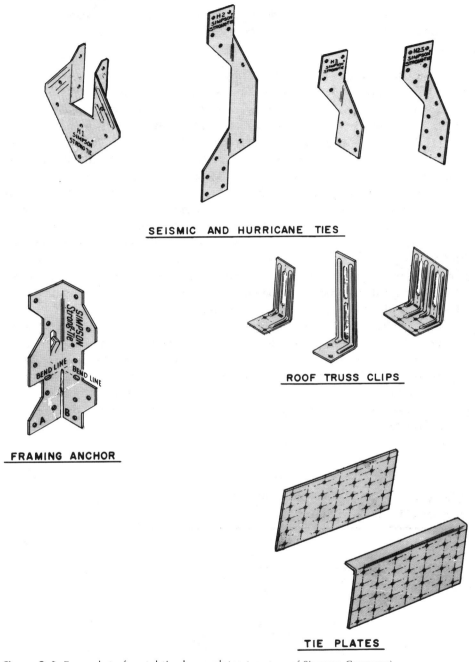

SEISMIC AND HURRICANE TIES

ROOF TRUSS CLIPS

FRAMING ANCHOR

TIE PLATES

Figure 8-4. Examples of metal tie-down plates (courtesy of Simpson Company).

Some nail quantities and uses that are encountered frequently are as follows:

1. To nail 2 × 4 studs in place we would use 500 16d common nails (about 12 lb) for each 1000 foot board measure (fbm) on the project.

2. For 1000 fbm of 2 × 10 joists we need 200 16d common nails (about 5 lb).

3. For bevel or lap siding (1 × 6 boards) we need 1500 gd coated nails (about 15 lb) for each 1000 fbm.

4. To fasten 100 ft² of individual asphalt shingles we would need 850 $\frac{7}{8}$-in. roofing nails (about 4 lb).

There are many sources for expanding this section. One old reliable source is the *Building Estimator's Reference Book* published by the Frank R. Walker Company.

Wood screws have greater holding power than nails, present a neater appearance, and usually will not greatly damage adjacent materials if removed or replaced. They are generally used for fastening trim hardware. There are three types of screw heads commonly made—slotted head, Robertson head, and Phillips head, with the slotted head being the most common. The slotted-head screw has a straight slot cut completely across the head and is driven with a standard screwdriver. The Robertson-head screw has a square hole in the head and requires a special screwdriver. The Phillips-head screw has an indented cross in the head and also requires a special screwdriver. Screw sizes are given by length in inches, and by gauge denoting the diameter such as a 1-in. No. 12 screw. They are purchased by the gross; therefore, the approximate number required for the material take off must be determined. When ordering screws, a list of the total number of each size, length, and type will be needed.

It should be noted that at one time or another, the quantities of nails, screws, and miscellaneous metal items will have to be determined. Usually, these quantities are not listed until an actual order list is prepared during the construction.

For the sake of time and expediency, it is recommended that the estimator plug in dollar allowances for these items. With experience relating to the size of the job, the estimator will eventually develop an accurate allowance figure to be used on any project.

Table 8-1
Number of Nails to the Pound

Size	Length (in.)	Common	Finishing	Casing
2d	1	850		
3d	$1\frac{1}{4}$	550	640	
4d	$1\frac{1}{2}$	350	456	
5d	$1\frac{3}{4}$	230	328	
6d	2	180	273	228
7d	$2\frac{1}{4}$	140	170	178
8d	$2\frac{1}{4}$	100	151	133
9d	$2\frac{3}{4}$	80	125	100
10d	3	65	107	96
12d	$3\frac{1}{4}$	50		60
16d	$3\frac{1}{2}$	40		50
20d	4	31		
30d	$4\frac{1}{2}$	22		
40d	5	18		
50d	$5\frac{1}{2}$	14		
60d	6	12		

MISCELLANEOUS METAL FRAMING ACCESSORIES

There are many metal items that can be a part of miscellaneous metal framing accessories. Plywood clips, T straps, L straps, and corner braces are a few of the common ones that may be encountered in building a home (see Figure 8-5). If the project involves any of the exterior site work, items such as post and beam caps, post anchors, and fence brackets (see Figure 8-6) will also be encountered.

The amounts and types of finish hardware items for the homes a contractor builds will vary greatly. Obviously, the more expensive and lavish homes will require more expensive finish hardware.

Finish Hardware

EXTERIOR AND INTERIOR DOOR HARDWARE

In Chapters 5 and 6, exterior and interior doors were discussed. It was indicated that prehung doors usually included locks and hinges. While this is generally true, the contractor may encounter a home that will require special finish hardware for doors. We will now discuss different types of door hardware.

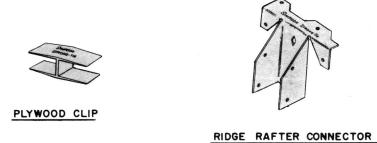

PLYWOOD CLIP

RIDGE RAFTER CONNECTOR

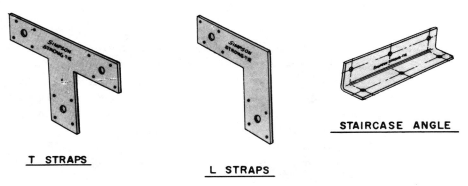

T STRAPS

L STRAPS

STAIRCASE ANGLE

Figure 8-5. Examples of miscellaneous metal framing accessories (courtesy of Simpson Company).

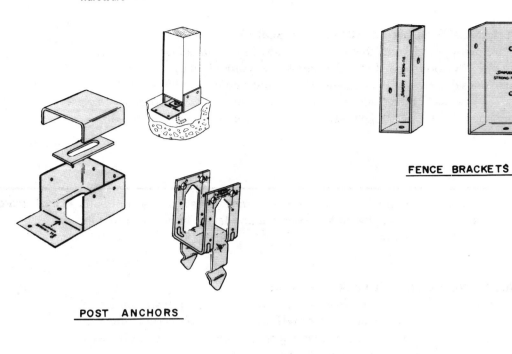

FENCE BRACKETS

POST ANCHORS

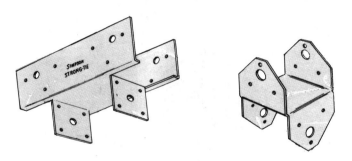

POST & BEAM CAPS

Figure 8-6. Examples of exterior site work miscellaneous metal framing accessories (courtesy of Simpson Company).

Hinges

The basic definition of a hinge, or butt, is that it is a movable joint used to attach, support, and permit a door to turn about a pivot. A hinge consists of two plates joined together by a pin that supports the door and connects it to a frame, thereby enabling it to swing open or closed. All exterior doors should be hung with a minimum of three hinges ($1\frac{1}{2}$ pairs) per door, properly aligned so the door will not twist out of shape. Interior doors under 7 ft 0 in. in height may be hung with two hinges (one pair). Since there are many hinge applications in residential construction consisting of wood doors and jambs, the estimator should become familiar with full-mortise and half-surface applications (see Figure 8-7).[9] The most popular

---

[9] Items shown in Figure 8-7 are illustrated in the *Catalog on Hardware Items* (New Britain, Conn.: Stanley Hardware).

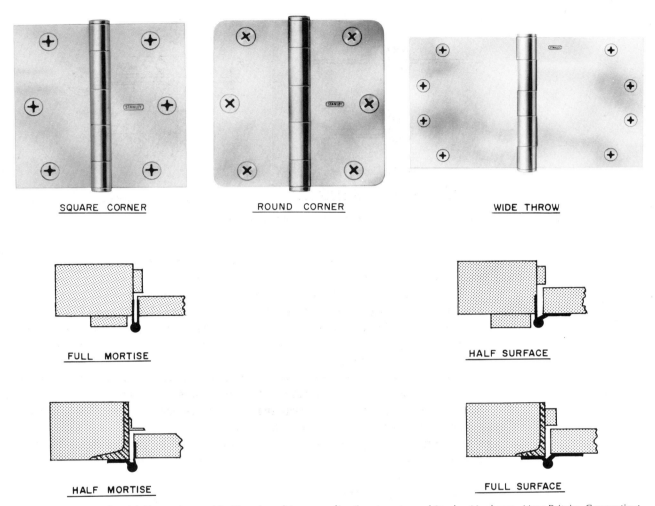

SQUARE CORNER   ROUND CORNER   WIDE THROW

FULL MORTISE   HALF SURFACE

HALF MORTISE   FULL SURFACE

Figure 8-7. Details of full-mortise and half-surface hinge application (courtesy of Stanley Hardware, New Britain, Connecticut 06050).

type is plain-bearing full-mortise hinges. See Figure 8-8 for the common residential door hinge details. When purchasing door butt hinges, state the size needed by giving the length of the joint first. Table 8-2 gives some basic data about hinge sizes required for various door thicknesses and sizes. The width of a butt hinge (when open) is determined by the thickness of the door and details of the door trim.

Keep in mind, when ordering hinges for residential construction, to order swaged hinges. Swaging is a slight offset at the barrel of the hinge that permits the two leaves to come closer together. A standard swaged full-mortise hinge provides a clearance of $\frac{1}{16}$ in. between the leaves when parallel. Swaged hinges are normally used for mortise application.

Locksets and Latchsets

A lockset or latchset is basically a device that is used to hold a door in a closed position. The lockset allows the locking of a door, which provides a certain

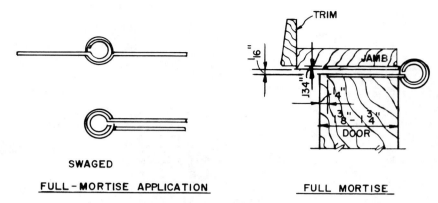

SWAGED

FULL-MORTISE APPLICATION   **FULL MORTISE**

Figure 8-8. Details of common residential hinges.

amount of security. Locksets are generally used on exterior doors. Latchsets are more commonly used on interior doors, where security is normally not required.

In residential construction the contractor will normally use cylindrical locksets or latchsets. Figure 8-9 shows the basic parts of a cylindrical set. These sets are also available with only one knob for use in such areas as closet doors. Generally, expect to use a standard "A" series lock for all interior and exterior doors in residential construction.

Exterior-door locksets are usually furnished with a key-locking mechanism from the outside and a turn-button locking mechanism from the inside. Interior-door locksets may be furnished with plain knobs (no locks) on each side or with a turn-button locking mechanism from either side.

When estimating materials for placing an order, the estimator should list the following characteristics of each item in the sequence listed below:

1. Quantity—number of units needed.

2. Manufacturer's catalog number.

3. Type of latch.

4. Style.

5. Type of finish.

**Table 8-2
Hinge Sizes**

Thickness of Door (in.)	Width of Door (in.)	Size of Hinge Length of Joint (in.)
$\frac{7}{8}$ or 1	Any	$2\frac{1}{2}$
$1\frac{1}{8}$	To 36	3
$1\frac{3}{8}$	To 36	$3\frac{1}{2}$
$1\frac{3}{8}$	Over 36	4
$1\frac{3}{4}$	To 41	$4\frac{1}{2}$
$1\frac{3}{4}$	Over 41	$4\frac{1}{2}$ heavy

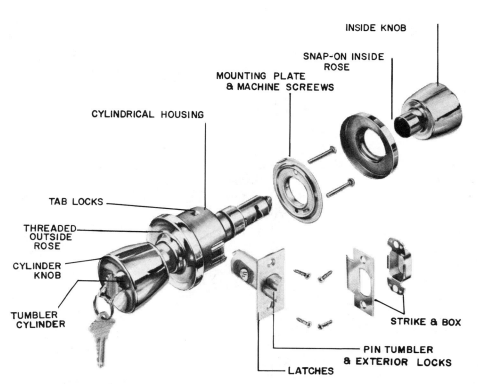

INSIDE KNOB

SNAP-ON INSIDE
ROSE

MOUNTING PLATE
& MACHINE SCREEWS

CYLINDRICAL HOUSING

TAB LOCKS

THREADED
OUTSIDE
ROSE

CYLINDER
KNOB

TUMBLER
CYLINDER

STRIKE & BOX

PIN TUMBLER
& EXTERIOR LOCKS

LATCHES

Figure 8-9. Cylindrical lockset details (courtesy of Schlage Lock Company, San Francisco, California 94119).

It is possible also to purchase special items, such as extra-long backset units, that will place the center of the knobs farther from the edge of the door. The designer may select to use a special escutcheon on doors rather than the standard types available. The escutcheon is the round flat plate surrounding the set, and it fits over the door cutout. If you are building a house with a very decorative entrance, the standard door knob can be replaced with a decorative entrance handle.

Figure 8-10 shows the recommended door hardware locations for standard residential doors.

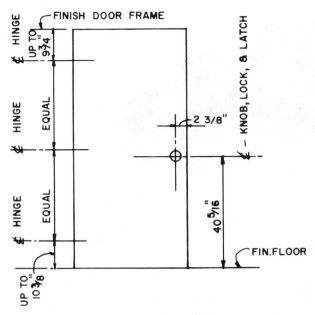

Figure 8-10. Recommended door hardware locations.

A greater degree of security can be obtained through the use of a *dead bolt* lock on exterior doors. The dead bolt serves the same function as the auxiliary latch shown on Figure 8-9. However, because it is larger, the dead bolt is a much more positive means of preventing unauthorized entry through the exterior door. Most frequently, the dead bolt requires a key on the exterior side and uses a simple turn-button locking mechanism on the inside. A dead bolt that requires a key to open or close the lock on both the exterior and interior sides of the door can also be obtained.

Sliding Doors
Usually, the tracks for sliding doors are made of aluminum. Sliding wood doors are suspended from overhead tracks and operate on nylon rollers that are attached to the door. Sliding operation does not provide a very high degree of privacy, sound isolation, or weather resistance, unless special engineering and custom hardware are used. The greatest advantage of any sliding door is that it eliminates door swings, which might interfere with the use of interior space.

Folding Doors
Folding doors are generally manufactured in flush, louvered, and paneled designs. They normally are provided in a bifolding design for use on closet areas, or in a multifolding design for use as a space divider. Another type of folding door is the accordian folding door. Accordian folding doors are generally made from either wood slats or strips that have been tied together with fabric tape or cording.

Most folding doors or accordian doors are suspended from overhead-mounted tracks and operate on nylon rollers or glides. Large door sections or multifolding doors may also require a floor track. In addition, folding doors will need 1½ pairs of light-weight butt hinges to hold the sections together. All folding doors or accordian doors will require a knob or handle to enable one to operate the door.

Screen and Storm Doors
Aluminum storm and screen doors are marketed prehung in an aluminum frame, with all hardware attached, and in an unassembled condition. The basic hardware that should be provided for any storm or screen door is 1½ pairs of butt hinges and a latch to keep the door in the closed position. The latch should have the capability of permitting locking from the inside. It is also advisable to provide a spring-loaded safety chain, which limits the door swing and cushions the impact caused by a sudden opening, such as that caused by a gust of wind. A door closer is highly recommended for closing the door when it is not in use.

Wood-frame screen and storm doors are also available to the builder. These normally come in an unassembled condition and will require the same hardware as an aluminum door.

Special Trim Hardware
Special trim hardware for doors would include such items as door knockers, special door pulls, door stops, automatic door closers, security vision glass, and special locksets. Figures 8-11 and 8-12 show typical examples of door stops and a door closer.

When preparing a material take off for special door hardware items, be sure to list each individual item with a full description. Unless something special is required, a standard prehung door will include all the required hardware.

Again, for expediency and speed in estimating, try to develop a feeling for allowances in the estimate. Quite often, the hardware selection has not been made at the early stage of estimating. Therefore, when selections are finally determined at a later time after construction starts, the estimator may make a final quantity take off and get quotations of cost against the allowance previously established.

WINDOW HARDWARE
In Chapter 5, a limited discussion of a material take off for the windows was started. At that time, the discussion was limited to the horizontal sliding-type aluminum window. It was indicated that the windows would be purchased as units, and no discussion of hardware was undertaken. It is now time to expand the discussion of windows a little further. There are basically two materials that constitute virtually all of the windows in residential construction. These materials are wood and aluminum.

The most common types of wood windows used in residential construction are fixed, awning, hopper, casement, single or double hung, horizontal sliding, and basement. In aluminum-window construction the most common types used in residential building are fixed, awning, projected, casement, single or double hung, horizontal sliding, jalousie, and vertical sliding.

Fixed windows usually consist of a frame and a glazed stationary sash. They are often used in conjunction with casement, awning, or hopper units to provide custom window designs. Casement windows have a side-hinged sash, which is

BASE   BOARD   APPLICATIONS

HINGE   PIN   APPLICATION

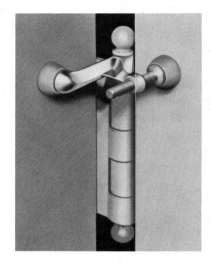

FLOOR   APPLICATION

Figure 8-11. Typical door stops (courtesy of Amerock Corporation, Rockford, Illinois 61101).

normally mounted to swing outward. Awning windows have one or more top-hinged, outward-swinging sashes. Hopper window units are quite similar to awning windows. They have one or more bottom-hinged, inward-swinging sashes. Projected windows are very similar to awning and hopper windows. The operation differs in that the hinged side of the operating sash moves upward or downward in a track. Basement windows usually belong in a class similar to the awning or hopper window.

Vertical-sliding windows and single- or double-hung windows are essentially the same in that they all move vertically within the main frame. Single- and double-hung windows utilize friction or a mechanical balancing system to keep the sash at the desired position. Vertical-sliding units utilize either friction or mechanical catches to retain the desired position.

Horizontal-sliding window units will normally employ one or more operating sashes that are designed to move horizontally within the window frame. Jalousie

Figure 8-12. (Courtesy of Scovill Security Products, Charlotte, North Carolina 28212.)

window units are constructed with a series of overlapping horizontal glass lou-vered sections that pivot together in a common frame.

Operating Devices

It becomes very apparent now, after a brief discussion of the different styles of windows and different modes of operation, that there must be a wide variety of mechanical operators available. Awning and hopper windows will generally be activated by rotary gear, push bars, and lever-type operators. These operators will cause the sash to move in sliding friction hinges. The operator will normally provide a weathertight closer; however, on large sash sections an additional awning lock may be needed. Casement windows utilize a rotary gear operator similar to the type used on awning windows. Casement movement will be assisted by either sliding hinges or extension hinges.

Sliding windows are often provided with a spring-cushioned metal or plastic track at the head, much like the sash guides provided with double-hung units. They are then normally provided with fixed metal or plastic tracks at the sill.

Double-hung windows are normally equipped with a balancing mechanism that will aid in raising the sash and then will hold the sash stationary in the opened position. In a smaller sash, the balancing mechanism may be abandoned in favor of friction fit.

Trim Items

In addition to the actual operating devices mentioned above, we still will need a few more hardware items to complete our discussion on windows. Large awning or hopper-style windows should have an awning lock for providing a weathertight closure. Casement windows will require one or more casement fasteners to pull long sash stiles tight against the frame.

Double-hung and horizontal-sliding window units will use a cam-action sash lock to draw the sash together and compress the weatherstripping. In addition, double-hung windows will require sash lift for easier operation.

Normally, all required window hardware will come with the window when the unit is purchased. Figure 8-13 shows some of the miscellaneous hardware items for windows that have been discussed. Now that we have described generally the types of window hardware available, note that almost all window manufacturers include hardware with their units. It is important that the estimator determine that such hardware is included when he/she gets quotations and places orders. The selection of hardware finishes is limited when furnished by the window manufacturer. Try to avoid custom-styled window hardware. One other window item to make note of is the removable muntin bars, which are used to simulate cut-up panes. These must be specifically ordered and are not included in base window quotation.

DOUBLE-HUNG SASH LIFT

DOUBLE HUNG WINDOW LOCK

CASEMENT WINDOW HINGE

CASEMENT WINDOW ROTO OPERATOR

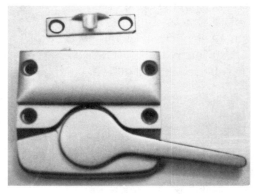

CASEMENT WINDOW SASH LOCK

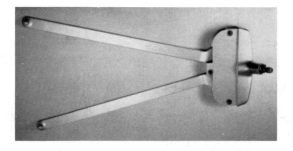

AWNING WINDOW ROTO OPERATOR

Figure 8-13. Miscellaneous window hardware (courtesy of Andersen Corporation, Bayport, Minnesota 55003).

MISCELLANEOUS HARDWARE ITEMS

These should include such items as cabinet hardware, drawer hardware, and closet hardware. There may be other incidental items that come up for any home for which the builder prepares an estimate. However, we will limit the illustrations to the three areas listed.

1. Cabinet hardware will include the hinges, latches, handles or pulls, locks (if necessary), and shelf brackets.

2. Drawer hardware will include slides, handles or pulls, and locks (if necessary).

3. Closet hardware will include such things as clothes rods, shelf brackets, and clothes hooks.

Figure 8-14 indicates some of the typical types of cabinet hardware that have been discussed in this chapter. Figure 8-15 shows some examples of typical closet hardware.

Our discussion of residential hardware requirements has been brief. It should not be assumed, however, that hardware is not a significant part of the estimate. The estimator should check the design drawings and specifications for all items of hardware required. In general, it should be noted that rough hardware is not always specified. This leaves the types and quantities up to the estimator to establish. The information about how residences are put together that this text has attempted to convey will be valuable to the estimator in determining these factors. On the other hand, finish hardware is generally called out in either the drawings or the specifications for the project.

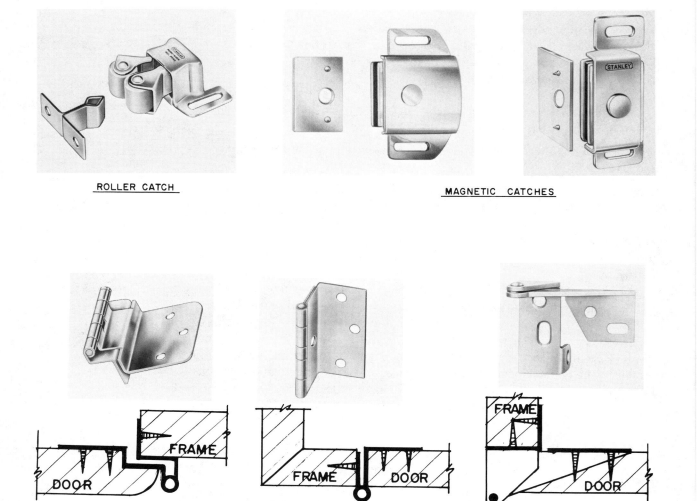

ROLLER CATCH   MAGNETIC CATCHES

LIPPED DOOR HINGE   SEMI-CONCEALED HINGE   PIVOT HINGE

DOOR KNOB

CABINET DOOR OR DRAWER PULL

Figure 8-14. Cabinet hardware (courtesy of Stanley Hardware).

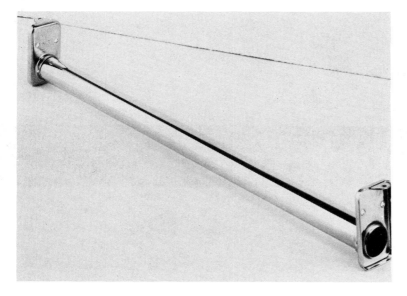

EXTENSION CLOSET ROD

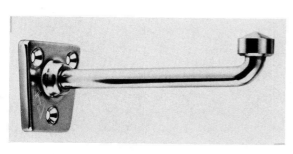

GARMENT BRACKET

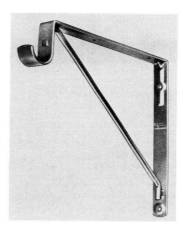

SHELF & ROD SUPPORT

Figure 8-15. Examples of typical closet hardware (courtesy of Knape & Vogt Manufacturing Company, Grand Rapids, Michigan 49505).

Chapter Nine

Mechanical Systems

This chapter discusses plumbing and heating systems. Since these two systems account for approximately 20% of the total cost of the house, the contractor is interested in obtaining economical as well as functional designs. This chapter will be broken down into two basic parts:

Part I: Plumbing
    Water Distribution
    Sewage Disposal

Part II: Heating, Ventilating, and Air-Conditioning

Requirements for all of these factors vary tremendously in different parts of this country. It is important for the estimator to know the requirements for the area in which he/she is working. Much of the estimate will involve equipment choices and piping connections. This chapter will try to illustrate the variety of choices available.

Part I

Plumbing

Plumbing codes govern the type of materials that may be used and the way in which the system must be designed and installed. Before tackling any plumbing or heating job, check local codes. The local authorities may not have jurisdiction in the use of wells or on-site septic systems. In that case, county or state authorization may govern.

Normally, at least three permits are required—one for plumbing, one for sewers, and one for water. Each community must be checked to see if other permits are required as well. Also, check with local authorities to determine if the water permit includes the price of the tap or the water meter. If the home is being built in a new development, chances are that a *water tap* has been provided for; however, there still may be a tap-in charge to the individual contractor.

Water Distribution

The water distribution system consists of supply pipes that conduct water from the water main or other source to fixtures and appliances. Lavatories, toilets, bathtubs, showers, laundry tubs, and kitchen sinks are fixtures. Clothes washers, dishwashers, garbage disposals, hot-water heaters, and the like are appliances. Some water-supply pipes end in outdoor faucets for garden hoses. A portion of this water or distribution system must be routed through a water heater to provide hot water. Most of the water piped into a building must also be drained out together with water-carried waste.

To understand the subject more clearly, this section will follow the travel of water from its source, through piping, fittings, and fixtures, to the point where waste disposal begins.

SOURCE

Water is supplied to most homes by private, public, or municipal water systems; some homes have their own systems, such as cisterns or wells. All water originates as rainfall or snow. Rainwater may be collected directly in cisterns or reservoirs; it may be found as surface water, as in lakes and rivers; or it may be obtained from wells (either shallow or deep) or springs.

All surface water must be treated to make it pure enough to drink, since rainwater or surface water almost always contains pollutants. The usual method of treating this water is by the addition of chlorine (normally at a water-supply system).

Most well water or ground water is pure enough to drink. Exceptions may be in shallow wells, where there may be surface contamination. The purity of the water in all wells must be determined by tests. Ground water often contains large amounts of dissolved or suspended solids—minerals—that make it "hard." Water softeners may be required to make well water more suitable for use.

PIPING

Of the wide variety of water-supply pipes available, copper tubing is generally used in residential work. In older homes, we might have seen water-distribution piping of wrought iron, galvanized iron, brass, copper, or lead. In today's residential piping, however, we would normally use copper or plastic piping. Plastic piping may not be permitted in some areas. Check with your local authority.

This book will review copper piping. Copper tubing is made as either hard- or soft-temper tubing. Hard-temper tubing is much stiffer than soft-temper tubing and should be used where rigidity is desired. Soft-temper tubing can be easily bent and therefore is generally used where bending during assembly is required.

**Table 9-1
Thickness of K, L, and M 1-in.
Nominal Copper Tubing**

| | Diameters | | | |
Temper	Inside	Outside	Thickness	Remarks
K	0.995	1.125	0.065	Thick
L	1.025	1.125	0.050	Medium
M	1.055	1.125	0.035	Thin

Neither hard- nor soft-temper tubing has the rigidity of iron or steel pipe and consequently must be supported at much more frequent intervals.

The nominal diameter indicates the approximate inside diameter of the tubing. The designations "K", "L", and "M" indicate wall thickness from heavy to light. See Table 9-1 for a comparison of nominal 1-in. copper tubing will illustrate how the thickness of the various tempers actually varies.

Code permitting, type M is normally adequate for house plumbing with soldered joints. For a line buried below ground or for one that may be subject to damage, use type K. Codes may require type L for standard runs. Type L is common for most commercial installations.

The designation "DWV" (drain–waste–vent) indicates a still-larger tubing intended for sewage disposal only. Copper-tubing joints are usually made with soldered joints, flared joints, or even compression joints. There are several types of flared joints, but the basic design of making a metal-to-metal joint is common to all. Fittings such as tees, elbows, and couplings are available for all joints. The advantage of flare and compression fittings is that any accessible joint can be taken apart at any time with a pair of open-end wrenches. The disadvantage is their relatively high cost compared to soldered fittings.

Soldered joints are also known as capillary joints, because the annular space between the tubing and the fitting is so small that the molten solder is drawn into the space by capillary action. The solder may be introduced through a hole in the fitting. Soldered joints may be made with soft solder (usually 50/50 or 60/40 tin and lead) or with silver solder. Silver solder has a higher melting point than soft copper, makes a stronger joint, and is suitable for higher operating temperatures.

Copper tubing of soft-temper material is available in straight lengths up to 20 ft or in coils of 60 ft. Hard-temper material is available in straight lengths only (also up to 20 ft), since it cannot be successfully coiled. Installation costs for coiled material are lower than for straight material, because of the fewer number of joints to be made.

Pipe is joined with couplings to connect straight runs or with elbows to connect 45 or 90° bends (see Figure 9-1). Tees are used for 45 and 90° branches. Unions are used where piping may require disassembling. Unions can be unscrewed for disassembling and reassembled by aligning and screwing the union nut. Adapters are used for joining screwed pipe or fittings to soldered, flared, or compression joints.

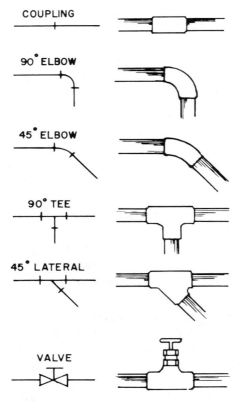

Figure 9-1. Pipe fittings.

VALVES

Valves are used to stop or regulate the flow of liquids in a pipeline. The more common types are globe valves, check valves, and gate valves. Other types of valves, such as pressure-reducing valves and safety valves, are special devices used to maintain a desired lower pressure on the downstream side of the valve automatically or to prevent undesirable overpressure, respectively.

Globe valves have approximately spherical bodies, with the seating surface at either a right or an acute angle to the center line of the pipe (see Figure 9-2). In such a valve, the flowing liquid must make abrupt turns in the body, thus resulting in considerably higher pressure loss than for a gate valve. Globe valves are commonly used where close regulation of flow is desired, because they lend themselves to this type of regulation and are less subject than gate valves to cutting action in throttling service. Faucets generally utilize the globe-valve principle. Valves of the inside-screw and outside-screw-and-yoke types are available. Angle valves and needle valves are special designs of the general class of globe valves.

Check valves are used to limit the flow of fluids in one direction only. The disk may be hinged, so as to swing partially out of the stream, or it may be guided in such a manner that it can rise vertically from its seat. The two types are called swing checks and lift checks.

Gate valves have full-sized, straight way openings that offer small resistance to the flow of fluids. The valve or disk may rise on the stem (inside-screw type, see Figure 9-2), or the gate may rise with the stem, which in turn rises out of the body

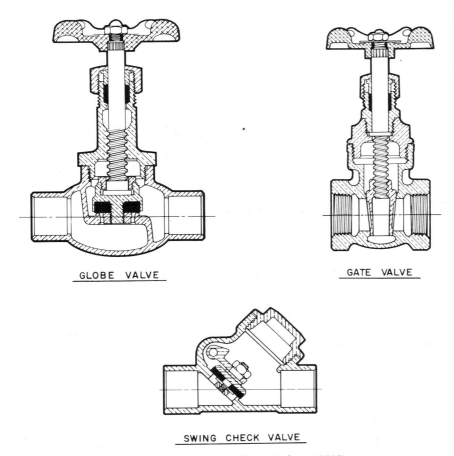

GLOBE VALVE   GATE VALVE

SWING CHECK VALVE

Figure 9-2. Valves (courtesy of Nibco, Inc., Elkhart, Indiana 46515).

(rising-stem or outside-screw-and-yoke type). Inside-screw-type valves are employed in the smaller sizes and lower pressures.

Most plumbing systems provide numerous shutoff valves for controlling water flow in the supply system. Sinks and lavatories have individual shutoffs for hot and cold water—toilets have just one. Generally, the hot-water supply for the entire house can be shut off at the hot-water heater. It is recommended that at least a single gate valve be installed on the cold-water supply inlet to the hot-water heater. There will always be a main shutoff valve near the water meter or at the wall where the main enters the house. This valve would shut off the water supply to the entire house, including the hot water, because the cold water obviously supplies the hot-water tank. Houses served by water mains have additional shutoff valves located underground near the sidewalk or lawn. Sometimes a special wrench is necessary to operate the valve, which is reached through a lined hole in the ground.

WATER SUPPLY

Let us trace the path of the water from the street main to a typical house (see Figure 9-3). The cold water main will enter the below-ground space as indicated on the sample crawl-space plumbing plan (see Figure 9-4).

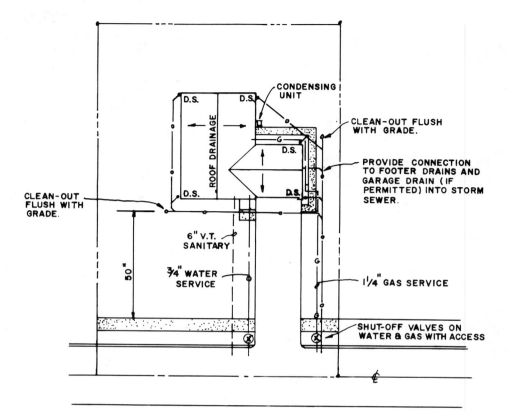

Figure 9-3. Sample mechanical site plan.

note: Be certain that all water piping outside the house foundations are installed below the *frost line* in the area of construction, or the piping must be insulated against freezing. This piping should also be insulated wherever it comes out of the ground to enter the house. Frost lines are generally denoted in the code that governs house construction in the area.

These two figures show an average house with a crawl space for plumbing lines. As shown, the figures assume that the house has a setback of 50 ft. Assuming that this house is being constructed in an existing neighborhood, the city water department would excavate the street to the public water main and install a tap to the property line. The city would install the tap, including a *gooseneck,* which is included to allow for future settling of the pipe. Two cocks are also installed on the tap—one close to the main (called a *corporation cock*) and another close to the property line (called a *curb cock*). The curb cock has either a long valve stem or a sleeve to reach to the valve-operating handle with a special wrench. The sleeve maintains a permanent vertical hole in the earth down to the valve.

The contractor will connect a ¾-in. copper tubing or plastic pipe to the curb cock and run the copper line in a trench below the frost line to the building. The cold water main enters the building through a caulked pipe sleeve and immediately passes through a service cock. The service cock is a gate valve that allows the owner to shut off the water throughout the building. From this point, the ¾-in. copper tubing would extend to the meter location. The sample plans indicate a

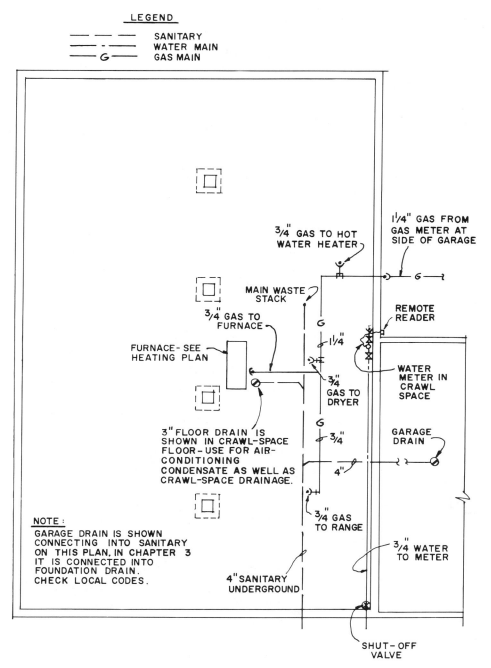

Figure 9-4. Sample crawl-space plumbing plan.

meter (a ⅝-in. meter is standard on residential construction) in the crawl space with a remote reader. The purpose of the remote reader is to permit the water department to read the meter setting from the exterior of the building without entering the structure.

If the water department does not provide this type of meter, the meter location becomes important because the water department needs to read the meter at regular intervals. Even with the remote reader, most water departments will require an annual reading of the meter itself.

If the local water department has the facility for remote readers, the water meter could probably be installed anywhere within the crawl-space area. If the remote reader is not available, the location of the water meter would probably have to be in the utility room or perhaps just below the access door in the crawl space. In some areas of the country where freezing is not a problem, a meter might be installed in the garage. Other water departments may require underground meters to be installed near the property line in a meter vault. The meter vault could be either a manhole-type structure (made of brick) or a precast concrete form. These meter vaults are very often used in commercial applications but seldom used in residential construction unless the property is very large.

There must also be a drain valve installed at the water meter. This valve is used when it is necessary to drain all of the water from the system. If a water softener is to be included in the project, the $\frac{3}{4}$-in. copper lines for the outside hose bibbs should be connected ahead of the water softener. The purpose of this is to save the wear and tear on the water softener, as well as saving the brine solution. If a water softener is required, it would normally be installed in a convenient utility room.

In determining piping needs for an actual project, it is important to note that the vertical riser running directly to each fixture always extends some 24 in. higher than the fixture connection. This extension is designed to provide an air chamber to reduce knocking or water hammer. *Water hammer* is a hammering sound in the piping that occurs when a faucet or automatic solenoid valve turns off rapidly. Water moving swiftly through the pipes while the valve is open comes to an abrupt halt as the valve is closed, and heavy pressure is put on the entire system. This pressure could cause the pipes to burst. To guard against this possibility, air chambers can be put on the tub fitting, the clothes washer fitting, the kitchen sink fitting, and the garage faucet. It is critical that air chambers be installed on connections to such items as clothes washers and dishwashers. These items have solenoid valves that open and close quickly and that in turn cause the water hammer or movement of the pipe.

The solution to water hammer is having properly operating air chambers. Since water is incompressible and air is compressible, the object is to provide a cushion of air in the top of the pipe. The air chamber lets rushing water bounce gently against the cushion of air when the valve closes, taking the strain off the pipes. Eventually, this type of air chamber will become waterlogged or filled completely as the air is absorbed into the water. In this case, the water lines should be drained completely with all valves open to allow these air chambers to be filled with air.

Commercial air chambers (also called water-hammer arrestors or air cushions) are available in several types. One type looks like a giant door knob, another consists of a rubber bag in a metal sleeve, and still another consists of compressed air in the top of a tube with a rubber or plastic diaphragm separating the water and the air. Another kind consists of flexible copper tubing wound in a spiral, with one end sealed and the other end connected to the cold or hot water main. All of the commercial air chambers work on the same principle of air cushioning.

Hot water may be generated by independent means, such as gas, electric, or even oil hot-water heaters. Other systems that utilize the boiler water to heat the domestic hot water are also available. These systems are recommended for use in conjunction with a separate hot-water heater that would be used for summertime operation. The use of a heating boiler to provide domestic hot water becomes quite inefficient for the light load in summertime application.

A hot-water heater is always full of water. Its temperature is controlled by a thermostat usually set between 120 and 180°. The government regulations of 1979 require commercial (not residential) water heaters to be kept at the much lower temperature of about 105°. Most people would find this temperature acceptable, because they like their showers or baths to be in the 100 to 110° range. The 105° water would be acceptable for washing hands and possibly for washing clothes as well. However, it must be noted that this temperature does not work effectively in a dishwasher since it is not hot enough to sanitize the dishes.

As the hot water is drawn off, cold water enters through a dip tube and flows to the bottom of the tank. There usually is a temperature/pressure relief valve installed on the tank. This relief valve should be piped to the nearest floor drain or at least down to 6 in. off the floor. Electric hot-water heaters do not require exhaust vents or flues. Draft diverter for gas or a draft regulator for oil is normally supplied with the heater and must be connected into the chimney or flue.

The home builder should fill the heater with water before lighting the burner or switching on the electric heater. This is done by turning on the water supply and opening a hot-water tap. When the water begins flowing steadily from the tap, it may be closed and the heater fired up. The thermostat should be set to a normal temperature (about 140°). If hot water runs low or you have a dishwasher, you may have to increase the setting.

A tee is installed on the $\frac{3}{4}$-in. cold-water supply line so that water is routed through a hot-water heater. A gate valve is installed on the supply line to the hot-water heater, so that it can be shut off for repair. If this valve is shut off, the entire hot-water system serving the house is shut off. A $\frac{3}{4}$-in. feeder with $\frac{1}{2}$-in. risers similar to those for the cold water are installed leading to each fixture (the bathtub/shower, the kitchen sink, the bathroom lavatory, the clothes washer, and the garage mixing faucet). The toilet requires only a cold water connection.

Several new versions of solar collectors have recently been introduced to hot-water heating. Solar collectors have many good applications, and the use of a solar collector for domestic hot-water heating can be more cost effective, especially if the cost of other fuels continues to rise.

Figure 9-5 shows an isometric riser diagram of the hot- and cold-water piping. It is unusual to have such a detailed water riser diagram in residential construction. However, this diagram will aid in illustrating how to estimate and evaluate the pipe location and the lengths of pipe. Proper sizing depends on a number of factors, such as the average water consumption, peak loads, available water pressure, and friction loss in long runs of pipe. For the average residence, though, this procedure may be simplified by the use of the minimum sizes recommended by the Federal Housing Administration, as shown in Table 9-2. Notice that this table shows the waste and vent stack sizes needed also. This latter information is needed to size the sewage-disposal system of this sample layout.

In the illustrated layout, supply lines to the hose bibbs and garage mixing faucet have stop and waste valves. The stop and waste valve is simply a gate valve

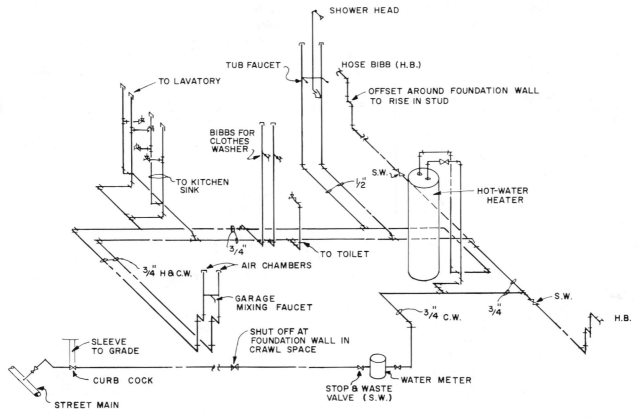

Figure 9-5. Sample hot- and cold-water riser diagram.

with a small petcock drain on the downstream side to allow the drainage of water from that side. This enables the water to drain out of the pipe between this shutoff valve and the hose bibb or the garage faucet, preventing the freezing of these pipes.

In the selection of faucets and shower heads, use energy conservation types that provide adequate functions with less water consumption.

PIPE INSULATION

Pipe insulation gives at least two kinds of protection. It will keep cold-water pipes from sweating in the warm weather and will reduce heat losses from the hot-water piping as well. It may also be used to dampen any pipe noises that might be caused by the expansion and contraction of piping. The insulation tends to keep the piping at a more uniform temperature and also provides a cushion for the pipe to rub against. Otherwise the pipe would rub against another pipe or beam and create noise.

Insulation comes in a number of forms. The form that is easiest to use and that is very effective for cold-water pipe is a liquid material containing finely ground cork. This is brushed on in one or more applications to build up the necessary thickness.

More effective is a self-sealing tape that has special insulating qualities. This

Table 9-2
Minimum Pipe Sizes

	Hot Water (in.)	Cold Water (in.)	Soil or Waste Branches (in.)	Vent (in.)
Supply lines	$\frac{3}{4}$	$\frac{3}{4}$		
Feeder lines				
Bathroom group plus one or more fixtures	$\frac{3}{4}$	$\frac{3}{4}$		
Three fixtures (other than bathroom group)	$\frac{3}{4}$	$\frac{3}{4}$		
Bathroom group	$\frac{1}{2}$	$\frac{1}{2}$		
Two fixtures	$\frac{1}{2}$	$\frac{1}{2}$		
Hose bibb plus one or more fixtures		$\frac{3}{4}$		
Hose bibb		$\frac{1}{2}$		
Fixture risers				
Toilet		$\frac{3}{8}$	3	2
Bathtub	$\frac{1}{2}$	$\frac{1}{2}$	$1\frac{1}{2}$	$1\frac{1}{4}$
Shower	$\frac{1}{2}$	$\frac{1}{2}$	2	$1\frac{1}{4}$
Lavatory	$\frac{3}{8}$	$\frac{3}{8}$	$1\frac{1}{4}$	$1\frac{1}{4}$
Sink	$\frac{1}{2}$	$\frac{1}{2}$	$1\frac{1}{2}$	$1\frac{1}{4}$
Laundry tray	$\frac{1}{2}$	$\frac{1}{2}$	$1\frac{1}{2}$	$1\frac{1}{4}$
Sink and tray combination	$\frac{1}{2}$	$\frac{1}{2}$	$1\frac{1}{2}$	$1\frac{1}{4}$

Source: Federal Housing Authority.

putty-like tape is wound spirally around the pipes and fittings and comes in different versions. Another kind that works well is asbestos tape wrapped over paste and molded in place. Better insulation qualities are obtained by using plastic foam air cells, asbestos wool-felt, or fiberglass pipe jackets. The thicker insulating sections are slit so that they can be slipped over the straight pipe runs. They are usually furnished in 3- or 4-ft lengths. Sections can be cut to length with a fine-toothed saw, such as a hack saw.

Example 9-1

The foregoing book material has been forming an example based on the sample home shown in Figures 9-3, 9-4, 9-5, and 9-6. Let us now take time to organize the plumbing material as it would be done in an estimate for plumbing. The material will be taken off of the cited figures and then tabulated on sample estimate sheets. The exterior water supply components are shown on Figure 9-7, whereas the interior water supply components are on Figure 9-8.

Segment 1
Exterior water and gas lines and fittings

$\frac{3}{4}$-in. water line from curb cock to shutoff	57 ft
$\frac{3}{4}$-in. water line shutoff to meter	27 ft
$1\frac{1}{4}$-in. gas line—curb to cock at meter	67 ft
$1\frac{1}{4}$-in. gas line—meter to crawl-space entrance	47 ft
One $\frac{3}{4}$-in. gate valve (water)	

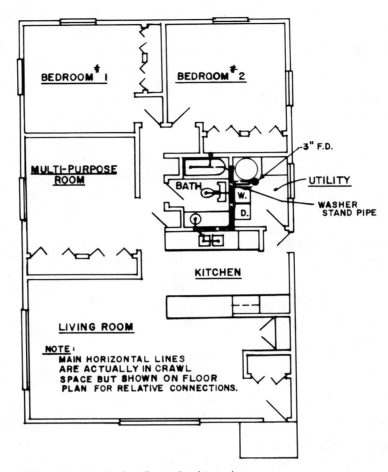

Figure 9-6. Sample first-floor plumbing plan.

One water meter plus remote reader
One gas meter assembly
One gas curb cock
Three 1¼-in. 90° elbows
Seven 1¼-in. 90° elbows

Segment 2
Interior water and gas lines and fittings

¾-in. water line—meter to hose bibb	35 ft
¾-in. water line—total to fixtures	76 ft
½-in. water-supply lines to fixtures	56 ft
1¼-in. gas line—entrance to hot-water heater, washer, and furnace	17 ft
¾-in. gas line—entrance to hot-water heater, washer, furnace, and range	49 ft

One ¾-in. gate valve (water)
One set tub faucets and shower head (for ½-in. pipe)
Five shutoff valves
Four stop and waste valves
One ¾-in. hose bibb

Estimate Sheet

PAGE NO. _____

JOB _____ LOCATION _____

DESIGNER _____ DATE _____

COST CODE	DESCRIPTION	QUANTITY		LABOR		MATERIAL	
		NO. OF UNITS	UNIT	UNIT COST	TOTAL	UNIT COST	TOTAL
	3/4" WATER LINE	84	FT.				
	1 1/4" GAS LINE	114	FT.				
	3/4" GATE VALVE (WATER)	ONE					
	WATER METER w/ REMOTE READER	ONE					
	GAS METER ASSEMBLY	ONE					
	GAS CURB COCK	ONE					
	1 1/4" - 90° ELBOW	10					

Figure 9-7. Sample estimate sheet (exterior water and gas lines and fittings).

Water line fittings

$\frac{3}{4}$-in. 90° elbows	23
$\frac{1}{2}$-in. 90° elbows	7
$\frac{3}{4}$-in. 45° elbows	6
$\frac{1}{2}$-in. 45° elbows	8
$\frac{3}{4} \times \frac{3}{4} \times \frac{3}{4}$-in. tees	5
$\frac{3}{4} \times \frac{3}{4} \times \frac{1}{2}$-in. tees	7
$\frac{1}{2} \times \frac{1}{2} \times \frac{1}{2}$-in. tees	9
caps	9

Gas cocks 4

Gas line fittings

One $\frac{1}{4}$- to $\frac{3}{4}$-in. reducers	1
$\frac{3}{4}$-in. 45° elbows	11
$1\frac{1}{4} \times 1\frac{1}{4} \times \frac{3}{4}$-in. tees	3
dirt legs	4

INSTALLATION

You must be a bit of a carpenter to do plumbing work. It requires considerable cutting through walls, joists, studs, and floors. In addition to the usual hand tools, an electric drill capable of driving a holesaw will not only make the job easier but neater as well. A hole drilled through a floor to pass a pipe makes a neater job than an irregular hole cut with a keyhole saw. Typical bathroom rough-in dimensions are shown in Figure 9-9. The $\frac{1}{2}$-in. hot- and cold-water risers will be roughed-in up to the walls to the points indicated on this figure.

If the project involves a basement, it may be necessary to notch floor joists for the piping. This will position the piping above the bottom of the joists (to permit the installation of a ceiling in the basement directly on the joists). Basic rules for notching joists are as follows:

1. Notch only in the end quarter of each joist.

2. Never notch near the center.

3. Never notch out more than one quarter of the joist depth (in a 2 × 8-in. joist, a 2-in. notch maximum).

4. Nail a steel brace or a 2 × 2-in. piece of wood across each notch, front and back.

Holes can be cut in the joist anywhere along its length if you center the holes between the top and the bottom no closer than 2 in. to the edge. The hole diameter should be less than one quarter of the joist depth.

Pipes across notched studs should conform to these rules:

1. Never notch deeper than two thirds of the stud depth ($2\frac{1}{2}$ in. on a 2 × 4 stud).

2. In the lower half of the stud, do not notch deeper than one third without reinforcing with a steel strap or with a wood brace across the notch.

Estimate Sheet

PAGE NO. _____

JOB _____ LOCATION _____

DESIGNER _____ DATE _____

COST CODE	DESCRIPTION	QUANTITY		LABOR		MATERIAL	
		NO. OF UNITS	UNIT	UNIT COST	TOTAL	UNIT COST	TOTAL
	3/4" WATER LINE	111	FF				
	1/2" WATER LINE	56	FT.				
	1 1/4" GAS LINE	17	FT				
	3/4" GAS LINE	49	FT				
	3/4" GATE VALVE (WATER)	ONE					
	TUB FAUCETS & SHOWER HEAD (1/2" PIPE)	ONE	SET				
	SHUT-OFF VALVES (WATER)	5					
	STOP AND WASTE VALVES (WATER)	4					
	3/4" HOSE BIBB	ONE					
	WATER LINE FITTINGS:						
	3/4" - 90° ELBOWS	23					
	1/2" - 90° ELBOWS	7					
	3/4" - 45° ELBOWS	6					
	1/2" - 45° ELBOWS	8					
	3/4" x 3/4" x 3/4" TEES	5					
	3/4" x 3/4" x 1/2" TEES	7					
	1/2" x 1/2" x 1/2" TEES	9					
	CAPS	9					
	GAS COCKS	4					
	GAS LINE FITTINGS:						
	1 1/4" TO 3/4" REDUCER	ONE					
	3/4" - 45° ELBOWS	11					
	1 1/4" x 1 1/4" x 3/4" TEES	3					
	DIRT LEGS	4					

Figure 9-8. Sample estimate sheet (interior water and gas lines and fittings).

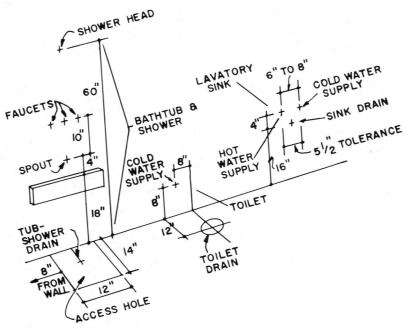

Figure 9-9.

3. In a nonbearing wall, which excludes most outside walls and center partitions, you can notch the upper half of the stud to half its depth if there are at least two unnotched studs left in the partition.

4. Pipes crossing under joists can be hung from perforated metal-pipe strapping that is cut to the proper length and nailed to the joist. Pipes running between two joists can be supported on wood braces nailed across the joist. A vertical run of pipe, such as a soil stack, is supported by resting the bottom fitting on a wood brace that is nailed into position. Other horizontal drain and vent lines entering the soil stack will also help support it.

note: Be careful in hanging copper piping from the building frame. The hangers must be copper strapping or plastic coated to prevent electrolysis between the copper and the hanger metal. Electrolysis between copper and steel will deteriorate the steel.

UNDERGROUND LAWN SPRINKLER SYSTEMS

In many areas of the country, it may be advisable or desirable to install an underground lawn sprinkler system. The sprinkler system may require a 1-in. water service instead of the normal ¾-in. size. The lawn sprinkler system can be simple or complex, depending on the area to be covered and the operational convenience desired. A fairly simple underground lawn sprinkler system might involve the use of shutoff valves in a utility room, or possibly the garage if freezing is not a problem. These valves feed multiple underground lines serving various parts of the yard. Each of these lines may have six sprinkler heads installed on the underground flexible plastic tubing. The simplest of the available sprinkler systems is a pop-up sprinkler head that attaches into a tee fitting in the underground line. More complex systems may have built-in pumps to pressure feed water to more sprinkler heads. Also available are such items as clock-operated programmers, which will turn separate zones of the system on and off according to a preset plan.

Sprinkler systems of the more complex variety must be fitted with antisiphoning valves. This will prevent submerged water-sprinkler heads from feeding contaminated water into the house water-supply system if a vacuum should occur in the house plumbing. Most sprinkler systems use flexible plastic pipe buried in trenches under the lawn. Flexible plastic polyethylene tubing comes in 100-ft coils. It is an "outdoor" pipe suitable for use in wells, underground sprinkler systems, and water service entrance lines. Polyethylene tubing should never be used for hot water.

Of the polyethylene tubing available, the best is rated to take pressures up to 125 pounds per square inch (psi). Medium quality, the one most commonly used, will withstand pressures up to 100 psi. The third grade, utility grade, should not be used for high pressure at all nor for drinking water. It is suitable, however, for underground sprinkler systems.

Polyethylene tubing is lightweight and easy to use. Since few joints are required in an installation because of its length, the tubing presents minimum resistance to water flowing through it. Tubing can be connected to threaded steel pipe and to itself with polystyrene fittings and couplings. Do not tighten plastic adaptors to a threaded fitting more than one turn beyond hand tight.

Stainless-steel spiral drive clamps are used to secure tubing to nonthreaded fittings. Joints can be loosened, pulled apart, and put back together as often as needed.

CROSS CONNECTION

A cross connection is any connection between water intended for drinking (in a water-supply system) and water that is unfit to drink. Almost every home has an example of cross connection. A faucet in a bathtub, sink, or lavatory that would be submerged if the basin should overflow is a cross connection. Should the bowl become filled with backed-up drain water, the contaminated water could be drawn into the water supply used for drinking. Siphonage can occur even through a closed faucet if there is a vacuum in the water supply. A vacuum could be caused by heavy water drawn elsewhere in the house or by a pressure drop from a nearby hydrant. Faucet outlets must be elevated above the flood level to create an air gap and prevent back-siphoning.

A water hose with its end left in a swimming pool or in a puddle of water is a cross connection. So is a hair-rinse hose that is left attached to the faucet and left lying in the bowl or tub. Similar reasoning is applied to the back-siphoning device installed on the underground sprinkler lines. Vacuum breakers must be installed on any faucet that has the provisions for a hose connection.

GAS PIPING

Gas piping from the street main to a building is run underground in a shallow trench 18 to 20 in. below the surface to a meter on the outside of the building. The meter setting requirements will vary quite substantially depending on the gas company involved. Some gas companies will require that the gas meter be installed at the street. Others might permit the installation of the gas meter around the perimeter of the house, with the provision that no more than one horizontal elbow be made between the street main and the gas meter. Still others may permit you to install the meter inside in a properly vented area.

The responsibility for maintaining the service pipe also varies. Generally, the gas company will maintain service responsibility of the pipe all the way to the meter, even though there may be a service charge involved.

All of the underground piping should be treated to prevent corrosion. This is usually accomplished by using black steel pipe and coating it with a plastic coating. Joints or fittings on the pipe also need an extra field wrap of the plastic coating. If the service line is very extensive, there may be need for cathodic protection (only required on steel pipe). The local gas company should be consulted for recommendations on types and methods of installations needed, since the requirements vary from area to area. A newer version of gas pipe would be the installation of direct-burial plastic tubing. Not all gas companies, or especially all communities, recognize the use of plastic tubing. However, plastic tubing has become very popular in residential construction in many areas of the country.

The gas line must enter the house above ground. It is then extended to the hot-water heater, furnace, clothes dryer, and range, or wherever the designer has specified gas appliances. Many personal preferences might be involved in the use of gas or electric for these particular items, or even to the hot-water heater and means of heat.

All gas connections to items of equipment must be made with a dirt-leg connection. A dirt-leg connection is a piece of pipe extending approximately 4 in. below the connection point with a cap on the end of the pipe. This dirt leg is to collect any rust, scale, or moisture before it enters the burner. All pieces of equipment must have gas shutoff valves and union connections for proper maintenance.

PLUMBING FIXTURES

Plumbing fixtures can vary tremendously depending on the decor or degree of elegance required. For example, bathtubs may range from strictly utilitarian-type tubs to much more fancy tubs including soaking tubs, whirlpool baths, and so forth. Some degree of elegance can be obtained by using utilitarian-type fixtures and highlighting them with fancier faucets. In the following discussion, we will describe the types of fixtures that might be expected in a standard, medium-priced house.

1. Bathtubs. Most varieties of bathtubs are 5 ft long. A major item of selection, though, involves the type of material the bathtub is to be made of; that is, fiberglass, enameled cast iron, or enameled steel. In any tub, pay special attention to the slip-resistant surface.

In the fiberglass tub, the owner may be interested in going a step further and purchasing an integral bath and shower with fiberglass surrounding the three walls. This unit provides a molded fiberglass panel that is water resistant. Therefore, there is no need to install ceramic tile or other wall material.

The next major item of selection is the control unit or the faucet to be installed on the tub. Keep in mind that this faucet will control both the tub spout and an overhead shower spraying into the tub. The type of faucet can vary substantially from an individually controlled hot- and cold-water mixing faucet to a thermostatically controlled single-lever faucet. Either kind would normally have diverting valves to direct the water from the tub to the shower. The decor or degree of elegance desired will usually help in the selection process. One option that is becoming more popular on a shower and tub combination is the use of the personal shower. The personal shower is a hand-held shower at the end of a flexible hose. Again, several varieties and adaptions of controls are obtainable.

When selecting the shower head, select an energy-efficient shower head that restricts the amount of water discharged. The energy efficiency comes not only in the amount of water discharged but in the amount of hot water consumed. The cost of taking a bath or shower equals the cost of the water used plus the higher cost of heating the necessary hot water.

2. Toilet (water closet). The toilet is probably the most noticeable item in the setting of the decor. Toilets are available not only in colors but in a variety of arrangements. In the residential-type water closet, the storage tank is required to store the water for flushing action. In the standard-type toilet, the tank is set above the flushing rim of the toilet. In a more deluxe variety, the tank is set lower or possibly even cast integrally with the bowl. In some cases, when the tank is integrally cast with the rest of the unit, the top of the tank is almost as low as the toilet seat.

Toilets are also available with wall outlets. In this case, the soil waste is discharged through an integral trap in the water closet and into a pipe buried in the wall. These types of fixtures require special wall-hanging brackets to support the unit. Their use, however, does make it easy to clean the floor. In the standard toilet, the waste will discharge through the floor approximately 12 or 14 in. away from the wall into the closet bend, which carries the waste into a soil stack.

note: The selection of a toilet seat also has a great deal to do with the decor you desire. Aside from the various colors, the material you select could be plastic, wood, or even padded with almost any degree of elegance you would like. Most residential toilet seats have a closed-front seat with a cover, as compared to a commercial seat, which very often has an open-front seat with no over.

3. Lavatory. House plans usually indicate a countertop-type lavatory as opposed to the standard-type lavatory seen in a commercial building. Countertop or vanity lavatories also come in a variety of colors, shapes, and sizes. The colors are fairly obvious; however, the shapes range from square or rectangular to round or oval.

Lavatories also have a variety of mounting techniques. A self-rimming lavatory basically sets into a hole in the countertop and is self-supporting and self-rimming from the countertop. This obviously creates a lip above the level of the countertop that may create somewhat of a cleanliness problem. Other types use a stainless-steel mounting rim that allows the lavatory to be installed almost flush with the countertop. Still others are installed to the underside of the countertop with a hole cut in the countertop opening into the lavatory.

In this case, either the countertop would be made of a material such as marble or if the countertop were made of standard material, the inside of the hole would have to be finished. The decor or the degree of elegance desired is instrumental in the selection of the faucets. The faucets may range from individual hot- and cold-water controls (either two separate faucets or a mixing faucet) to a single lever-type control with the integral faucet. Most of these faucets can be obtained with integral pop-up drain controls. The degree of elegance determines the selection of finish and the handles. For example, you might select glass handles on a chrome-plated faucet or you may go to a very fancy gold-plated-type faucet. Lavatories are made of vitreous china, enameled cast iron, or enameled steel.

4. Kitchen Sinks. Kitchen sinks come in a variety of colors, arrangements, and materials. The arrangements vary from a single-compartment sink, a double-compartment sink, or even a triple-compartment sink with a small sink in the center that might be used for such special purposes as garbage disposal. Generally, a garbage disposal can be installed in any of the sink compartments.

The material selection, ranging from stainless steel to enameled cast iron or enameled steel, can have a great deal to do with the setting of the decor of the kitchen. The stainless-steel sink is available only in the stainless-steel finish. If a colored sink is desired, either the enameled steel or the enameled cast iron would have to be used. Faucets range from individual hot- and cold-water supplies, to a mixing faucet and discharge spout, to a single-lever control mixing faucet and discharge spout. Most of the faucets are available with a hand hose and spray attachment.

5. Garage mixing faucet. A garage mixing faucet should have extra support, such as a wall bracket, to help support the unit. In this case, individual hot- and cold-water controls are used to supply a mixing faucet and threaded discharge. When a discharge is threaded for a hose connection, we must also have a vacuum breaker on the faucet (also required on hose bibbs for garden hoses) to prevent backflow into the supply piping system.

6. Clothes washer faucets. Clothes washer faucets can be individual hot- and cold-water hose bibbs with threaded connections to connect the washer hoses, or they may go through a special laundry valve, that, with a single-lever control, turns off both the hot and cold water to the washer. These valves are normally mounted on the surface of the wall. However, if the special laundry faucet is selected, there are available special boxes to recess the faucet into the wall. Some of the recess boxes also have available a standpipe discharge connection to conceal the waste outlet into the wall.

Much of the choices we have just indicated are actually the province of the designer of the residence. The builder, of course, can make recommendations to the designer and/or client on choices that will make a difference in costs.

Let us trace the path of the waste water from the fixtures to the public sewer shown on the sample sanitary isometric (Figure 9-10). Also refer to the typical bathroom roughing-in diagram shown in Figure 9-9 and the riser isometric in Figure 9-5 shown earlier. The drainage system is completely separate. Drain pipes are larger than incoming water-supply pipes, varying from an inside diameter of $1\frac{1}{4}$ to 4 in. The drainage system handles drain water removal, waste removal, and venting. As a result, it is called the *drain–waste–vent,* or DWV system. These items are shown in Figure 9-10.

At each fixture the drain passes through a U-shaped bend called a *trap.* The trap retains water that acts as a seal to prevent gases, bacteria, and vermin from entering the house. Lavatory and bathtub traps are installed in the fixture branch lines; toilet traps are cast as a part of the fixture.

Vent pipes carry off sewer gases and keep the whole DWV system at atmospheric pressure. A sudden discharge of waste water causes a suction or siphon action that may empty the trap. To prevent this, vent pipes are connected beyond the trap and extended through the roof to open air. Vent stacks should be installed not less than 6 in. or more than 36 in. from the trap. Vent stack sizes may be obtained from Table 9-2. The portion extending through the roof is increased to 4 in. in diameter to prevent stoppage by snow or frost. The 4-in. section should

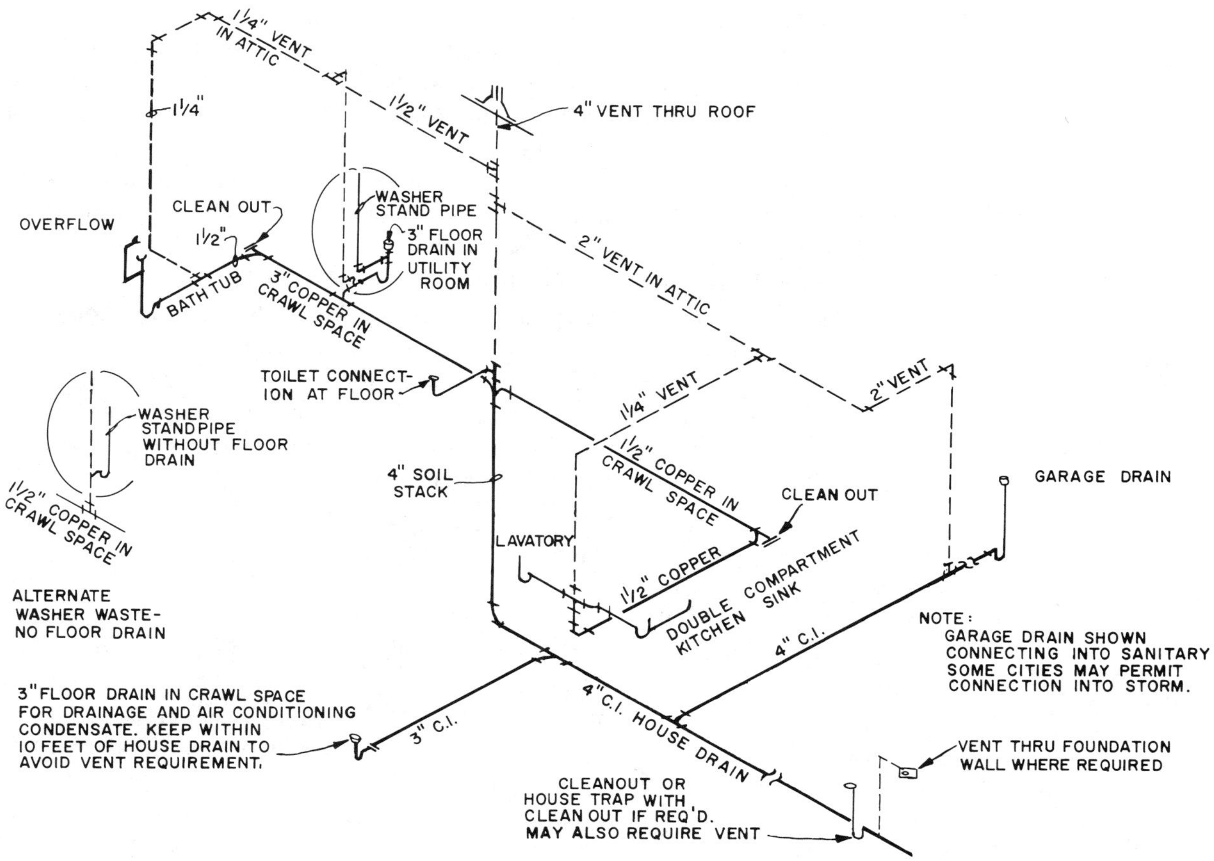

Figure 9-10. Sample sanitary isometric diagram.

begin at least 1 ft below the roof and be no closer than 10 ft to ventilators or higher windows.

Main vents serving the toilets, and secondary vents serving other fixtures are shown extended through the roof to open air. This sample building has a rather compact plumbing system, and therefore all of the vents or revents are shown connected to one vent that extends through the roof. As a result of remote fixtures, some systems may have separate venting through the roof; however, if there were adequate space to run the vent as well as have proper vent sizing, that vent may also be brought back to the main vent stack. Codes require that at least one main stack run full size through the roof. In this sample building, the main vent stack is shown behind the toilet (often referred to as the *water closet*). It is the only vent stack needed on this small building.

Waste pipes carry waste away from each fixture by gravity. It would be very costly to carry each fixture branch separately to the sewer; therefore, the fixture branches are collected and run to the large vertical pipe. This pipe is called a waste stack if it receives discharge from a toilet with or without other fixtures. Soil stacks are usually 4 in. in diameter, but waste stacks could be smaller.

The soil and waste stacks usually discharge into a house drain, which is a horizontal run under the house and runs to 5 ft past the foundation wall. The house drain is then connected into the house sewer, which may be of 4-in. cast iron or 6-in. vitrified clay pipe. Both the house drain and the sewer must be sloped a minimum of $\frac{1}{8}$ in./ft (or preferable $\frac{1}{4}$ in./ft or more) to the public sewer.

Every DWV system should have plugged openings called cleanouts. There would normally be at least one cleanout for each horizontal run in a drainage line. Cleanouts provide access to the inside of the DWV system for removal of blockage. Threaded plugs are used to close the openings on the sewer line. In some cases, easily removable fixtures can be utilized as cleanouts. It is best to include cleanouts at the foot of each waste or soil stack and at each change in direction of the horizontal run. In most cases, the cleanout will also be required on the house drain just before it exits the building.

In instances where a house trap is required, it would be located on the main house drain just before it exits the building. The house trap furnishes a water seal to prevent gas from entering the building piping from the public sewer. Cleanouts are located at the top of one or both sides of the trap. A vent on the house drain may also be required; however, this vent does not normally go through the roof, but just to a small vent through the foundation wall just above grade.

PIPING

Whereas some kinds of pipe will serve for both water supply and drainage, the fittings will not. Drainage fittings have smooth inner contours, so nothing will hamper the movement of solids through them. In a DWV system, regular fittings can only be used on the vent system where no liquids flow (see Figure 9-11).

Cast-iron fittings are used for drainage only. Galvanized steel, copper sweat-type, and solvent-welded plastic fittings come in either regular or drainage types.

Cast-iron pipe is the most popular pipe for soil and waste stacks. It is available in service weight as well as the heavy grade. Service- or standard-weight pipe can be cut with a hack saw. Extra-heavy cast-iron pipe is cut with a cold chisel and hammer.

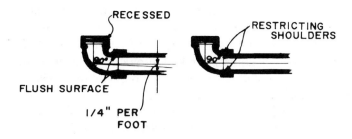

RECESSED

FLUSH SURFACE

1/4" PER FOOT

RESTRICTING SHOULDERS

DRAINAGE FITTING   **WATER-SUPPLY FITTING**

Figure 9-11.

Cast-iron soil pipe has a bell-shaped hub at one end and a ridge around the other end called a spigot, which fits into the hub of the same size pipe. Because the fit is loose, the joint must be *caulked*. The space is first filled with oakum, a stringy fiber with tar, which is wrapped around the inner pipe and packed down to within an inch of the top of the hub. Molten lead is then poured into the hub over the oakum to complete the seal. An important rule when working with hub-type pipe is to install it so the hub faces up, never down. This will prevent solid matter from becoming lodged at the joint.

Installation is simpler with new no-hub pipe and fittings. Instead of caulked joints, neoprene gaskets that permit slight misalignment of pipes and fittings without leaking are used. There are also fewer wasted pieces, as cutoff sections are usually usable. Any accessible no-hub joints can be taken apart for repairs or additions just by loosening the clamp screws. To take hub-type pipe apart, the lead must be melted with a torch, or the pipe cut on both sides of the fitting. After a hub-type system has been opened up, no-hub fittings and pipes are compatible with it (provided the local plumbing code approves). No-hub pipe can also be used below grade if the code permits. No-hub pipe comes in 2-, 3-, and 4-in. diameters and 5- and 10-ft lengths. There is no required direction of flow to the pipe as there is with hub-type pipe. The fittings must be arranged, however, so the flow follows the smooth inner curves. No-hub-type pipe can be used on the soil stack and sanitary sewer to a point 5 ft outside the building. The plumber will then usually change to 6-ft vitreous tile pipe to extend to the street sewer. Copper piping is used on the smaller waste fittings connecting to the lavatory, bathtub, and so forth.

Most codes permit the use of hub-type cast iron, no-hub cast iron, copper, or plastic for the soil stack and sanitary sewer. The no-hub cast iron is simpler to install than the hub-type cast iron. It is heavier and has better sound-adsorbing qualities than either the copper or plastic pipe. Copper pipe with soldered fittings on the waste system is easier to install than galvanized steel pipe. Plastic piping has also become very popular for use in waste systems where permitted by code.

The student/builder should look next at the various types of plastic pipes available. Basically, there are three types of rigid plastic pipe produced for use in home plumbing. These are designated PVC (polyvinyl chloride), ABS (acrylomitrile butadiene styrene), and CPVC (chlorinated polyvinyl chloride). Local codes often forbid their use behind or within walls, though most codes would permit the use of plastic pipe for lawn sprinkler systems.

All three types of plastic piping can be used for cold-water supply and drainage systems. Only the CPVC, rated to take 100 pounds of water pressure per square inch (psi) at a temperature of 180°, can be used for both hot- and cold-water piping, again provided that local codes permit the use of plastic piping. To use the CPVC on hot water, be certain that the temperature pressure relief setting on the hot-water heater is less than 100 psi and 180°. A special connection must be used to connect to hot-water heaters to absorb the heat from the tank wall. Plastic piping expands and contracts more than other pipes, and special hangers should be used to permit movement without damage to the pipe.

All types of rigid plastic pipe can be joined by plastic fittings by means of a special cement that is solvent-welded. Plastic pipe cannot be solvent-welded at temperatures below 40°. In addition, separate solvents are used for the ABS and PVC types. This solvent comes in a single can. The CPVC solvent-welding process takes two steps: first, a cleaning agent is used and second, the solvent-welding material is applied.

Rigid plastic pipe can be joined to copper tubing by means of flare fittings. To be joined with rigid copper pipe or steel, a special adapter threaded on one end to accept the steel or copper adapter may be used.

INSTALLATION

DWV assembly is done first, starting at the toilet drain. The connection to the toilet or closet vent and the sanitary tee into which it connects should be suspended. Next, the work from the sewer or building drain back to the closet is done. Make sure to install accessible cleanouts as required.

If the drainage portion of the soil stack must be offset to clear an obstruction, use two ⅛ bends; if the bent portion must be offset, use two ¼ bends.

Because of cramped space involved when installing a closet bend, many plumbers use a lead pipe for the connection between the toilet and the drain. The lead pipe permits fittings into awkward areas with slight bending and straightening—after the closet bend is in place. The joint between the lead and the cast-iron drain is made by a process called *wiping,* using molten lead to make the connection. Build the soil stack up from the toilet and out through the roof for venting. Work out from the stack, building the branch waste and revent lines.

Pipes through walls need ample clearance. DWV sizes up to 3 in. in cast iron, plastic, copper, or steel will fit into a standard 2 × 4 framed wall. All threaded pipes must be given sufficient additional space to allow for tightening. The entire DWV system should be tested for leaks. It is normally done by temporarily capping all of the outlets at the wall and using a garden hose to fill the system from the vent through the roof.

SEWAGE TREATMENT

A public sanitary sewer system is much more efficient than private disposal. In a collective sewer system the drain water and waste enter a network of pipes from each house and flow, most often by gravity, to a sewage treatment plant.

Modern sewage treatment plants then aerate the sewage to hasten bacteriological action and breakdown, to settle out the remaining solids, and to dry them, selling the residue for fertilizer. The effluent is further aerated, filtered, and chlorinated to kill any remaining bacteria. When the process is complete, the water is pure enough to drink, and it is discharged into a nearby stream. Most private sewage disposal systems serve one family and consist of a septic tank and disposal field. The septic tank breaks down the sewage into liquids and solids by bacteriological action. Solids settle to the bottom of the tank and must be cleaned out every few years. Effluent runs out of the tank and is distributed throughout a system of underground trenches or pits, where it seeps into the soil. In time, all septic disposal fields become clogged by suspended solids in the effluent, and they have to be enlarged. Better, but more expensive, are one-family disposal treatment systems that work much like collective sewage treatment plants but on a smaller scale.

Any private sewage disposal system must be specifically approved by the correct agencies, often a county board of health under the direct supervision of the Environmental Protection Agency. They will normally give exacting recommendations and requirements for any private treatment plant if no public system is available.

STORM SEWERS

For this discussion, refer to the mechanical site plan (see Figure 9-3) for the storm sewers. The storm sewers carry away the rainwater generally collected on the roof. Gutters collect the water from the roof and run it to the vertical collector called the downspout. The downspouts will then drain into underground drain tiles, which are storm sewers.

There must be at least one downspout for every straight section of gutter. In general terms, one downspout could serve a gutter of up to about 30 ft. The gutters and downspouts are usually installed by someone other than the plumbing contractor because they cannot be installed until the building is almost completely finished. By that time, the plumber has completed all of his/her work and left the site. The underground drains are installed by the plumber.

Generally, we are concerned with only two sizes for the underground storm sewer, since we are using vitreous tile pipe. Vitreous tile pipe is obtainable in most areas as 4- and 6-in. pipe; however, some communities still require a 5-in. vitreous tile pipe, which is used on a very limited basis for sanitary sewer connection. The plumber provides vertical inlets into which the downspout discharges.

In some areas of the country, the use of PVC piping is permitted for use in storm sewers. The pipe forms are very similar to vitreous tile piping. The joints are cemented together to form an impervious connection. The use of PVC units is spreading. Some of its advantage stems from its light weight, its ease in cementing, plus the ease in cutting pieces to proper lengths.

SPECIAL INSTALLATION CONSIDERATIONS

1. The excavation for the water line, gas line, sanitary sewer, and storm sewer may likely be done by a separate excavation contractor. The gas piping is relatively shallow and can be installed in a much smaller trench than would be required for the sanitary or storm sewers. The water pipe must be installed much deeper (at least below the frost line); however, if coiled copper tubing is used, a smaller trenching machine could also be used for this excavation. We have discussed excavation in Chapter 3. Most of this work would be done by an excavation subcontractor. In working with the excavation subcontractor, remember that the sewers and water line in the street are installed deeper than required for the lines around a home.

2. Backfilling of the trenches for the excavations mentioned previously should be considered a part of the excavation contract. Most plumbing contractors will have excavation equipment available for this type of work.

3. If no storm sewers are available in the community, water runoff is onto the ground or to a trench that drains to the street. Downspouts will spill onto splash-blocks and then spread onto the ground.

4. If a well is required (no city water is available), the well can be installed at any time. This will require a well driller who drills the well, installs the pump and a storage tank, and runs the line between the pump and the well. The plumber usually connects to the storage tank and extends the lines to the fixtures.

5. If a septic tank is required, it will probably be done by a specialist contractor who installs such systems. It is recommended that the builder consult such a specialist contractor and the approval agency before starting any work.

6. If a well and septic system are both required on the lot, there are minimum clearance dimensions required between each system, house, street, and so forth. Consult with local authorities.

7. Bricklayers usually install the perimeter drain tile and slag, as well as waterproof the foundation wall. Under certain conditions, the downspout drains (storm sewer) can be placed on top of the slag, over the perimeter drains, instead of farther away from the wall as indicated on our plans. Consult with local authorities.

8. If the street sewer is higher than the outlet of the house sewer, a sewage-ejector pump will have to be installed. A special residential-size sewage-ejector sump and pump can be installed in the lowest level of the house to push the sanitary waste to the street sewer.

9. If a building is set farther away from the street, some communities might require additional manholes at points such as where the slope of the sewer changes, the direction of the sewer changes, or the distance that they want between manholes has been exceeded.

10. General timing of the plumbing contractor would be in the approximate sequence listed below:

    (a) The excavations for sewer and outside utilities can be brought from the street to the building line while the foundation walls are being constructed.

    (b) The plumber must wait until the foundation walls are up. Then he/she will install the storm sewer around the building and put the risers in for the downspouts.

(c) Then the plumber must wait until the house is completely roughed-in before proceeding.

(d) After the house has been roughed-in, the waste vents and water lines can be installed. The house drain is usually installed after the installation of the waste lines. If the plumber is required to install the house sewer before the rest of the house is built, the house drain could be installed to the point of the soil stack.

(e) As the walls are roughed-in in the bathroom, but before they are finished, plan to set the bathtub, shower bases, or special faucet mounting that must be built into the walls. The plumber then usually leaves the job until the house is completely finished.

(f) The plumber returns to install the plumbing fixtures as well as to make the final connections.

(g) The plumber installs and makes the final gas connection to the furnace, range, and so forth.

(h) As a variation to this procedure, the gas-line excavation is done completely separately and usually to about the point of rough-in connections. The plumber will purchase and install the arm for the gas meter. The interior gas piping might be done with the rest of the rough-in piping; however, a special trip might be required to connect the furnace in colder climates, where it is required to provide heat for construction.

11. Inspections by the proper authorities will be required throughout the job. Make certain that the inspections are done before installing interior wall material—drywall or gypsum plaster.

Summary of Part I

In summary, the plumbing requirements of a home are governed by many code restrictions. Restrictions can be set in the form of

1. Codes—local, statewide, and/or national.

2. Area-wide customs and/or zoning restrictions.

3. Cost limitations imposed by authorities and/or clients.

The best summary can be done in an example.

Example 9-2

Again let us look at the structure shown in Figures 9-3, 9-4, 9-5, and 9-6. This time let us determine the waste-line piping, fittings, and fixtures needed. The results are to be entered onto a standard material take off sheet. The waste lines' take off will be summarized in Figures 9-12a and b and 9-13. See Figures 9-9, 9-10, and 9-11 for some of the components discussed here.

Segment 1

Sanitary waste and vents—all copper lines

3-in. diameter pipe	7 ft
$1\frac{1}{2}$-in. diameter pipe	34 ft
2-in. diameter pipe	20 ft
$1\frac{1}{4}$-in. diameter pipe	21 ft

Fittings

3-in. diameter—90° elbows	3
2-in. diameter—90° elbows	2
1½-in. diameter—90° elbows	6
1¼-in. diameter—90° elbows	1
3-in. diameter—45° elbows	1
1½-in. diameter—45° elbows	1
3 × 3 × 3-in. tees	1
1½ × 1½ × 1½-in. tees	1
2 × 1½ × 2-in. tees	1
3 × 3 × 1½-in. tees	1
3 × 1½ × 3-in. tees	3
1½ × 1½ × 1½-in. tees	2
3-in. diameter traps	1
3-in. diameter floor drains	1

Traps

Tub	1
Lavatory	1
Sink	1 double
Cleanouts—3-in. diameter	1
1½-in. diameter	1
1½ × 4 in. crosses	1

Segment 2
Sanitary and storm sewers

6-in. diameter vitrified tile (VT)—street to 5 ft from house	62 ft
4-in. diameter cast iron (CI)—from VT to house trap	7 ft
4-in. diameter CI interior lines	52 ft
3-in. diameter CI to floor drain in crawl space	5 ft
6-in. diameter VT storm sewer lines	60 ft
4-in. diameter VT storm sewer lines	190 ft

Fittings

6-in. diameter VT sanitary elbows	8
4-in. diameter VT storm elbows	8
4-in. diameter CI sanitary elbows	1
4 × 4 × 4-in. CI sanitary tees	1
4 × 2 × 4-in. CI sanitary tees	1
4 × 3 × 4-in. CI sanitary tees	2
6 × 4 × 4-in. VT storm tees	1
4 × 4 × 4-in. VT storm tees	7
4-in. diameter CI house trap, cleanout, vents	1
4-in. diameter CI trap and floor drains	1
3-in. diameter CI trap and floor drains	1
4 × 3 × 1½ × 4-in. (CI) crosses	1
4-in. diameter exterior cleanouts (VT)	2

Estimate Sheet

PAGE NO. _____

JOB _____ LOCATION _____

DESIGNER _____ DATE _____

COST CODE	DESCRIPTION	QUANTITY		LABOR		MATERIAL	
		NO. OF UNITS	UNIT	UNIT COST	TOTAL	UNIT COST	TOTAL
	<u>COPPER LINES:</u>						
	1¼" PIPE	21	FT.				
	1½" PIPE	34	FT.				
	2" PIPE	20	FT.				
	3" PIPE	7	FT				
	<u>COPPER FITTINGS:</u>						
	1¼" - 90° ELBOW	ONE					
	1½" - 90° ELBOW	6					
	1½" - 45° ELBOW	ONE					
	1½" x 1½" x 1½" TEE	3					
	2" - 90° ELBOW	2					
	2" x 1½" x 2" TEE	ONE					
	3" - 90° ELBOW	3					
	3" - 45° ELBOW	ONE					
	3" x 3" x 3" TEE	ONE					
	3" x 3" x 1½" TEE	ONE					
	3" x 1½" x 3" TEE	3					
	1½" x 4" CROSS	ONE					
	1½" CLEANOUT	ONE					
	3" CLEANOUT	ONE					
	3" TRAP	ONE					
	3" FLOOR DRAIN	ONE					
	TUB TRAP	ONE					
	LAVORATORY TRAP	ONE					
	SINK TRAP (DOUBLE)	ONE					

(a)

Figure 9-12a. Sample estimate sheet (sanitary waste and vents—interior—copper).

Estimate Sheet

PAGE NO. _____

JOB _____ LOCATION _____

DESIGNER _____ DATE _____

COST CODE	DESCRIPTION	QUANTITY		LABOR		MATERIAL	
		NO. OF UNITS	UNIT	UNIT COST	TOTAL	UNIT COST	TOTAL
	CAST IRON LINES:						
	3" PIPE	5	FT.				
	4" PIPE	52	FT.				
	CAST IRON FITTINGS:						
	4" ELBOW	ONE					
	4" x 4" x 4" TEE	ONE					
	4" x 3" x 4" TEE	2					
	4" x 2" x 4" TEE	ONE					
	3" TRAP WITH FLOOR DRAIN	ONE					
	4" HOUSE TRAP WITH CLEANOUT VENT	ONE					
	4" TRAP WITH FLOOR DRAIN	ONE					
	4" x 3" x 1½" x 4" CROSS	ONE					

(b)

Figure 9-12b. Sample estimate sheet (sanitary waste—interior—cast iron).

Estimate Sheet

PAGE NO. _____

JOB _____ LOCATION_____

DESIGNER_____ DATE_____

COST CODE	DESCRIPTION	QUANTITY		LABOR		MATERIAL	
		NO. OF UNITS	UNIT	UNIT COST	TOTAL	UNIT COST	TOTAL
	Vitrified Tile (V.T.) Lines:						
	4" Pipe	190	FT.				
	6" Pipe	122	FT.				
	V.T. Fittings:						
	4" Elbow	8					
	4" x 4" x 4" Tee	7					
	4" Cleanout	2					
	6" Elbow	8					
	6" x 4" x 4" Tee	ONE					
	Cast Iron Lines:						
	4" Pipe	7	FT.				

Figure 9-13. Sample estimate sheet (sanitary and storm sewers—exterior).

Part II

Heating, Ventilating, and Air-Conditioning

All heating and air-conditioning systems have a common purpose—treating air to maintain comfortable levels of temperature and humidity (moisture content). In the past, houses were heated by an open fireplace or stove, and ventilation was accomplished by opening doors and windows. Today, more attention is being given to maintaining the proper temperature in a house and the correct moisture content in the air as well.

Air-conditioning means different things to different people. The person on the street thinks of air-conditioning as the cooling of a building on a hot day. The heating-, ventilating-, and air-conditioning-oriented person considers air-conditioning to mean heating *and* cooling, in addition to humidity control, ventilation, filtering, and other processing. All of these elements are essential to human comfort and should be considered when planning a building.

Heating   It is important to know a few facts about heat. For example, it is constantly on the move in one of the following three ways:

1. Conduction. Heat will always leave an object that is warm for one that is less warm, and it will always flow in the direction of the cooler object. When heat passes through the walls and roof of a house, it travels by "conduction."

2. Convection. Air tends to rise when it is heated, so warm air always rises to the ceiling of a room whereas cold air drifts down. The current formed by warm air's tendency to rise is called "convection."

3. Radiation. The traveling, or transference, of heat from one object directly out into the air is known as "radiation." The sun's rays give off heat through radiation.

These three characteristics of heat are the basis, in varying degrees, of all our present home heating and cooling systems.

Many heating systems create the heat for an entire building at one central point. The heat is then delivered to the places where it is required. These heating systems are called central systems. One type of central system uses ducts to carry the heated or cooled air to the various rooms. Another uses pipes to carry hot water or steam to radiators or other types of room units.

Most central heating systems burn coal, oil, or gas or are powered by electricity. The system to be used will depend very much on the local availability of energy. Coal, gas, and electricity are burned or consumed directly. Oil is changed into a fine mist that burns when it is mixed with air. Most central heating systems today are automatically controlled by a thermostat. When the temperature drops below a certain point, the thermostat makes an electrical contact that turns the burner or heater on. When the temperature reaches a higher point, the thermostat turns the heat source off or down.

To get maximum comfort from such systems, the house must be insulated. Insulation is a thermal barrier that keeps heat in during cold weather and out during hot weather. Besides installing insulation to reduce heating and cooling loss, the owner can save money in other ways:

1. Develop good heat conservation habits. Pull sash tightly together to lock windows. Close fireplace dampers, except when a fire is burning. Close draperies at night, open them on sunny days.

2. Use storm windows or insulating glass. Double-thickness glass resists heat loss almost twice as much as single-thickness glass.

3. Use storm doors, and keep them tightly latched.

4. Weatherstrip windows and doors to keep warm air in, cold air out.

5. Caulk cracks around the outside of window and door frames.

6. Have a serviceperson clean and adjust the furnace and check the balancing of the heat distribution system to make sure no room gets more heat than it needs.

7. Clean or replace furnace filters. Dirty filters can severely hinder movement of warm air.

8. Set the thermostat back at night, but only 6 or 7°. A greater setback will require extra fuel for morning pick-up. Always set the thermostat back if you are going away for a weekend or longer.

9. Turn off heat in rooms that are not used. If the house has zone thermostats to control heating, consider keeping bedrooms at a lower temperature during the day.

10. Install a humidifier. When relative humidity is high, the house occupants will be comfortable at a lower temperature.

Fuel costs amount to several hundred dollars a year. With proper application of a heating (and air-conditioning) system and good conservation, a large percentage of the fuel costs can be saved.

Systems

There are several types of heating systems available. Some of the advantages and disadvantages of common systems are shown in Table 9-3. There are literally dozens of variations of each type. The type selected should be based on the size of the building, the amount of zoning desired, the location of the building, the orientation of the building, the type or types of occupancy, the type of construction (amount of glass, insulation, and doors), the climate, and so forth. This book will confine itself to a forced warm-air system for all its illustrations and examples.

Warm-air systems can be operated by furnaces using gas, oil, coal, or electricity as fuel. Furnaces also are available in several arrangements. An up-flow model brings return air in low (through side or bottom of unit) and discharges air out the top.

Table 9-3
Comparison of Heating Systems

Heating System	Advantages	Disadvantages
Warm air[a]	Quick heat No radiators or convectors to take up floor space Air-conditioning and humidification possible Cannot freeze Low installation cost	Ducts take up (basement) headroom Ducts convey dust and sound Flue action increases fire danger Separate hot-water heater required
Hot water[a]	Low-temperature heat possible for mild weather	Retains heat during periods when no longer required Slow to heat up Radiators require two lines Must be drained to avoid freezing when not in use
Radiant[b]	No visible heating device Economical operation Good temperature distribution	Slow response to heat needs Air-conditioning must be separate unit Repair costly
Steam (one pipe)[a]	Radiators require only one line	Large size pipes required Sloping pipes take up (basement) headroom Inefficient; time and pressure required to vent air from radiators Water hammer
Electric resistance[c]	No visible heating device Low installation cost Individual room control Clean, silent operation	Operation cost high in many locations Heavy insulation required
Solar	Low operation cost	Supplemental heating system necessary System not fully developed High costs

note: Heat pumps generally fall into the warm-air classification. In warmer climates, supplemental heating may not be required. Electric resistance heaters are added in unit when supplemental heat is required.

[a] Systems could use gas, oil, coal, or electricity for fuel.
[b] Systems could be electric or hot water.
[c] Not a central system.

Example 9-3

Use the floor plan in Figure 9-14 to investigate possible alternate heating systems. This home is to be built over a crawl space. The room dimensions of this home are shown in Figure 6-6.

Trial I—Up-Flow Model: There is physically not enough height in the crawl space for this installation. If it were installed in the utility room, the return air would have to go through the crawl space and the supply duct

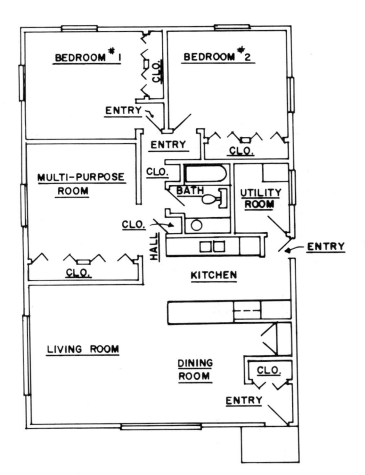

Figure 9-14.

in the attic, requiring the duct to be insulated. It would also utilize valuable floor space in the utility room.

Trial II—Down-Flow Model: A down-flow furnace could be installed in the utility room with a similar sacrifice in floor space. The return air ductwork could be installed in the attic from a central return air grille in the hallway to the top of the furnace. The supply air would be discharged from the bottom of the unit to the crawl space and ducted to registers in each room.

Trial III—Horizontal Model: A horizontal furnace could be located in the crawl space with both the supply air and return air ducted in the crawl space. This solution reduces the loss of space and also reduces the length of duct runs to be insulated. A layout of the ductwork for the crawl-space heating and air-conditioning plan is shown in Figure 9-15. A detailed sketch of the horizontal furnace is shown in Figure 9-16. Figure 9-17 illustrates the main-level heating and air-conditioning plan and shows the location of supply and return register locations.

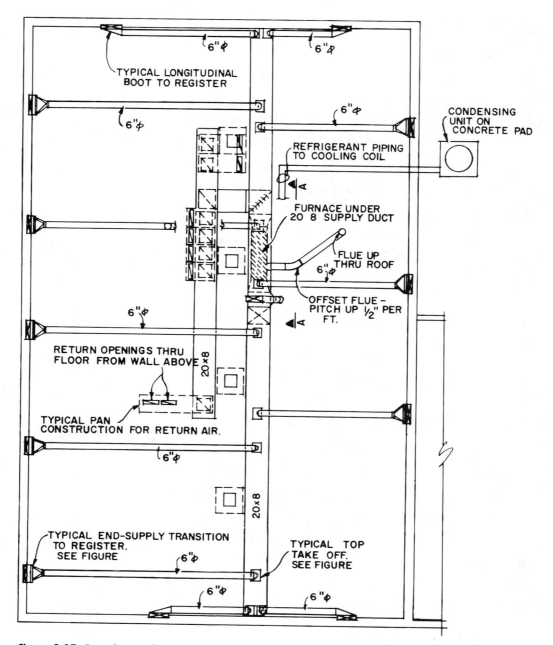

Figure 9-15. Sample crawl-space HVAC plan.

Example 9-4
Use standard estimate sheet(s) to illustrate the take off of ductwork needed for the horizontal furnace discussed in the previous example (see Figure 9-18).

The horizontal furnace of Figure 9-16 can be gas fired, oil fired, or have an electrical heating coil. An oil- or gas-fired furnace requires a flue or chimney to carry the particles of combustion (smoke) through the roof. Make sure the flue or

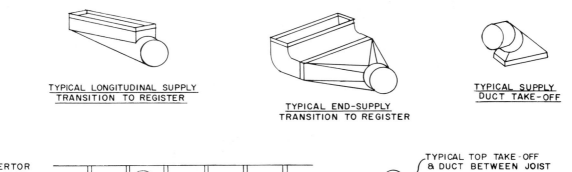

TYPICAL LONGITUDINAL SUPPLY
TRANSITION TO REGISTER

TYPICAL END-SUPPLY
TRANSITION TO REGISTER

TYPICAL SUPPLY
DUCT TAKE-OFF

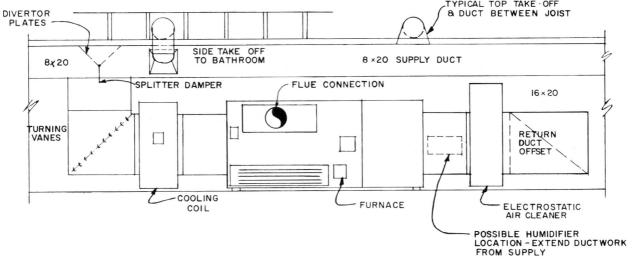

Figure 9-16. Longitudinal section "A-A" at furnace.

chimney is designed to take the proper temperature flue gases, according to the size and type of furnace selected. A flue or chimney is also required for the gas-fired hot-water heater and can be connected into the furnace flue. Flues are generally metal with dual walls, whereas chimneys are generally considered masonry. Electric furnaces do not require flues.

Note that when gas-, oil-, or coal-fired furnaces and hot-water heaters are used, some means of bringing air for combustion must be developed. In a crawl space such as is in our sample project, the combustion air can be brought in by providing louvered (and screened) openings in the foundation wall. If the unit is in an enclosed area, outside air for combustion must be ducted in from the outside of the structure.

Table 9-4 is a work sheet to illustrate the take off of ductwork on a project. The results are then tabulated on estimate sheets, as shown in Figure 9-18.

The air-conditioning is accomplished by adding a cooling coil on the discharge side of the furnace. This coil (evaporator coil) is connected by copper tubing to a condensing-unit setting outside by the patio. The condensing unit has a condenser fan that blows air across the condenser coil. This in turn causes the refrigerant in the coil to "boil," giving off heat. A compressor in the condenser compresses the vaporized refrigerant and "pumps" it into the evaporator coil at the furnace. At this point, the refrigerant condenses, collecting heat that is taken

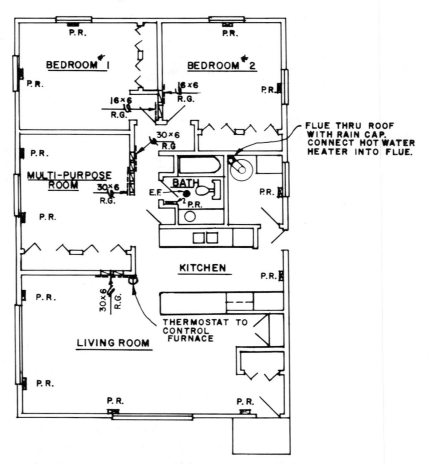

Figure 9-17. Sample first-floor HVAC plan.

back to the condensing unit. The heat is then released and the cycle starts all over again.

A gravity-type furnace (as opposed to forced air) is not applicable in a one-story home, as it relies on air temperature differential for air movement. The furnace would have to be installed low, with all ductwork supplies off the top to the registers. In the home shown, there is not enough height in the crawl space for such a furnace or the larger ductwork system.

A heat pump is applicable in any of the forced-air furnace applications discussed. Simply substitute the blower unit (the inside unit of a split system) in place of the furnace.

Estimate Sheet

PAGE NO. _____

JOB _____ LOCATION_____

DESIGNER_____ DATE_____

COST CODE	DESCRIPTION	QUANTITY		LABOR		MATERIAL	
		NO. OF UNITS	UNIT	UNIT COST	TOTAL	UNIT COST	TOTAL
	SUPPLY MAIN:						
	20" x 8" DUCT	50	FT.				
	TAKE-OFFS	13					
	LONGITUDINAL BOOTS	5					
	END BOOTS	8					
	PERIMETER REGISTERS	13					
	DUCT DAMPERS	13					
	ADJUSTABLE ELBOWS	8					
	6" ⌀ PIPE	150	FT.				
	RETURN AIR:						
	20" x 8" DUCT	24	FT.				
	PAN MATERIAL	40	FT.				
	PAN ENDS	16					
	30" x 6" RETURN GRILLES	3					
	16" x 6" RETURN GRILLES	2					
	FURNACE						
	SUPPLY:						
	TRANSITION - FURNACE TO COOLING COIL	ONE					
	COOLING COIL DISCHARGE w/ TURNING VANES	ONE					
	TRANSITION - ELBOW TO SUPPLY DUCT	ONE					
	DIVERTER PLATE						
	SPLITTER DAMPER	ONE					

(a)

Figure 9-18a. Sample estimate sheet (ductwork).

Estimate Sheet

PAGE NO. _____

JOB _____ LOCATION _____

DESIGNER _____ DATE _____

COST CODE	DESCRIPTION	QUANTITY		LABOR		MATERIAL	
		NO. OF UNITS	UNIT	UNIT COST	TOTAL	UNIT COST	TOTAL
	FURNACE CONT.						
	RETURN :						
	EXTENSION TO 20" X 8" DUCT	ONE					
	ELBOWS	2					
	EXTENSION TO FURNACE ELBOW	ONE					
	TRANSITION TO ELECTROSTATIC AIR CLEANER	ONE					
	TRANSITION TO FURNACE INLET	ONE					
	FLUE :						
	DOUBLE - WALLED VERTICAL	16	FT				
	RAIN CAP	ONE					
	ROOF SUPPORT W/ FLASHING	ONE					
	CEILING SUPPORT	ONE					
	FLOOR SUPPORT	ONE					
	TEE - BREECHING CONNECTION	ONE					
	SINGLE - WALLED STOVE PIPE	8	FT				
	SINGLE - WALLED - 45° ELBOW	ONE					
	SINGLE - WALLED - 45° ADJUSTABLE ELBOW	ONE					
	BATHROOM EXHAUST FAN (TO ATTIC SPACE)	ONE					
	KITCHEN RANGE EXHAUST :						
	36" HOOD WITH FAN & LIGHT	ONE					
	ROOF JACK WITH FLASHING	ONE					
	12" X 3¼" DUCT	5	FT.				
	TRANSITION TO ROOF JACK	ONE					
	CLOTHES DRYER VENT : WITH 9' FLEX. DUCT	ONE					

(b)

Figure 9-18b. Sample estimate sheet (ductwork).

Table 9-4
Ductwork Take Off

Supply main
  50 ft of 20 × 8-in. duct
  13 take offs
   5 longitudinal boots
   8 end boots
  13 perimeter registers
  13 duct dampers
   8 adjustable elbows (allowance of 5 extra for unforeseen offsets)
  150 linear ft 6-in. round pipe—allow 10% for joints
Return air system
  24 ft of 20 × 8-in. duct
  Pan material—7 pans indicated—assume 2 may require additional pans because of stud
    space not lining up with joist space
  Use 40 linear ft plus 16 ends
  Three 30 × 6-in. return grilles
  Two 16 × 6-in. return grilles
Furnace with cooling coil and electrostatic cleaner
Supply
  Transition between furnace and cooling coil
  Cooling coil discharge to elbow with turning vanes
  Transition from elbow to supply duct
  Divertor plates
  Splitter damper
Return
  Extension to 20 × 8-in. return duct
  Elbow
  Extension to furnace elbow
  Elbow
  Transition to electrostatic air cleaner
  Transition to furnace inlet
Flue
  Double-walled vertical flue—16 ft
  Rain cap—**note:** Check to see if more-fancy chimney covered desired
  Roof support with flashing
  Ceiling support
  Floor support
  Tee—for breeching connection
  Single-wall stovepipe—allow 8 ft with 45° elbow and adjustable 45° elbow at vertical
Bathroom exhaust fan
  Ceiling exhaust fan discharging to attic—attic is vented
Kitchen range exhaust 36-in. packaged hood with internal fan and lights, discharge
    through roof with roof jack
  Hood
  Roof jack with flashing
  5 ft 12 × 3¼-in. duct
  Transition to roof jack
Clothes dryer vent
  Package vent system with flexible duct through crawl space to wall cap on foundation
    wall

Distribution System   Usually, the only parts of a warm-air heating system visible in the room are the registers that distribute the heat. Registers in a heating or heating/cooling system can be of the type that are in the floor, at the intersection of floor and wall, or in the wall (Figure 9-19). Refer to Figure 9-17.

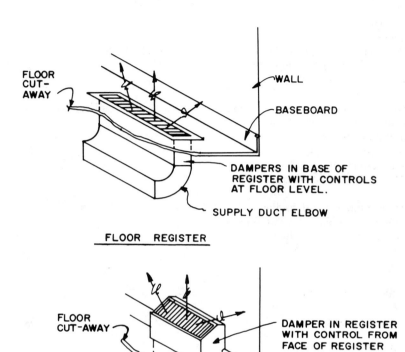

FLOOR REGISTER

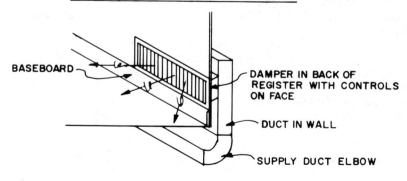

WALL/FLOOR OR PERIMETER REGISTER

WALL REGISTER

Figure 9-19.

In forced warm-air heating, diffusion-type registers are recommended. They distribute the air evenly and without drafts. These are best located so that the room's occupants are not in the direct path of the warm-air supply. The supply registers of a modern forced warm-air system may be in any of a room's walls, though perimeter walls are preferred; if not in the baseboard, they should be low on the wall. If the primary objective is cooling, registers should be located in the high wall or the ceiling. The cold-air return intakes are best located at or near the baseboard or in the floor, but not too close to the supply grilles.

The ductwork is, of course, crucial to a warm-air distribution system. Whereas furnace location and the layout of the house determine its exact routes, two basic systems, the radial and the extended plenum, are often used.

In the radial system, warm-air outlets are located around the perimeter of the house, along each room's outside walls. Each run of ductwork extends, as directly as possible, outward from the furnace plenum to the room register. The return is usually led back through inside wall registers.

In Example 9-4, we have selected an extended-plenum system. Refer to the crawl-space heating and air-conditioning plan in Figure 9-15. With the extended-plenum system, a large rectangular duct extends in a straight line from the plenum. From it, smaller ducts lead to individual registers. This system, while more costly to install, permits better register placement, and the large duct means less resistance to the flow of air.

Either rectangular or round metal ducts may be employed. Round ducts (like stovepipe) are easier to install but their use is limited. Rectangular ducts are more popular for larger installations and for those systems where air-conditioning is planned.

Humidity Control

As far as human comfort is concerned, temperature and humidity are inseparable. In dry air (low humidity), perspiration evaporates readily and cools the skin. Consequently, winter heating should be accompanied by humidification. In moist air (high humidity), perspiration will not evaporate, and the skin and clothing become wet and uncomfortable. Summer cooling, then, can be aided by dehumidification.

It is generally agreed that a comfortable winter temperature is 72°, with a relative humidity (relative humidity is the ratio of the quantity of water vapor actually present to the greatest amount possible at that temperature) of between 20 and 30%. Lower humidity will dry furniture and house members, causing them to crack and warp. A higher humidity causes condensation on windows and possibly on walls. A summer temperature of 76° at a relative humidity under 60% is desirable. Indoor temperatures in the summer should not be lowered more than 15° below the outdoor temperatures to prevent an unpleasant chill upon entering or the feeling of intense heat upon leaving the building.

In addition to thermostats for controlling temperature, some systems are provided with hygrostats (also called humidistats), which are sensitive to and control the humidity of the air. Separate humidifiers and dehumidifiers in portable units are also available. Humidifiers are commonly installed at the furnace.

Ventilation Temperature, humidity, and ventilation are all important to human comfort. A warm to hot room having a gentle air motion may be more comfortable than a cooler room containing still, stale air. For air motion, a velocity of about 25 ft per minute is considered satisfactory. Much higher velocities cause uncomfortable drafts. Air-conditioning systems in large buildings continuously introduce some fresh outdoor air and exhaust stale air containing excess carbon dioxide, reduced oxygen, and unpleasant odors. Air from toilets, kitchen, and smoking and meeting rooms is not recirculated but exhausted directly. A complete air change every 15 min is recommended for most activities. In uncrowded homes, natural infiltration provides a satisfactory amount of fresh outdoor air. In windowless bathrooms, exhaust fans must be used.

Filtering Air contaminated with dust, smoke, and fumes can be purified by filters and air washers of many designs. The most commonly used air filters are dry filters, viscous filters, and electric precipitators. Dry filters are pads of fibrous material, such as spun glass or porous paper or cloth, that must be cleaned or replaced to remain effective. Viscous filters are screens coated with viscous oil to trap dust. They may be cleaned by air or water and recharged by dipping in oil. Electric precipitators (electrostatic air cleaners) remove particles by passing the air through a high-voltage field. This charges the particles, which are then attracted to plates of opposite polarity. Electric precipitators are more effective in dust control and very beneficial for persons with allergies to dust or pollen. These filters remove up to 95% of the particulates in the air, compared to about 10% for the standard throw-away filter.

Cooling Heat will transfer from a warm surface to a cooler surface. Air cooling may be accomplished by transferring heat from the air to the cooler surface of evaporator coils in a refrigerating unit. A compressor circulates a refrigerant between two sets of coils, evaporator coils and condenser coils. In Example 9-4, the evaporator coil is connected to the furnace and the condenser coil is in the condensing unit placed outside. This is called a split system.

Air-conditioning systems are designated central or unit systems. A central system may be designated as part of the heating system, using the same blower, filters, ducts or pipes, and registers. Or it may be separate from the heating system, having its own distribution method. In general, a single, combined, all-season system is more economical than two separate ones that must duplicate equipment.

This split-type of central unit is suitable for most forced warm-air heating systems. The condensing unit is located outdoors at the most convenient place and connected by small-diameter copper tubing to the evaporator cooling coil at the furnace, using the furnace blower and ducts for summer cool-air distribution. In this example, a horizontal evaporator (cooling coil) installed at the air-discharge outlet of a horizontal furnace will be used. The vertical air-flow evaporator, or cooling coil, is installed on top of the air-discharge outlet of an upflow-type forced-air furnace. The downflow evaporator is placed underneath a downflow furnace and is commonly used in slab construction and basementless houses or in houses that are built above a crawl space.

For homes with nonducted heating systems, a special blower is used; it may have its own duct system or discharge cool air directly into the room through a directional air-flow grille. These independent units are ideal for installation in central hallways, attics, or closets. They often offer an optional electric heat module for winter/summer operation.

In some cases, exhaust fans are used to remove hot air that accumulates in the attic during hot weather. Sometimes these exhaust fans are connected to a thermostat for automatic control. This is a desirable feature in areas subject to excessively hot summers.

Although more expensive than a single-package unit, the split system automatically eliminates exterior noise and the need for large holes through an exterior wall (necessary to accommodate the connecting duct in a single-package, outside installation). Split systems are the dominant choice for installation in new and existing homes.

For greater accuracy of control, it is often desirable to divide a building into zones for cooling as well as for heating. Frequently, the sections of a house vary in the amount of heating and cooling required because of different exposures to prevailing winds and sun, varying construction materials, and different uses. Thermostats are placed in each zone. The zones may be groups of rooms or individual rooms each with their own thermostat controlling the air-conditioning.

Cooling systems may be combined with most heating systems. The forced warm-air system can supply cooled air as well as heated air (as was done in Example 9-4). Chilled water can be circulated through the same pipes used for hot water in hot-water heating systems. In this case, the room convectors are equipped with blowers to circulate the warm room air over the chilled coils. The operation of the heat pump can be reversed to either supply or withdraw heat as required.

Self-contained, room size unit systems are particularly effective in buildings with naturally defined zones. The units may be controlled automatically or manually as desired. Room units are built into the exterior walls in new construction and installed in window openings in existing dwellings.

Special Installation Considerations

Some of the following notes will help in planning a good mechanical system in a home:

1. The furnace and ductwork should be installed after the house is completely framed in.

2. Following is a guide for ductwork installation:
   (a) All work shall be properly performed.
   (b) Gauge of metal—round pipe:

Less than a 12-in. diameter	30 gauge
12 to 14 in.	28 gauge
Over 14 in.	26 gauge

(c) Gauge of metal—rectangular pipe:

Less than 14-in. maximum dimension	28 gauge
14 to 24 in.	26 gauge
Over 24 in.	24 gauge

(d) Furnaces shall be erected in a level and plumb manner approximately $1\frac{1}{2}$ in. off basement floor. In some areas, local codes require furnaces located in garages to be mounted 18 in. above the floor on a platform.

(e) Plenum and extended plenum should be down 1-in. minimum from joist.

(f) Supply and return ducts in cold space shall be insulated with a minimum of 1-in. insulation.

(g) Round pipe shall be joined with one screw and tape or three screws per joint.

(h) Round pipes larger than 8 in. shall have screws spaced no farther than 10 in. apart at joints.

(i) Square and rectangular ducts shall have clip and drive or slips on all sides.

(j) All warm-air supply openings shall be fire-stopped.

(k) Return air in wall and joist space shall have cold-air blocks installed properly.

(l) All kitchen and toilet exhaust ducts shall be vented to outside.

(m) All hangers shall be plumb, uniform length, and fastened to duct with screws.

(n) All heat runs shall have volume dampers.

(o) Panning shall be nailed every 3 in. or fastened with angle rail $1\frac{1}{2} \times 1\frac{1}{2}$ in. Panning attached to cold-air return trunk shall be mechanically fastened. (*Panning* refers to areas of joist spaces turned into ducts by closing off the space with sheet metal panels.)

(p) Gauge of smoke pipe and hot water vents:

Up to and including 6 in. diameter	26-gauge metal
7 in. up to and including 10 in.	24-gauge metal

(q) Smoke-pipe joints shall have three screws per joint. Pipe shall not extend beyond the inner wall of chimney flue.

(r) Square-throat supply elbows 4 in. or larger shall have turning vanes.

(s) Take off fitting for extended plenum shall be 50% larger than extended trunk.

(t) Take off fitting from extended plenum shall be 50% larger than heat run.

3. If the house is constructed with a slab on grade with underground ductwork, use the following ductwork installation guide:

(a) A moisture barrier shall be placed under all material used in slab construction.

(b) Minimum gauge for ducts in slab construction shall be 26 gauge. Ducts over 14 in., 24 gauge; over 24 in., 22 gauge.

(c) All round metal joints shall be metal screwed or tack soldered.

(d) Extended metal plenum shall be stiffened every 2 ft with $1 \times 1 \times \frac{1}{8}$ angle, screws every 6 in.

(e) Asbestos pipe shall be connected with coupling and wrapped with tape or drawn bands and tape. Minimum length of draw band is 6 in. Minimum length of metal coupling is 4 in.

(f) Ceramic pipe shall be butted and taped, or installed with tapered draw band and tape.

(g) Asbestos cement pipe and ceramic pipe with proper trade identifications shall be covered with $2\frac{1}{2}$ in. concrete on top; all other material shall be encased with minimum of $2\frac{1}{2}$ in. above and 2 in. under.

4. After the furnace system (with rough-in for cooling coil) has been installed, the air-conditioning portion will be added. Note that the furnace may be required for temporary heat. The condensing unit will be installed, and insulation added on ductwork and refrigeration tubing. This installation may take place after the house is basically complete.

5. Following is an installation checklist for the air-conditioning system:

(a) In most units, heat is dissipated from the condenser by a stream of air directed over the coils by a fan. Other models require special cold-water connections and a drain-off water evaporator "tower" outside. In these devices, cold water in a jacket around the coils removes heat created by compressed refrigerating gases. Check local ordinances. They may prohibit this arrangement because of the excessive water use and loss involved.

(b) Ductwork passing through areas that are not air-conditioned should be insulated to prevent condensation problems and heat gain. Also, if furnace ductwork is to be used for cold air, check the size. Warm and hot air can travel in ducts smaller than those usually required for cold air. Ducts should be insulated.

(c) Some air-conditioners require 230 V to operate the motor. This generally necessitates a special line to the fuse box. A separate line should always be run from the fuse box to the air-conditioner regardless of the unit's voltage requirements. This prevents the overloading of other household circuits.

(d) The condensing unit should be located, if possible, where it will receive a minimum of direct sunlight. There should be at least 10 ft between the condenser air discharge and any wall or obstruction that might return heated discharge air to the air intake. The air intake should be at least 12 in. from any obstruction.

(e) Electrical wiring and refrigerant tubing should be installed so they are protected against being walked on or accidentally damaged in any way.

(f) The blower coil can be used when it is not practical to use the furnace blower for air-conditioning as well as heating. The blower coil is mounted in its own duct along with its own blower and connected to the main duct of the heating system. A damper (usually it will be a sliding type) shuts off the distribution system during the winter, when the heating system is in operation.

(g) Be sure that a proposed installation satisfies local building codes and FHA requirements.

(h) Check whether draining of evaporator condensate could present any problems.

(i) Care should be taken in locating and mounting the condensing unit, so that the operating vibrations (even though slight) are not exaggerated by the building construction or by the mounting mechanism.

(j) If the cooling coil is to be installed in the furnace, the cooling coil should be placed on furnace discharge.

In summary, the mechanical systems in a residence are an important part of the cost of the residence. It is generally more economical for a contractor to engage an HVAC subcontractor to do this work. The subcontractor is more intimately familiar with the materials, installation methods, and costs of this aspect of construction.

We feel, however, that the contractor and estimator should be familiar with this material so that a subcontractor's bid and/or work can be better evaluated.

Chapter Ten

Basic Electrical

The estimating of the electrical work required for any house involves a considerable amount of design capability and a knowledge of the National Electrical Code (NEC), as well as of any local or state electrical codes that might be in force. Most building codes include the current issue of the NEC as the electrical portion, but many municipalities have also included special rules that alter the effect of some portions of the NEC.

This book does not intend to turn the estimator into an electrician or an electrical engineer. The authors will try to give the reader an idea of the electrical work involved in the construction of a residential structure. With this background, the estimator can judge the validity of an electrical subcontractor's estimate of a particular project.

General Discussion

There are many approaches to the actual estimating of the electrical portions of a job. Each estimator develops a particular technique, tricks, and shortcuts that depend upon the estimator's background and experience.

Three main styles of estimating are commonly used. These are

1. The square-foot approach, in which the experienced estimator is familiar with the type of work in a given area or neighborhood and with the complexity of the electrical system. Because of this familiarity, the cost (on a per square-foot basis) will not vary greatly from house to house. The estimator can thus determine a square-foot price for the job based on the square-foot costs of previous installations for which the estimator has recorded (and stored) accurate figures. Obviously, this method is a great time-saver, although subject to inaccuracies. It also has the drawback of not producing a usable bill of material. This shortcoming is no handicap, though, if the electrical contractor's field personnel order the material as required.

2. The completely detailed take off method wherein each item is carefully counted, measured, and dutifully recorded. This method is used most frequently in larger commercial and industrial work. It tends to be needlessly exact and time-consuming for residential estimating.

3. The outlet method, which relies on an exact count of important items and adds approximations of other materials based on that count. This is the method probably most used, and the one that will be used in this book.

Procedure   To make a good estimate, the estimator should first review the entire set of drawings to become familiar with the type of construction involved and the various materials necessary. He/she should also judge the extent of the electrical work involved. In addition, the appliances and mechanical equipment that are to be provided must be determined. Any peculiarity of the site location, or of the construction that might affect the installation of the work and the working conditions for the workers, should also be determined at the beginning. To illustrate the procedure to be followed, the authors will study a sample project that is a one-floor wood-frame structure with a crawl space below and attic space, with access, above. This structure also has an attached garage with concrete floor on grade. The interior is drywall throughout.

Local codes have been checked, and it has been found that the city in which this house is to be built follows the NEC without exception. This permits the use of Romex as a wiring method. Romex is a type of cable dealt with in the NEC under the heading of "nonmetallic sheathed cable." It consists of two or three circuit conductors and a bare ground conductor all enclosed by a "nonmetallic" fiber or plastic covering or *sheath*.

Furthermore, it has been noted that homes in this area are served with overhead drops by the power company from poles along the rear lot line. The layout of the sample home is illustrated in Figure 10-1.

After becoming familiar with the plans, the next step is to make a take off of the visible electrical items that are shown in symbol form on the drawings. Keep a separate count for each different type of device. A typical legend describing the more common symbols is shown in Figure 10-2. The result should appear similar to the sample take off sheet as indicated in Figure 10-3.

The next step is to list the one-of-a-kind items or any items that are required even though they don't appear on the drawings. These are listed on the sample take off sheet in Figure 10-4. Knowing which items to include is the mark of a seasoned estimator. At this point, most experienced estimators have all the data they need to figure a price.

Some of the components with which the estimator must be familiar include

1. An outlet box, usually of stamped galvanized steel, or plastic. Several types are shown in Figure 10-5.

2. A box support, such as a bar hanger, that spans two studs, or a box with a built-in cleated strap that can be nailed to a stud. A common bar hanger is shown in Figure 10-6.

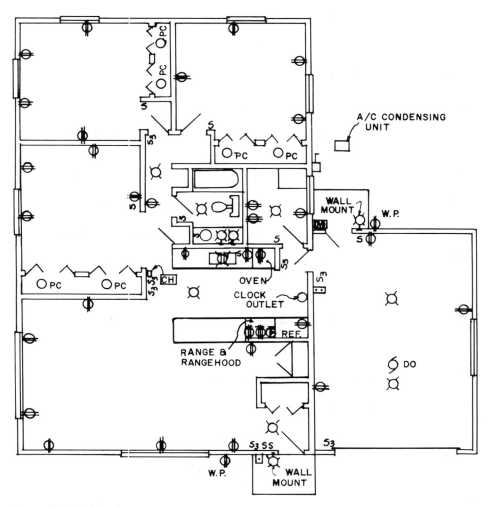

Figure 10-1. Floor layout.

3. A duplex receptacle.

4. A receptacle plate.

5. One or more Romex connectors, used to make a permanent, slip-proof connection of the Romex cable to the outlet box. Most commonly, a box with built-in connectors is used in Romex work.

6. A quantity of Romex, determined by experience and by averaging the amount of Romex used on previous similar houses.

Similarly, the service-entrance ground connection will consist of a ground lug at the panel, a ground clamp at the water line, and a length of wire between, along with a cable jumper around the water meter (see Figure 10-7). Obviously, these items, which vary little from unit to unit and job to job, easily lend themselves to this type of take off.

This method may be taken one step further by using selling-price figures in place of cost figures for each of these unit items.

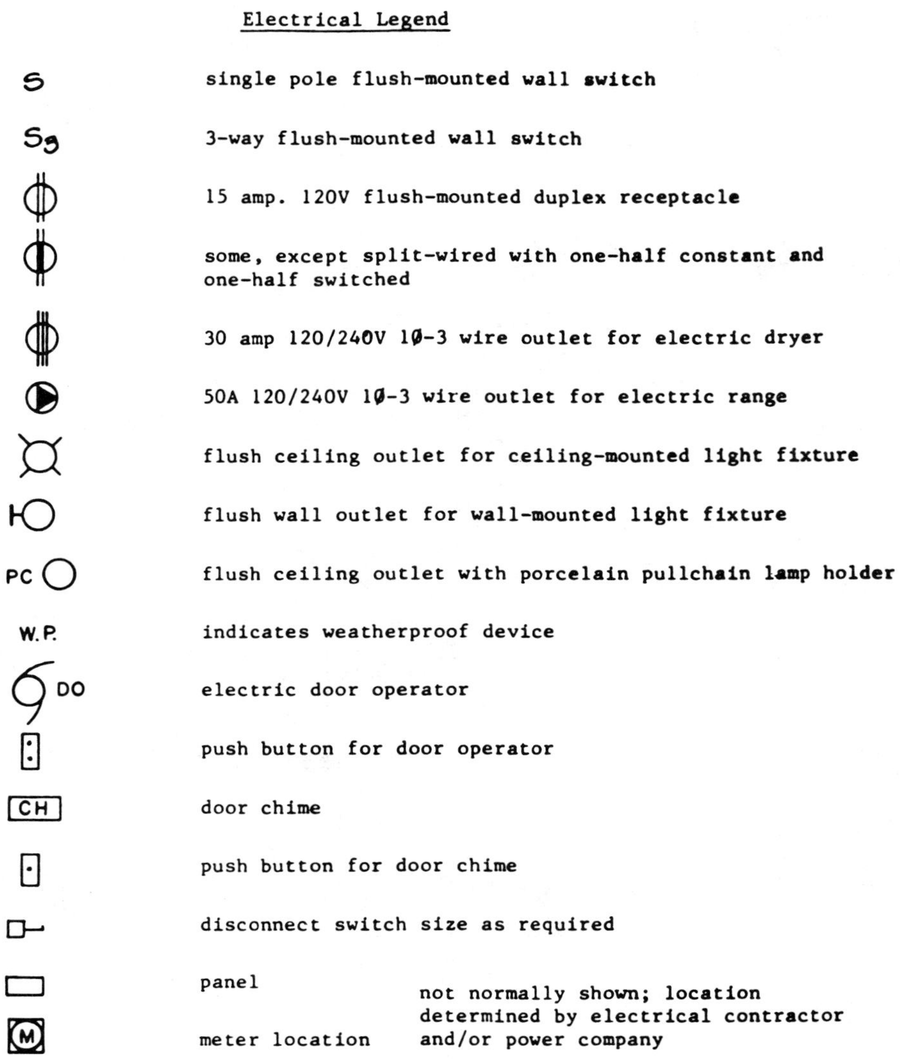

Electrical Legend

S	single pole flush-mounted wall switch
S₃	3-way flush-mounted wall switch
⌽	15 amp. 120V flush-mounted duplex receptacle
⌽	some, except split-wired with one-half constant and one-half switched
⌽	30 amp 120/240V 1∅-3 wire outlet for electric dryer
◉	50A 120/240V 1∅-3 wire outlet for electric range
⌧	flush ceiling outlet for ceiling-mounted light fixture
⊢○	flush wall outlet for wall-mounted light fixture
PC ○	flush ceiling outlet with porcelain pullchain lamp holder
W. P.	indicates weatherproof device
⟲ DO	electric door operator
▯	push button for door operator
CH	door chime
▯	push button for door chime
⊡⊢	disconnect switch size as required
▭	panel
Ⓜ	meter location

not normally shown; location
determined by electrical contractor
and/or power company

Figure 10-2.

In order to establish a useful bill of material, it is necessary to break down each assembly into its components, as in the example of the receptacle above. The result is shown on the take off sheet illustrated in Figure 10-8. Note the following on this figure:

1. Generally, dryers, ovens, and ranges require different receptacles depending on voltage and amperage rating. Some may require a solid connection from the junction box rather than a receptacle.

2. Multigang switch plates must be determined by reviewing the drawing.

3. Clock outlets include a finish plate.

4. The junction box outlet is included for kitchen hood.

Estimate Sheet

PAGE NO. _____

JOB _____ LOCATION _____

DESIGNER _____ DATE _____

COST CODE	DESCRIPTION	QUANTITY		LABOR		MATERIAL	
		NO. OF UNITS	UNIT	UNIT COST	TOTAL	UNIT COST	TOTAL
S	SINGLE POLE SWITCHES	10					
S₃	3 WAY SWITCHES	6					
⌀	DUPLEX RECEPTACLE	25					
⌀WP	DUPLEX RECEPTACLE-WATERPROOF	2					
⌀	DUPLEX RECEPTACLE-SPLIT WIRED	4					
⌀	DRYER OUTLET	ONE					
⌀	OVEN OUTLET	ONE					
⌀	RANGE OUTLET	ONE					
⌀	WALL OUTLET	4					
⌀	CEILING OUTLET	7					
PC O	PORCELAIN PULL CHAIN LAMPHOLDER	6					
	RANGE HOOD	ONE					
	CLOCK OUTLET	ONE					
S D.O.	OVERHEAD DOOR OPERATOR	ONE					
▯	OVERHEAD DOOR PUSHBUTTON	ONE					
CH	DOOR CHIME	ONE					
▯	DOOR CHIME PUSHBUTTON	ONE					
⊡WP	A/C DISC. SWITCH (60 AMP-ZP)	ONE					

Figure 10-3. Sample estimate sheet (visible electrical items).

Estimate Sheet

PAGE NO. _____

JOB _____   LOCATION _____

DESIGNER _____   DATE _____

COST CODE	DESCRIPTION	QUANTITY		LABOR		MATERIAL	
		NO. OF UNITS	UNIT	UNIT COST	TOTAL	UNIT COST	TOTAL
	SERVICE MAST ASSEMBLY W/10' OF 1¼" CONDUIT	ONE					
	METER SOCKET	ONE					
	PANEL:	ONE					
	100A-2P MAIN BRANCH CIRCUIT BREAKER (C/B)	ONE					
	30A-2P BRANCH C/B (DRYER)	ONE					
	30A-2P BRANCH C/B (OVEN)	ONE					
	50A-2P BRANCH C/B (RANGE)	ONE					
	20A-1P BRANCH C/B (FURNACE)	ONE					
	50A-2P BRANCH C/B (A/C CONDENSING UNIT)	ONE					
	20A-1P BRANCH C/B (APPLIANCE CCTS)	2					
	20A-1P BRANCH C/B (LAUNDRY OUTLET)	ONE					
	20A-1P BRANCH C/B (LIGHTS & RECEPTACLES)	6					
	20A-1P BRANCH C/B (GFI TYPE FOR BATHROOM & EXTERIOR RECEPTACLES)	ONE					
	SERVICE ENTRANCE GROUND CONNECTION	ONE					
	WATER METER JUMPER	ONE					
	FURNACE & THERMOSTAT CONNECTION AND CONTROL WIRE CONNECTION TO A/C UNIT	ONE					
	POWER CONNECTION TO A/C UNIT	ONE					
	BATHROOM FAN CONNECTION & INSTALLATION	ONE					
	LIGHTING FIXTURE ALLOWANCE						
	TEMPORARY LIGHT & POWER ALLOWANCE						
	PERMITS						

Figure 10-4. Sample estimate sheet (hidden electrical items).

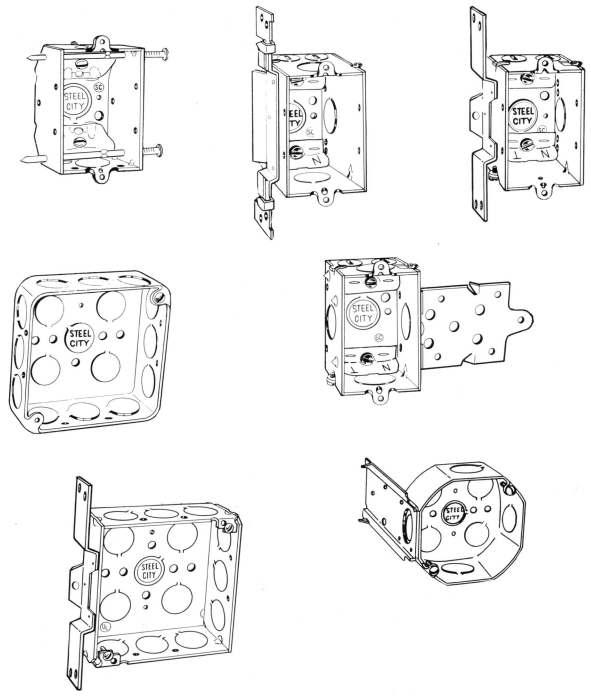

Figure 10-5. Electrical boxes and mounting brackets (courtesy of Midland-Ross Corporation, Pittsburgh, Pennsylvania 15230).

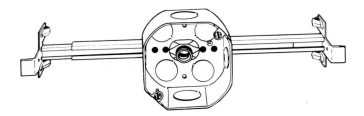

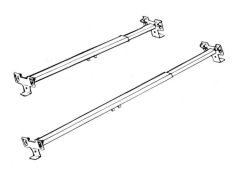

Figure 10-6. Example of bar hanger box support (courtesy of Midland-Ross Corporation).

Details to be Noted

For bill-of-material purposes, split-wired receptacles are no different from any other. The difference is accomplished during installation, when the factory connection between the two sides is removed. Note also that this receptacle requires three circuit wires (a neutral, a constant hot leg, and a switched leg). The column totals from Figure 10-8 are then included in the bill of material. Without quantity amounts from previous projects to go on, the quantity of Romex or wire is simply measured from the drawing, using a scale to determine the horizontal runs and allowing for vertical runs.

Quantities already on hand in Figure 10-8 can be helpful in determining a vertical allowance. For instance, a switch height of 4 ft and a ceiling height of 8 ft yield a vertical distance of 4 ft. Allowing 1 ft for slack and $1\frac{1}{2}$ ft for connections results in a vertical allowance of $6\frac{1}{2}$ ft of Romex for each individual switch.

It is generally more cost-effective to install two, two-conductor Romex runs to a double or a three-way switch rather than introduce a small quantity of three-conductor cable to the job. Also note that normally receptacles may be wired with No. 14 wire on 15-A circuits. A laundry receptacle requires No. 12 wire on a 20-A circuit. NEC also calls for two 20-A appliance circuits in the kitchen, pantry, and breakfast room.

The range and the condensing unit are wired with No. 8 wire on 50-A

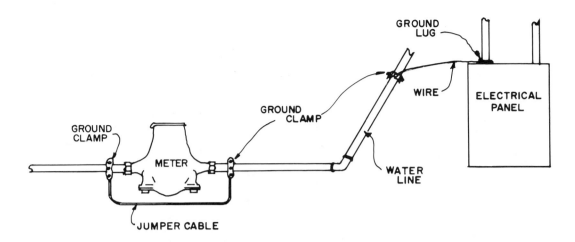

SERVICE ENTRANCE GROUND

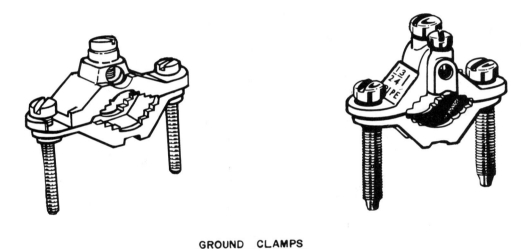

GROUND CLAMPS

Figure 10-7. Service entrance grounding details (courtesy of Midland-Ross Corporation).

circuits. Note that conduit must be provided to physically protect the wiring where it would otherwise be exposed and subject to damage.

Other code rules cover exposed wiring in attics and basements, and when runs through studs or other framing materials are used. Total wire requirements for the example house are shown on Figure 10-9. Note that "2/c" (two conductor) and "3/c" (three conductor) indicate only the number of circuit conductors in Romex and do not count the ground conductor, which must be included.

Returning to the sample take off sheet in Figure 10-4, we shall comment on some of the items that are shown on the take off. The service mast may be made up from individual parts, but it is generally sold as a package that includes conduit, weatherhead, roof flashing, and so forth (see Figure 10-10).

The meter socket is sometimes provided by the power company, but in any case must meet its requirements. The panel size is determined by the number of

Estimate Sheet

PAGE NO. _____

JOB _____ LOCATION_____

DESIGNER_____ DATE_____

	OUTLETS									DEVICES					PLATES						
	1GANG WALL	3GANG WALL	LTG. CLG.	LTG. WALL	30A	50A	J	⊕	⊕	S	S₃	⊘	⊕	⊕	P.C.	S	SSS	⊕ WP	⊕	⊕	⊕
SWITCHES	12	2								10	8					12	2				
S₃'S																					
⊖'S	25							25											25		
WP ⊖	2							2										2			
⊕	4							4											4		
DRYER					1								1							1	
OVEN					1								1							1	
RANGE						1			1					1							1
CEILING LIGHTS			7																		
WALL LIGHTS				4																	
P.C.			6												6						
HOOD	1						1														
CLOCK	1											1									
TOTALS	45	2	13	4	2	1	1	31	1	10	8	1	2	1	6	12	2	2	29	2	1

NOTE: PROVIDE APPROPRIATE SUPPORT FOR EACH OUTLET BOX.

Figure 10-8. Sample estimate sheet (electrical components).

Estimate Sheet

PAGE NO. _____

JOB _____ LOCATION _____

DESIGNER _____ DATE _____

COST CODE	DESCRIPTION	QUANTITY		LABOR		MATERIAL	
		NO. OF UNITS	UNIT	UNIT COST	TOTAL	UNIT COST	TOTAL
	WIRE:						
	2/c #14 ROMEX	1400	FT.				
	2/c #12 ROMEX	200	FT				
	2/c #10 ROMEX (OVEN & DRYER)	40	FT				
	3/c #8 ROMEX (RANGE)	30	FT				
	2/c #8 U.F. (TO A/C)	20	FT				
	1/c #3 THW (SERVICE ENTRANCE)	60	FT				
	LOW VOLTAGE WIRE:						
	FOR THERMOSTAT	40	FT				
	FOR DOOR CHIME	90	FT				
	ADD 5% TO COVER WASTE						

Figure 10-9. Sample estimate sheet (wiring).

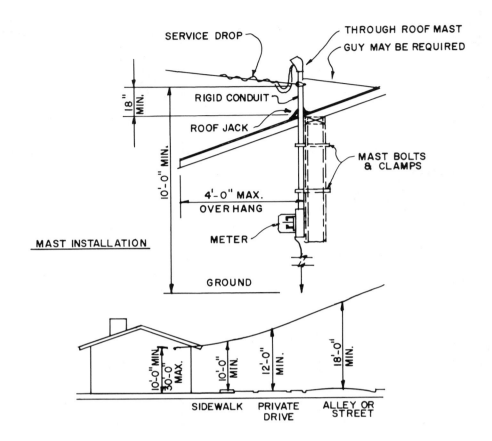

MAST INSTALLATION

MINIMUM SERVICE DROP CLEARANCE

Figure 10-10. Service mast details.

circuits required. The NEC permits 10 receptacles per circuit (4 only in kitchen and dining room areas). The ground-fault-interrupting (GFI) breaker is a code requirement for bathroom and exterior receptacles. This requirement may also be met by providing self-contained GFI-type receptacles, made by most manufacturers of wiring devices.

The service-entrance ground has been discussed previously. A fixture allowance is generally determined by the builder or designer; the furnace and bathroom fan are just additional connections to be made. Fans may be furnished by the general, mechanical, or electrical contractor. This must be determined.

The air-conditioning unit (condensing unit) generally sits outside on a concrete pad and requires a weatherproof disconnect switch and type VF wire. This is a plastic-jacketed waterproof type of nonmetallic cable, another type of code-approved weatherproof wiring.

The temporary electrical service for construction-related power and lighting requirements, along with the necessary panel and outlets, may be included as a requirement. A permit and/or inspection fee is generally a requirement of each individual municipality.

Another item that should be included in the final estimate summary is a listing of miscellaneous materials. This is usually a lump sum figure that covers minor items, most of which do not require separate labor units. This figure would include such items as pipe clamps and supports, and conduit nipples for meter socket and mast. For wire protection you would need wire connectors, tape, woodscrews and nails, Romex mounting staples, and expendable tools such as drill bits and hacksaw blades.

Some additional electrical items that are not included in the sample house but that might be included in any given house are

Countertop built-in mixer	Gutter snow-melting cables
Instant hot-water unit	Lightning rods
Dishwasher	Electric heat
Disposal	TV antenna system
Microwave oven	Electrically operated draperies and
Water softeners	curtains
Well pump	Low-voltage lighting control sys-
Sump pump	tems
Sewage pump	Landscape lighting
Attic fan	Swimming pool lighting
Central vacuum system	Tennis court lighting
Intercom and/or built-in music	Dimmers
systems	Telephone outlets
Smoke detectors	Recessed lighting fixtures, which
Snow melting—driveway and/or	may need to be supplied by the
entrance steps	electrical contractor

Many of these items are subject to specific code rules and the estimator should become familiar with the pertinent sections of the code when confronted with any of these items. If not, the estimator may find that the installation has been rejected by an inspector. This rejection usually requires a great deal of costly additional work to be done prior to acceptance by the authorities. Furthermore, some of these items will require the electric service to be larger. Again, the NEC can be used as a guide by the electrical estimator.

This has been a brief overview of residential electrical needs. It is, of course, a very important aspect of the cost of the residence. The electrical wiring and outlets must be installed before the interior wall- and ceiling-covering materials can be put into place.

Chapter Eleven

Putting It All Together

As stated throughout this book, our purpose in preparing this material was to illustrate how to determine quantities of materials needed in the construction of a residential structure. In addition, we have tried to show the builder or the student the various components needed in a structure of this type. A proper understanding of this material should enable a builder to put together a reasonably accurate estimate of the projected cost of the building before construction starts.

Let us review the construction aspects that have been covered to this point.

Chapter 1—Introduction and General Information
This chapter dealt with the various items such as permits, building codes, and licenses that should be understood before beginning the estimating take off. A brief review of the mathematics needed for quantity take off of construction material was included in this chapter.

Chapter 2—Earthwork Operations
This chapter illustrated the methods of determining the quantities of earth to be excavated, transported (moved), and replaced.

Chapter 3—Foundation Work
This chapter dealt with the various types of foundations generally used in the construction of residential structures. It also discussed how the quantities of these various foundation types are determined.

Chapter 4—House Framing
In this chapter, we covered the construction of the shell of a residential structure. Regular and shortcut methods of determining quantities needed were covered in

examples and text. Many of the details of constructing the frame were also discussed.

Chapter 5—Roofing and Exterior Finish Materials
The exterior of the frame developed in Chapter 4 was covered in this chapter. We discussed the materials needed, how they were installed, and how the required quantities were determined.

Chapter 6—Insulation and Interior Finishes
The subject of energy conservation in home construction was touched on in this chapter. The method of insulating and quantitating the insulation requirements was also covered. The discussion then went on to analyze the interior finishes and trim needed to produce a nearly finished product.

Chapter 7—Decorating
The subject of this chapter was making the structure pleasing to the eye. The main questions considered were what and how much to use.

Chapter 8—Hardware
Hardware, both finished (exposed) and rough (concealed), is necessary for components of the structure to function as designed. What to use, how much is needed, and how it is installed were questions that this chapter addressed.

Chapter 9—Mechanical Systems
This chapter discussed methods of supplying water and disposing of waste, as well as ways of heating and ventilating the structure. In addition, we gave some insight into the problem of providing for air-conditioning of the structure. A subcontractor licensed in this field should be consulted before finalizing an estimate that includes plumbing, heating, and air-conditioning.

Chapter 10—Basic Electrical
A very specialized subject in home construction is the determination of the electrical components needed. This chapter summarized most of the basic requirements and referred to national codes that must be satisfied in residential construction. Again, the services of a licensed contractor will be needed to do the installation of the electrical components called for in even the most basic and ordinary plan.

The first 10 chapters of this book covered the major portion of the material take offs for almost any residence to be built. In addition to these material evaluations, the final price of the building will be affected by three other items. They are miscellaneous materials, labor, and overhead and profit. Before continuing with the summary, let us provide some background for the three areas just noted.

Miscellaneous Materials   The following discussion focuses on many of the miscellaneous material items that may be encountered by a residential contractor. This is an important part of our estimate inasmuch as there are many material items that were not discussed in the previous chapters. We will cover these materials in this category.

EARTH BACKFILL

The steps and procedures involved in backfilling were covered in Chapter 2. One possible cost item that was not covered, however, was the condition that occurs when there is not enough soil available from the on-site excavation to fill all the areas needing to be filled.

The contractor will have to determine the total quantities required by using the procedures outlined in Chapter 2. After determining the quantities (in cubic yards), he/she should enter them on a take off sheet.

When you eventually put costs to these materials, remember to provide for the cost of the earth backfill that may not be available on the job site. This purchase price may or may not include the cost of delivering the material to the site. Be sure to verify what is included in this price when you obtain it.

CHIMNEY ACCESSORIES

If the home being estimated has a chimney, possibly with a fireplace, determine the material requirements such as masonry, flue liners, dampers, clean-out doors, insulation next to wood framing, the mantle, and hearth.

The masonry quantities for chimneys can be obtained in the same manner as was discussed for foundation walls. Do not forget to include fire brick and chimney flues in your take off. Chimney flues are purchased by standard units.

The hearth will usually be constructed with a concrete base and will be finished with stone, brick, or tile. Figure 4-11 shows the basic details of a hearth. Remember, concrete is purchased by the cubic yard. Don't forget to include reinforcing steel. The mantle will usually be built of stone or wood. We have already discussed how to estimate each of these materials in previous chapters.

Dampers and clean-out doors are standard-size shelf items. The insulation comes in rolls as discussed earlier, and generally one roll would be sufficient.

STAIRS

If the home has more than one floor level, you will need to provide stairs to gain access to the different levels. Most residential stair construction is of wood. Chapter 4 thoroughly describes the procedures for lumber take offs.

The basic elements of any stair are as follows:

1. Tread. This is the portion of the stair upon which a person steps.

2. Nosing. This is the portion of the member forming the tread. It projects in front of the riser board.

3. Riser. This is the vertical member at the back edge of the tread extending upward to the next tread.

4. Carriage. This is more commonly referred to as a "stringer." It is the member at the sides of the stair that provides support for the treads and risers. (See Figure 4-11 to see how the carriage relates to the floor framing.)

5. Glue block. This is a triangular piece of wood about 4 in. long that is glued at the underneath side of the intersection of the tread and the riser.

Figure 11-1 shows the elements of the stairs just discussed. One thing to keep in mind when building stairs is always to provide a positive method of supporting your treads. This can be accomplished by notching the stringers and resting the tread on the notch, or by securing a cleat to the side of the stringer with wood screws to support the tread. Never depend on nails or wood screws that go only from the stringer into the end of the tread to do the job. The notch or cleat assures the safety of the tread-to-stringer assembly.

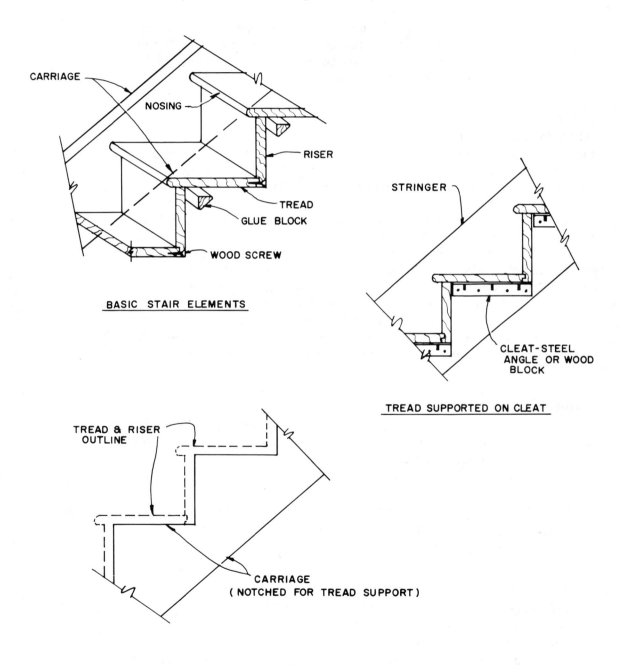

BASIC STAIR ELEMENTS

TREAD SUPPORTED ON CLEAT

TREAD SUPPORTED ON NOTCH

Figure 11-1. Basic elements of a stair.

An integral part of any stair is the handrail. Handrails may be supported by either wall brackets or by newel posts. Newel posts are placed in a vertical position and are usually located at the first step or at a landing. Handrails are normally located at a height of 36 in. above landings. They will be sloped at the same angle as the stringer and will be located at a height of 32 in. above the surface of the tread. Codes generally require that handrail ends be returned to the wall. This is a safety precaution. Figure 11-2 shows the handrail components noted.

CEILING ACCESS PANELS

Most residential construction utilizes the open space between the ceiling joists and roof rafters for miscellaneous storage. In most instances, this space is not large enough to warrant loss of usable floor space to build a standard stairway up to the area. There are two common ways to provide access into this space. The less expensive way is simply to provide an access opening through the ceiling of one or more closets. The other method is to frame out an opening in the ceiling joists, normally in a hallway large enough to install a commercially available pull-down folding ladder. This ladder is sold as a unit, and when not being used it folds up and is concealed by a solid wood panel that is built flush with the ceiling. The details of such a ladder are shown in Figure 11-3.

FLOOR TRAP DOORS

If the residential structure is to be built over a crawl space (not high enough to warrant a regular stair), a trap door through the floor in a utility room might be the best solution to provide access to the crawl-space area. Such doors are generally built to fit a particular situation. Again, review the framing hints given in Chapter 4 to estimate material quantities needed for this application. In split-level-type homes, the crawl space under one level may be reached by a wall access panel from another level. Access to crawl spaces can also be made from the exterior of the structure by a wall access panel. Check for these constructions carefully on your project drawings.

CAULKING AND WEATHER STRIPPING

These material costs are not major expense items; however, you could possibly forget to include the labor costs involved if you neglect to include the material.

Caulking is a resilient mastic compound that is used to seal cracks and fill joints. It is used to prevent air leakage and to provide a watertight joint at the transition of different materials.

Weather stripping is used to seal the joints around doors and windows to prevent the entry of water, snow, and cold air. It also aids in preventing heat from escaping. Weather stripping can be made of strips of wood, metal, neoprene, or felt.

BUILT-IN APPLIANCES AND SPECIALTY ITEMS

The items that could be included here are unlimited. Remember, if you agree to provide them in the home that you have contracted to build and then forget to

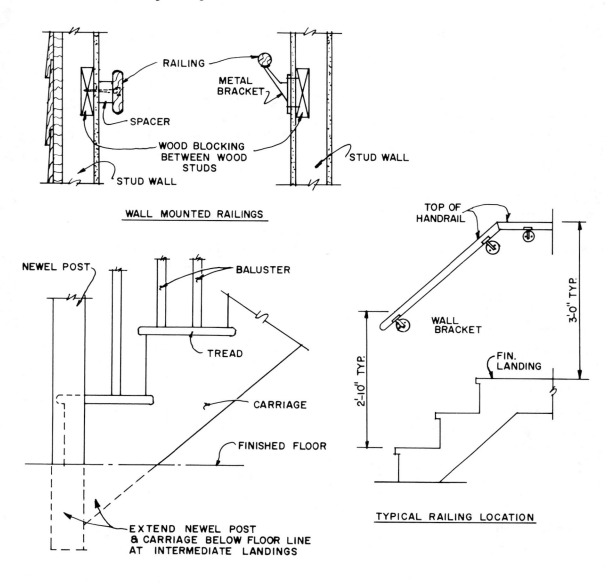

WALL MOUNTED RAILINGS

NEWEL POST & BALUSTER

TYPICAL RAILING LOCATION

Figure 11-2. Basic handrail components.

include them in your estimates, you will be expected to pay for them out of your profits. When listing them on a material take off, it would be a good idea to prepare your take off on a room-by-room basis. In this manner, you can provide a check on yourself to help assure that you have included all items. These items can and should be separated into interior and exterior items.

Interior items would include such items as the following:

1. Living room or family room. Drapery rods, chimes or doorbells, built-in cabinets or shelves, telephone outlets, cable TV connection, and intercom system.

2. Kitchen. Drapery rods, built-in cabinets or shelves, dishwasher, oven,

Figure 11-3. Pull-down folding ladder (courtesy of Bessler Stairway Corporation).

range, range hood and fan, exhaust fan, garbage disposal unit, telephone outlets, and intercom system.

3. Bedrooms. Drapery rods, built-in chests, cabinets, or shelves, cable TV connections, intercom systems, and telephone outlets.

4. Bathrooms. Medicine chests, towel bars, soap dishes, toilet-paper holders, grab bars, shower curtains and rods or sliding doors, mirrors, shelving for linen closets, exhaust fans, and intercom systems. Backing or blocking should be provided in the wall framing to provide anchorage for some of these accessories.

5. Utility rooms and garages. Utility sinks, water supply, drains, soap dishes, towel bars, intercom systems, telephone outlets, folding stair, and shelving.

Many of these items may and will occur more than once in a home. For example, many homes are built with more than one bath, perhaps even a bath off the master bedroom. Since most homes have more than one bedroom, take off the materials on a room-by-room basis.

Exterior items would include such things as lighting, mailboxes, mail chutes, letter drops, door bells, door knockers, and milk boxes. Other exterior items, not necessarily built in, would include storm doors and screens, storm windows and screens, louvers, and exhaust fans.

The foregoing list of miscellaneous material items is not complete; however, it is indicative of the types of things to look for. Again, before completing the estimate, double-check all plans to be sure that no item has been omitted. It is very difficult, if not impossible to add the cost of any items after the job estimate has been accepted by the client.

Labor   We have not dealt with the labor costs at any time in this book. As indicated in Chapter 1, this was not intended to be a "costing book." Rather, our main purpose was to show how to prepare a material take off. However, the estimator should be aware that labor is a major factor in the final cost of any residential structure. With this in mind, we have included some labor time tables in the appendixes as guides in making complete estimates.

There are several reasons for not including labor costs. For one thing, different parts of the country have different wage rates. The estimator may be faced with union and nonunion laborers. Also, each contractor will have different skilled laborers on the firm's permanent payroll. In addition, some unions or geographical locations will require workers to have more training than others.

All of these factors will affect the labor costs for any individual project. It is strongly recommended that the estimator establish labor cost standards for the firm by keeping good records for each job performed by the firm's craftworkers or subcontractors used on a repeated basis.

Overhead and Profit   Overhead expenses and profit are two items that are quite often inadvertently omitted from many estimates. When this happens, the contractor could end up with a disaster. Basically, there are two types of overhead: individual job overhead expenses and general overhead expenses.

Individual job overhead expenses are those cost items that are directly chargeable to each individual project. These items will probably be different for each contractor. Some items that you would normally expect to find on individual job overhead expenses are as follows:

1. Salaries of field personnel, such as project supervisor, craftworkers, and equipment operators.

2. Temporary buildings, if the project is large enough to require a field office.

3. Legal fees for services directly related to the project.

4. Building permits and licenses, including costs for obtaining permits for installing plumbing, electrical lines, and in-house electrical inspection, as well as heating system inspections.

5. Utilities, including tie-in costs for water and sewers, gas lines, and electrical service.

6. Testing, including the cost of testing materials such as concrete and all plumbing and electrical service.

7. Progress reports, which may simply be in-house reports.

8. Professional services for engineering and surveying services.

9. Protection of finished work, including the protection of finished floors and masonry during the balance of construction.

10. Completion date penalties, which, although more prevalent under commercial project construction, may be applied in housing developments.

11. Final clean-up.

General overhead expenses are those expenses that cannot be charged to a particular project. These items are prorated, and a proportionate amount is charged to each project. Some examples of this type of expense could be

1. Expenses incurred by the office of the firm that must be covered in some way, such as rentals, office utilities, and so forth.

2. Salaries of staff including executives, secretarial help, estimators, draftworkers, and so forth.

3. Costs of advertising and such literature as brochures.

4. Travel expenses.

5. Costs of tools and equipment.

The estimator or other firm official should review the firm's general expenses at the end of each fiscal year or on a frequent basis. At that point, all necessary adjustments should be made.

Profit is an item that will vary with each project or type of work involved. Quite often the percentage of profit may be subject to change according to the competition on a project. Profit will normally be the last item entered on the bid or estimate. Do not forget it, since the firm's growth is related to the net profit margin received from all the projects undertaken by the firm.

Summary

Now that the estimator has completed the material take off sheets, the next step is to enter the costs of all materials. The materials must be purchased from several sources, so it would be advisable to divide the material list into groups. This will make it easier to get separate quotations for the different items.

The estimator may obtain quotations based on unit prices. These must be extended to obtain totals. Quite often, he/she will find that bulk or lump sum quotations are generally lower than unit quotations. When starting to price out the materials, make a notation at the bottom of each estimate sheet to add sales tax and, if applicable, any delivery and/or freight costs as well.

If a quotation is far below that of the estimator or other sources, review the list of materials. Quite often, an item may inadvertently be omitted. The supplier is obligated to ship only the items on his/her list of materials. If this list is incomplete, the contractor will have to pay for ordering the missing items.

Now that the estimator has accumulated the individual costs, he/she must transfer these costs to a summary sheet (see Figure 11-4). Summary sheets cover most items required for construction. By using these sheets as a checklist, the estimator will minimize the possibility of omitting any substantial items.

Common Estimating Errors

Throughout this manual we have cautioned the estimator to be accurate and to double-check all calculations. Now we are going to discuss some of the most common sources of errors in estimating. These are common errors that are quite often made not only by beginning estimators but by experienced estimators as well.

1. Errors with figures. The most common source of error in all estimating results from sloppy, illegible figures. Quite often numbers are misread because of the carelessness of the individual writing them.

The simplest of arithmetical calculations—addition, subtraction, multiplication, and division—very often can result in errors of grave consequences. Even with calculators or computers, there is the possibility of error. Machines will produce correct answers only if they have been given the proper information.

Another common error occurs when transferring numbers from one piece of paper to another. One example of this would be as follows: Assume that you had a dimension of 83 ft 0 in., and you transposed the numbers when copying them and wrote 38 ft 0 in. This is a difference of 45 ft 0 in. If this were a calculation to determine the amount of concrete needed for a floor, you might be multiplying this by a number such as 60 ft 0 in. Since most residential floors are 4 in. thick, you would end up with a difference in volume of $45 \times 60 \times \frac{4}{12}$ ft, or 900 ft³. This would amount to $33\frac{1}{3}$ yd³ of concrete. At today's prices this would be a significant error.

2. Poor practices. Become familiar with the site on which the structure is to be built. If you do not visit the site, you cannot possible know the shape of the land or the topography. Location, both of the site and on the site, may also have a bearing on travel and hauling expenses.

Make a checklist of items that are essential to the construction of a home. Do not forget to include costs of labor and materials that may be required in the building of temporary runways for wheelbarrows and buggies. Most lumber for this can be used only once. The cost of scaffolding and its maintenance is an item that can easily be forgotten.

When making your estimate, never throw away any calculation sheets

ESTIMATE SUMMARY

MEANSCO
FORM FME110

PROJECT	TOTAL AREA	SHEET NO.
LOCATION	TOTAL VOLUME	ESTIMATE NO.
ARCHITECT	COST PER S.F.	DATE
OWNER	COST PER C.F.	NO. OF STORIES
QUANTITIES BY PRICES BY	EXTENSIONS BY	CHECKED BY

NO.	DESCRIPTION		MATERIAL	LABOR	SUBCONTRACT	TOTAL	ADJUSTMENT
	SITE WORK						
	Demolition, Clear & Grub						
	Excavation & Fill	✓					
	Caissons & Piling						
	Drainage & Utilities	✓					
	Sewage Treatment						
	Roads, Walks & Walls	✓					
	Lawns & Plantings						
	Termite Control						
	CONCRETE						
	Formwork						
	Reinforcing Steel & Mesh	✓					
	Foundations	✓					
	Superstructure						
	Floors & Finish	✓					
	Precast Concrete						
	Cementitious Decks						
	MASONRY						
	Brick	✓					
	Block	✓					
	Stonework						
	Mortar & Reinforcing						
	METALS						
	Joists						
	Structural Steel						
	Miscellaneous Metal						
	Ornamental Metal						
	Fasteners, Rough Hardware						
	Metal decks						
	CARPENTRY						
	Rough Carpentry	✓					
	Finish Carpentry	✓					
	Cabinets & Counters	✓					
	Laminated Construction						
	MOISTURE PROTECTION						
	Water & Dampproofing	✓					
	Insulation	✓					
	Roofing	✓					
	Siding	✓					
	Sheet Metal Work						
	Roof Accessories						
	DOORS, WINDOWS, GLASS						
	Doors & Entrances	✓					
	Windows	✓					
	Glass & Glazing						
	Weather stripping						
	Finish Hardware	✓					
	PAGE TOTAL						

R.S. MEANS CO., INC. KINGSTON, MA. 02364

Figure 11-4. Sample estimate summary sheet (courtesy of Robert S. Means Company, Inc.).

until the estimate is complete. Don't use shortcuts when taking off material quantities. The best way to take off materials is in the order in which they are to be used. Some common oversights are omitting items like bridging, headers in rough carpentry, wall framing, and steel lintels for masonry wall framing.

Another error in judgment occurs when you as an estimator do not provide yourself with adequate time to prepare the estimate. This will quite often cause you to omit the check against project specifications and the estimator's own guide list. Do not let yourself be put in the position of not having enough time to check your take offs completely.

In addition to skipped items, lack of time, and numerical transposition, you must constantly pay attention to the correct placement of decimals.

Another common area for error is in double take offs. Two examples of this are flooring and base boards. Quite often, these double coverages are small items and may be forgotten. However, on large projects or on repetitive work they could become sizable quantities and could result in estimates being too high. This could result in the loss of the project.

Summary Sheets

Most summary sheets are divided according to the various segments of the construction of a building. Each segment is given a code number for ease in checking and to ensure that no items are forgotten in the take off. You will note that the segments are organized roughly in the order in which they fit into the actual construction of the building. One set of segments is as follows:

Code Number	Phase (Subject)
1.00	General conditions
2.00	Site work
3.00	Concrete work
4.00	Masonry
5.00	Metals
6.00	Carpentry
7.00	Moisture protection
8.00	Doors and windows
9.00	Finishes
10.00[a]	Specialties
11.00[a]	Equipment
12.00[a]	Furnishings
13.00[a]	Special construction
14.00[a]	Conveying systems
15.00	Mechanical
16.00	Electrical

[a] These items generally would not be required in residential construction.

The foregoing tabulation has been adapted from the master format of the Construction Specifications Institute. Other tabulations can be obtained, such as the one in the American Institute of Architect's sample specifications. The general conditions referred to in this tabulation cover common items that appear in specifications. These include such items as

Summary of work.

Special project procedures.

Coordination of work.

Regulatory requirement (permits, licenses, and so forth).

Alternates.

Methods of measurement and payment.

Construction facilities and temporary controls.

Contract closeout.

Figure 11-4 shows one section of a typical summary sheet. You will notice that there are small check marks next to some of the code numbers. These indicate those items that apply to your estimate and will serve as an additional safeguard against any errors of omission. Before you have completed your estimate, you should have a total dollar amount listed for each item you have checked.

Conclusion

This completes our treatise on material estimating for house builders. You should now have the basic tools and knowledge that are needed to prepare material quantity take offs. We recommend that you keep this book (and its related manual) close at hand for easy reference. The only remaining aspect of training that you will need to become a good estimator is practice.

If you will remember to follow the basics of estimating that we have stated and the following general rules, you should be able to provide complete, accurate results:

1. Prepare and follow a general guide list that is applicable to the firm's individual type of work.

2. Always use a sharp pencil and write your numbers clearly.

3. Always double-check calculations and the numbers that are entered on take off summary sheets.

4. Know your suppliers and check their quotations in detail.

5. Visit each site to become familiar with the location and special considerations for each project.

6. Provide adequate time to prepare each statement properly.

7. Do not try to prepare an estimate if you are overtired. Fatigue produces errors.

8. Make sure the company is qualified and capable of performing the work on a project before making the estimate.

9. Invest in a calculator with a tape—don't rely on handwritten or mental arithmetic calculations.

(One thing you must keep in mind, however, is the fact that human beings frequently make errors. The estimator should try at all times to minimize these mistakes.)

Epilogue   Estimating is a vital and necessary procedure in the construction business. It is important for the estimator to realize that many of his/her efforts will be offered in competition with other firms. Therefore he/she should learn to work carefully. Remember, when an estimate is the lowest offered in the bidding process, the employer will want to be assured that no significant error or omission was made. Of course, if a firm loses the bid because the estimate is high, explanations may well be in order. To recap, the successful estimator is careful with his/her figures, knowledgeable in material take offs and cost records, and knowledgeable in construction processes.

Symbols and Abbreviations

π	pi is an abstract number that relates the circumference of a circle to its diameter; circumference = π × diameter; π = 3.14, or approximately $\frac{22}{7}$
x°	degrees
ABS	Acrylo-mitrile butadine styrene (plastic pipe)
cl	cast iron
CPVC	chlorinated polyvinyl chloride (plastic pipe)
fbm	foot board measure (M-fbm = 1000 board feet)
ft	foot = measure of length
ft^2	square foot = measure of area
ft^3	cubic foot = measure of volume
h	height
hp	horsepower
HVAC	heating–ventilating–air-conditioning
in.	inch = measure of length
in.^{2}	square inch = measure of area
in.^{3}	cubic inches = measure of volume
L	length
lb	pound = measure of weight
lf	linear foot

NEC	National Electrical Code—a standard for anything related to electricity
oc	on center
psf	pounds per square foot (load or stress)
psi	pounds per square inch (stress)
PVC	Polyvinyl chloride (plastic pipe)
r	radius
R	a value used to measure insulating capabilities
V	volume
VT	Vitrified tile
w	width
wwm	welded wire mesh
yd	yard = measure of length
yd^2	square yard = measure of area
yd^3	cubic yard = measure of volume

Appendixes

Appendix A

Earthwork

Table A-1
Earthwork Labor Rates

Equipment	Size	Typical Crew	Daily Output (yd^3/hr)
Backhoe	$\frac{1}{2}$ yd^3	1 Equipment operator 1 Oiler	20
Backhoe	1 yd^3	1 Equipment operator 1 Oiler	45
Dozer	75 hp 50-ft haul	1 Equipment operator 1 Oiler	50
Dozer	75 hp 150-ft haul	1 Equipment operator 1 Oiler	25
Front-end loader (wheel mounted)	$\frac{3}{4}$ yd^3	1 Equipment operator 1 Building laborer	45

Source: Adapted from *1982 Building Construction Cost Data* published by Robert S. Means, Inc.

Table A-2
Volumes of Excavation (5-ft 0-in.
Average Depth of Excavation)

Plan Dimensions (ft)	Plan Dimensions (ft)					
	20	22	24	26	28	30
16	59	65	71	78	83	89
18	67	73	80	87	93	100
20	74	82	89	97	103	111
22	82	90	98	106	114	123
24	89	98	107	117	125	134
26	97	106	116	125	135	144
28	103	114	124	135	145	156
30	111	123	133	144	156	167
32	118	130	142	156	167	178
34	126	138	151	165	176	189
36	134	147	160	173	187	200
40	148	163	178	193	207	222

note: Volumes are rounded off to next full cubic yard value. Other values for depth can be proportioned to the 5-ft depth used in the table above. See Example 2-1 for actual method of calculating all earth volumes.

Appendix B

Concrete Work

Table B-1
Estimated Weight of Welded Wire Fabric[a] (Approximate
Weight in Pounds per 100 ft² Based on 60-in. Fabric
Width Center to Center of Outside Longitudinal Wires)

"W" or "D" Wire Size Number	Nominal Weight (lb/lin ft)	Spacing and Weight of Longitudinal Wires (in.)								
		2	3	4	6	8	9	10	12	16
31	1.054	653	443	337	232	179	162	148	126	100
30	1.020	632	428	326	224	173	156	143	122	97
28	0.952	590	400	305	209	162	136	133	114	90
26	0.884	548	371	283	194	150	139	125	124	106	98	78
24	0.816	506	343	261	180	139	125	115	105	90	71
22	0.748	464	314	239	165	127	115	105	95	82	65
20	0.680	422	286	218	150	116	104	95	86	73	58
18	0.612	379	257	196	135	104	94	86	76	65	52
16	0.544	337	228	174	120	92	83	76	67	57	45
14	0.476	295	200	152	105	81	73	67	57	49	39
12	0.408	253	171	131	90	69	63	57	52	45	36
11	0.374	232	157	120	82	64	57	55	50	43	34
10.5	0.357	221	150	114	79	61	55	52	48	41	32
10	0.340	211	143	109	75	58	52	50	45	39	31
9.5	0.323	200	136	103	71	55	50	47	43	37	29
9	0.306	190	129	98	67	52	47	44	40	35	27
8.5	0.289	179	121	92	64	49	44	42	38	33	26
8	0.272	169	114	87	60	46	42	38	33	26
7.5	0.255	158	107	82	56	43	39	36	31	24
7	0.238	148	100	76	52	40	37	33	29	23
6.5	0.221	137	93	71	49	38	34	31	27	21
6	0.204	126	86	65	45	35	31	29	24	19
5.5	0.187	116	79	60	41	32	29	26	22	18
5	0.170	105	71	54	37	29	26	24	20	16
4.5	0.153	95	64	49	34	26	23	21	18	15

(continues)

Table B-1 (Continued)

"W" or "D" Wire Size Number	Nominal Weight (lb/lin ft)	Spacing and Weight of Longitudinal Wires (in.)								
		2	3	4	6	8	9	10	12	16
4	0.136	84	57	44	30	23	21	19	16	13
3.5	0.119	74	50	38	26	20	18	17	14	11
3	0.102	63	43	33	22	17	16	14	12	10
2.9	0.098	61	41	31	22	17	15	14	12	9
2.5	0.085	53	36	27	19	14	13	12	10	8
2	0.068	42	29	22	15	12	10	10	8	6
1.5	0.051	32	21	16	11	9	8	7	6	5
1.4	0.049	30	21	16	11	8	8	7	6	5

Source: Tech Facts (TF501) of the Wire Reinforcement Institute.
[a] For estimating purposes only

Table B-2
Labor Times for Concrete Work

Item	Unit	Time Required (hr/unit)
Footings—18 × 9 in.	Cubic Yard	0.35
4-in. ground slab—exclude finish	Cubic Yard	0.17
Finishing—steel trowel for finish floor	100 ft²	1.45

Source: Adapted from Section 3.3 of 1982 Building Construction Cost Data, published by Robert S. Means, Inc.

Table B-3
Labor Times for Masonry Work

Item	Unit (ft²)	Time Required (hr/unit)
Standard brick (running bond)	100	3.5
8-in. concrete block	100	4.0

Source: Adapted from Sections 4.2 and 4.3 of 1982 Building Construction Cost Data published by Robert S. Means, Inc.

Appendix C

Lumber-Related Tables

The following sketches show typical cross sections of many types of millwork that are available in the United States. Sections shown are a composite of the output of many forestry products suppliers.

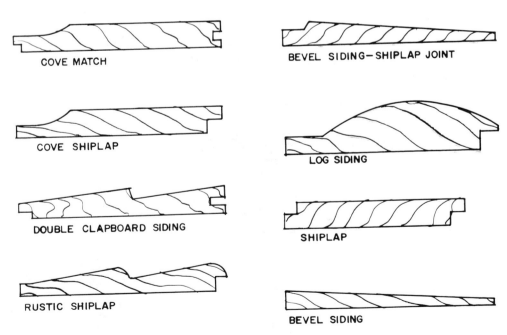

COVE MATCH

BEVEL SIDING—SHIPLAP JOINT

COVE SHIPLAP

LOG SIDING

DOUBLE CLAPBOARD SIDING

SHIPLAP

RUSTIC SHIPLAP

BEVEL SIDING

Figure C-1. Examples of wood siding.

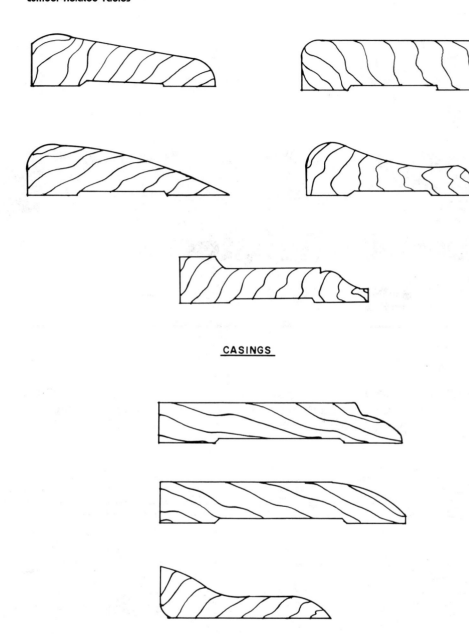

CASINGS

BASES

Figure C-2. Examples of interior wood trim—casing and base material.

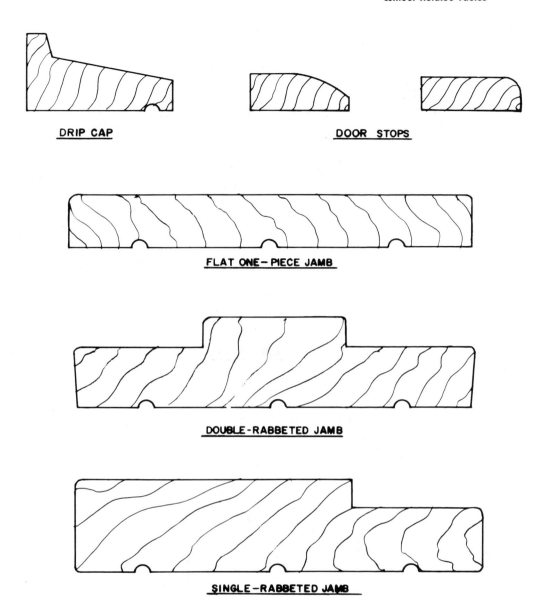

DRIP CAP   DOOR STOPS

FLAT ONE–PIECE JAMB

DOUBLE–RABBETED JAMB

SINGLE–RABBETED JAMB

Figure C-3. Examples of wood door and window trim.

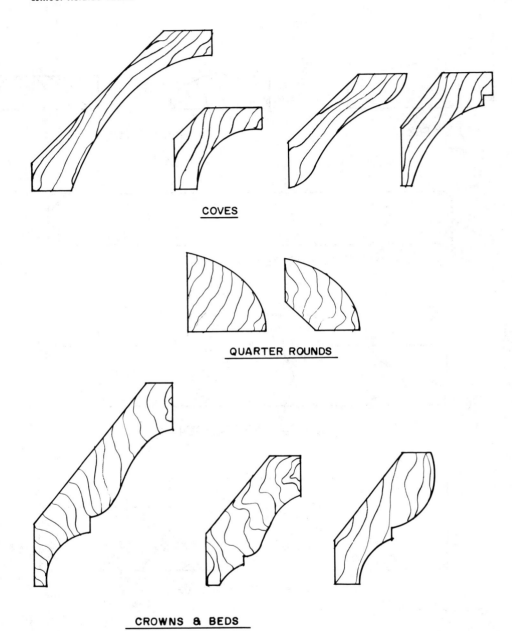

COVES

QUARTER ROUNDS

CROWNS & BEDS

Figure C-4. Examples of interior wood ceiling moldings.

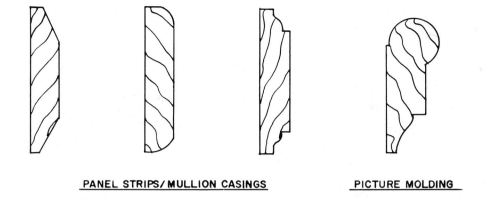

PANEL STRIPS/MULLION CASINGS   PICTURE MOLDING

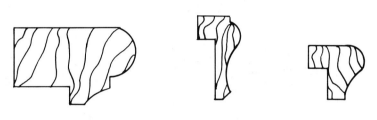

WAINSCOT PLY CAP MOLDINGS

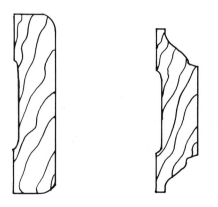

CHAIR RAILS

Figure C-5. Examples of miscellaneous wood trim moldings—normal interior use.

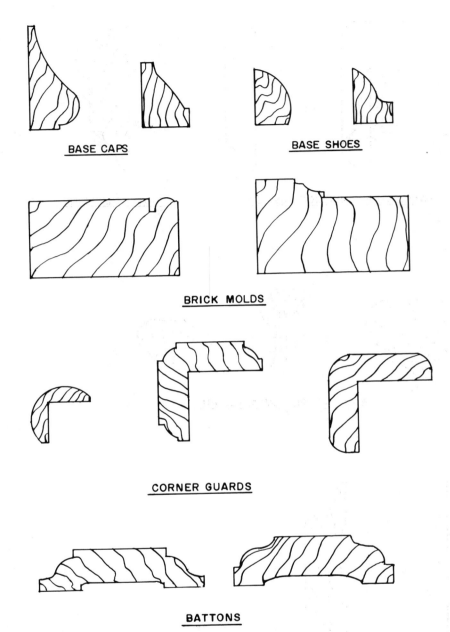

Figure C-6. Examples of miscellaneous wood trim moldings—normal exterior use.

Table C-2
Permissible Spans (in ft) for Timber
Trusses Each 2 ft 0 in. oc

Pitch	Chord Sizes (nominal in in.)		
	2 × 4 Top and Bottom	2 × 6 Top 2 × 4 Bottom	2 × 6 Top and Bottom
$\frac{2}{12}$	28	29	42
$\frac{3}{12}$	34	39	52
$\frac{4}{12}$	40	47	59
$\frac{5}{12}$	43	54	65
$\frac{6}{12}$	45	59	67

Lumber properties:

2 × 4	2 × 6
$f_b = 1850$ psi	$f_b = 1600$ psi
$f_t = 1050$ psi	$f_t = 1050$ psi
$f_c = 1450$ psi	$f_c = 1450$ psi

Modulus of elasticity
for all lumber
$E = 1.8 \times 10^6$ psi.

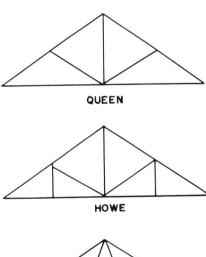

QUEEN

HOWE

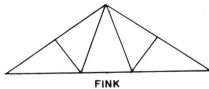

FINK

Figure C-7. Examples of common residential wood roof trusses.

Source: Alpine Engineered Products, Inc., Pompano Beach, Fla.

Table C-3
Labor Times for Carpentry Work

Item	Unit	Time Required (hr/unit)
Rough carpentry		
Light framing (average for all framing)	M-fbm	7.6
Joists 2 × 8 in. (fir)	M-fbm	6.4
Plates 2 × 6 in. (treated)	M-fbm	9.4
Stud walls 2 × 4 in. (8 ft-height)	M-fbm	11.4
Rafters, to $\frac{4}{12}$ pitch, 2 × 8 in. ordinary	M-fbm	8.4
Subfloor, $\frac{5}{8}$ in.-thick plywood	100 ft^2	0.6
Finish carpentry		
Paneling, prefinished, $\frac{1}{4}$-in.-thick, 4 × 8-ft sheets	100 ft^2	2.3
Miscellaneous trim	100 lf	3.2
Siding, cedar bevel A-grade ($\frac{1}{2}$ × 8 in.)	100 ft^2	2.9
Exterior molding (average)	100 lf	3.2

Source: Adapted from Sections 6.1 and 6.2 of *1982 Building Construction Cost Data* published by Robert S. Means, Inc.

Appendix D

Finish-Related Tables

Table D-1
Labor Rates for Applying Coats of Paint and Performing Other Decorating Operations

Operation	Rate (ft²/hr)		
	Brush	Other	Roller
Exterior			
Oil paint on new siding and trim	105		110
Oil paint on primed siding	200		300
Oil paint on trim only	80–95		
Oil paint on shingle or rough-sawn siding	150–200		200–250
Staining on shingle or rough-sawn siding	150–185		200–240
Oil paint on common brick	100–140		275–320
Oil paint on medium-texture siding	100–175		200–250
Interior			
Sanding for painting		215–140	
Doors	125–175		275–300
Windows (no frame)	150–90		
Paint on smooth plaster or wallboard	175–220		300–320
Stippling	200		
Paint on textured plaster or wallboard	110–135		375
Seamless floors			
Concrete etching and neutralizing		200	
Base coat, 18 in. roller, also first flood coat		200	
Chip coat, by hand		400	
Sanding and wiping by machine		400	
Second flood coat—18 in. roller		600	
Three finish glaze coats, 18 in. roller		800 (each)	
To prepare plywood for base coat		200	

Source: Adapted from *1982 Estimating Guide* of the Painting and Decorating Contractors of America.

Table D-2
Labor Times for Finishing Work

Item	Unit	Required Time (hr/unit)
Gypsum lath, $\frac{3}{8}$ in. nailed to wood studs	100 yd^2	9.40
Gypsum plaster—2 coats on wells	100 yd^2	7.60
Drywall, $\frac{3}{8}$ in. (no finish)	100 ft^2	0.36
Taping and finishing drywall joints	100 ft^2	0.40
Suspended ceilings, including suspension system	100 ft^2	2.10
Carpet, stretched and edge fastened	yd^2	0.20
Resilient tile, vinyl 12 × 12 in., $\frac{1}{8}$ in. thick	100 ft^2	2.10
Parquet wood flooring, including finish	100 ft^2	10.70

Source: Adapted from Sections 9.1, 9.2, 9.5 and 9.6 of *1982 Building Construction Cost Data* published by Robert S. Means, Inc.

Glossary

Aggregate Particles of inorganic minerals of various sizes; broken rock or soil.

Backfill(ing) Fill (or filling) used in areas where existing ground elevation is below the desired final elevation.

Backhoe A tractor-type piece of construction equipment with booms and a bucket that can be used to dig trenchlike excavations.

Backup Stud A stud added to a wall frame where a partition meets the exterior wall; is needed to back up the interior finish material.

Balloon-Framing A construction system in which the exterior wall is framed to its full height and carries intermediate floor frames on "ribbons" let into the wall frame.

Bank Measure The volume occupied by earth before being dug out.

Base Coat The first layer of plaster or stucco (sometimes called a "brown coat").

Basement Living quarters whose floor level is more than 3 ft below the exterior grade.

Bearing Partition A partition used to transmit loads to lower levels.

Bearing Post The vertical member used to transmit floor- or roof-framing loads to a lower level or a foundation.

Bevelled Siding Wood, steel, or aluminum members set horizontally to act as an exterior covering for a structure (see appendixes for shapes commonly used).

Birdsmouth The cut made in a rafter so that it will sit securely on the wall plate (see Figure 4-24).

Board Measure The term used in lumber purchases that refers to the size of lumber *before* surface finishing of any kind. One foot board measure = $12 \times 12 \times 1$ in. thick. Thus a nominal 1×6-in. board (actual $\frac{3}{4} \times 5\frac{1}{2}$ in.) contains 0.50 board measure per foot of length although it covers only a $5\frac{1}{2} \times 12$-in. area.

Bonding Obtaining an "insurance" policy to guarantee proper performance of all phases of a construction project.

Box Sill The end-closure member at right angles to the joists in a floor frame.

Brick A construction unit made of pulverized, mixed, and molded clay or shale that is then burned in a kiln.

Bridging Minor structural floor members used to prevent twisting of a joist (see Figure 4-9).

Brown Coat See **Base Coat.**

Butt Joint Joint formed when members are placed end to end and held together by splice plates on both sides (see Figure 4-6).

Casement Windows Windows with sections that open using vertically placed hinges.

Casing Wood trim (see appendixes for shapes) used to finish the opening for a door or window.

Clapboards A form of siding (usually of wood).

Caulking Generally, a putty-like substance used to seal a joint.

Cement The pulverized product of a burned (calcined) mixture of clay and limestone.

Clearing and Grubbing The removal of underbrush, trees and stumps, large boulders, and man-made structures from a project site.

Closet Bend The elbow-shaped fitting under a water closet.

Concrete The hardened product that results from mixing coarse and fine aggregates with a portland cement and water paste.

Concrete Block A masonry unit made of concrete.

Conduit A tube or trough for electric wires.

Construction Documents A term referring to all the documents involved in a construction contract, including drawings, specifications, change orders, and addends.

Corner Beads Strips of metal used to reinforce the outside corners of plastered construction.

Cornice Another term for fascia board.

Crawl Space The space below habited areas of a structure that is too shallow to permit persons to stand.

Cripple A wall stud used to fill in the space below and above wall-frame openings.

Curing The process of keeping concrete wet until it has hardened (hydrated) properly.

Cutting Action The erosion of the inside of a valve that results from the high-velocity of the water passing through gate valves as the valve is initially opened.

Datum Plane The basic level surface from which changes in elevation (vertical measurements) are measured.

Double-Hung Windows Windows in which both sashes can be moved vertically.

Downspouts Galvanized metal or aluminum tubes used to carry rainwater from gutter to ground level or into underground drainage lines.

Earthwork All operations involved in the movement of earth; includes excavating, grading or leveling, transporting or moving, backfilling, and so forth.

Escutcheon A plate or cast-metal decorative piece that fits over the door cutout for a door-locking mechanism.

Estimate The projected cost of constructing a building.

Fascia An edge piece used to finish off the edge of a roof frame.

Faucet A device with hand-operated valves for regulating the flow of a liquid.

Fiberglass An insulating material consisting of spun glass fibers; comes in the form of rolls or batts.

Finished Grade Final surface of ground at a site.

Finishing (Concrete) Putting the desired surface finish on a wet concrete surface.

Fire Stop Wood blocking in joist or stud spaces to delay passage of smoke or flames through the spaces.

Fixed Sash A section of window that is fixed in position and cannot be opened.

Flashing Sheets of metal or other material used to waterproof joints or holes in roofs.

Flitch-Plated Beam A beam or girder consisting of a steel plate bolted between two or more wood boards.

Flue A tube, pipe, or shaft for the passage of smoke or hot gases, as in a chimney.

Formwork Wood or metal components used to hold plastic concrete in the desired shape until it hardens.

French Drain A drainage trench filled with coarse, broken stone or gravel to permit flow of water through the ground without using any kind of pipe.

Front End Loader A tractor-type construction unit with a bucket at the front that can be used to excavate earth materials and deposit them into a truck for disposal.

Frost Line The underground level below which frost action will not penetrate; any construction that sits above the frost line is subject to damage by the freezing and thawing action in the soil.

Gable A roof construction in which the roof slopes up from only two opposite walls (see Figure 4-17); also refers to the vertical wall at the ends of this roof.

Gauging Plaster A pulverized gypsum product mixed with cement, sand, and water to control the setting time of the mortar formed.

Gin-Pole A simple piece of timber held almost vertical by four guy wires about 90° apart; has an attached hoisting mechanism that is used to lift construction materials.

Girders Main horizontal structural members that carry the joists in a floor frame and are supported by bearing posts of wood, steel, or brick/block piers.

Glue-Laminated Girders Built-up beams consisting of layers of structural lumber boards that are glued together under pressure; enable the builder to get larger beams than are normally available.

Gooseneck A flexible connection in piping that permits differential settlement of two sections of pipe.

Grade Surface of ground; also refers to the process of leveling an area.

Ground (Strip) A wood strip (usually $\frac{3}{4} \times \frac{3}{4}$ in.) used at the floor line and at openings in walls to be plastered; sets the thickness of the plaster on a wall.

Gutter Metal trough to gather water running off a roof (see Figure 5-2).

Gutter Boards Wood boards used at the sides of roof framing as attachment points for gutters.

Header A structural unit used to frame a floor or wall opening; rungs are at right angles to floor joists or wall studs.

Hinge A movable joint to attach, support, and permit the turning of a door about the hinge as a pivot point.

Hip Roof A roof construction in which the roof slopes up from exterior walls (see Figure 4-19); see also Figure 4-20 for the various components of a hip roof.

Hose Bibb A faucet whose nozzle is bent downward and is used for supplying water to flexible hoses.

HVAC The abbreviation for heating–ventilating–air-conditioning.

Hydrated Lime A pulverized limestone product used as an ingredient for plaster and/or stucco.

Isometric A three-dimensional figure showing the three dimensions without fore-shortening (see Figure 1-2).

Jamb The vertical support member at the sides of openings such as doors or windows.

Joist A direct load-carrying structural member that is normally horizontal.

Joist Hanger A piece of sheet metal formed to support the end of a joist and attach it to a wall or girder.

Laminated Beams Structural members made from thin strips of material glued under pressure to improve load-carrying ability of the basic material.

Lap Siding A form of wood or metal strip that sets horizontally and is used as exterior finish on a structure (see appendixes for typical shapes).

Ledger A structural member attached to a wall or girder and used to support floor joists.

Lintel A structural member used to carry loads over an opening such as a window or a door.

Louvers A window or opening set with a series of sloping slats arranged to admit air and light but to shed rainwater outward.

Masonry Cement A cementing material specifically formulated to use as a mortar for masonry construction.

Mastic A pastelike mixture (usually with an asphalt base) used to glue two materials to each other, such as rigid insulation boards to block walls.

Material Take-Off A tabulation of the types and quantities of materials needed to complete a project that is prepared by the estimator from construction documents.

Meter An instrument that measures the quantity of gas, electricity, or water passing through it.

Millwork A term used for finished wood products such as doors, trim, and baseboards.

Moldings Shaped wood or plastic items used to trim edges of paneling, frame around openings, and so forth (see the appendixes for typical shapes).

Mortar A mixture of cement, hydrated lime, sand, and water used to cement brick or block units into a solid structure.

Panning Refers to areas of joist spaces turned into ducts by closing off the joist spaces with sheet-metal panels.

Partition A vertically framed wall used to divide a structure into functionally useful areas.

Pilaster A projecting structure built into a masonry wall that is used to add strength to the wall at points of concentrated loads.

Pitch A method of stating the slope of a roof; equals the unit rise over the unit span of the roof.

Plate A horizontal member used at the bottom and top of wall studs.

Platform-Framing A construction system in which the one-story wall units act as the support for the floor/roof frame for the next level (see Figure 4-13).

Plumb Cut The vertical cut of the notch on roof rafters (see Figure 4-24).

Plyscord Plywood made with exterior-grade glue that has one face of C grade and the other of D grade; used for sheathing (wall or roof) and as subflooring material (term not presently used in some areas).

Plywood Wood sheets made of three or more thin layers (veneers) of wood that has been glued together under pressure.

Plywood-Boxed Girders Large beams formed by glueing structural boards to plywood webs; the boards forming the flanges.

Portiere A heavy curtain hung in a doorway.

Portland Cement See **Cement.**

Prehung A term used to describe an assembly consisting of a door and a door frame connected by hinges and that is ready to position into the door opening of the wall framing.

Quicklime A product consisting chiefly of calcium oxide (lime) and that is used in plaster and/or stucco.

Rafter The sloped structural member that supports the roof.

Ribbon A structural unit used in balloon-frame construction to support intermediate floor frames.

Ridge The apex, or high point, of a section of roof frame.

Rim Joists Joists at end of a joist run (see Figure 4-4).

Rise The vertical distance measured from the top of the wall plates to the point where the center line of the roof rafters hits the ridge of the roof.

Roofing Felt A building material consisting of coarse paper impregnated with bituminous material; comes in rolls and is used to waterproof roofs and underground walls.

Rough Sill The structural member that forms the bottom of a window opening in a wall frame.

Run The horizontal distance from the outer face of the wall framing to the point below the ridge (or peak) of the roof.

S4S A lumber term used to indicate that the four sides of a board have been planed; stands for "surfaced four sides."

Scratch Coat The first layer of plaster in a wall; also called "brown coat."

Seepage Water that penetrates through a wall that has not been properly waterproofed.

Sheathing Material used to cover the outside of a wall stud frame or a roof rafter frame.

Shingles Prefabricated wall or roof facing materials usually made of wood, asphalt, or slate.

Shiplap Form of edge treatment for boards to form tight joints.

Sill The horizontal (flat) member on a wall to which the floor joists are attached.

Sillcock A faucet or valve usually exterior for regulating the flow of a liquid.

Single-Hung Window A window unit in which only the lower section is made to slide up and down.

Soffit Undersurface of any overhanging building element.

Specifications A written set of instructions on the types of material and/or equipment that are to be used in the construction of a building.

Splash Block Usually a concrete pad or trough set on the ground surface that receives the flow from downspouts; prevents erosion of the soil.

Square Term used in finish work; 1.0 square = 10 × 10 ft = 100 ft^2 of surface area.

Standard "A" Series Door Lock The industry standard lock for residential and light commercial buildings.

Stucco A plaster mixture used as an exterior finish on the walls of a structure.

Studs The vertical framing members used in walls and partitions.

Styrofoam A trademark for a rigid, lightweight, cellular polystyrene used as insulation material.

Subcontractor A person or firm that specializes in one (or more) facets of construction.

Subflooring The material covering floor joists that is used as a base for the finished flooring material.

Sump A floor drain set in a depressed well in a slab on the ground, usually in a basement; collects excess water and prevents it from spreading throughout the floor.

Sump Pump An automatically controlled pump that is used to lift water from a sump and discharge it into a drain line.

Swell The percentage change in the volume of earth when it is removed from its original position.

Tail Joist A short segment of joist that extends from a floor header to a support point (see Figure 4-4).

Tap in A place in a water line or gas line where a connection can be made.

Tongue and Grooved Lumber with edges treated to provide tight joints in floor, wall, or roof construction.

Trimmer A piece of wall stud that forms the jamb of a wall opening.

Trimmer Joists Joists in a floor frame that form the sides of a floor opening (see Figure 4-4).

Underlayment A fiberboard or plywood cover of a subfloor that provides a smooth surface on which to place the finish floor material.

Unit Rise The rise (vertical distance) of a roof rafter in a horizontal distance of 12 in.

Unit Run A 12-in. section of the run (horizontal distance) of a roof rafter.

Valve A unit for controlling the flow of water or gas through pipes.

Veneer A single thickness of masonry wall used as an architectural facing on the wall.

Vent Stack A vertical pipe used to permit passage of gas from a drainage/sewage system; prevents buildup of gas pressure.

Waste Excess earth material.

Water Hammer A hammering sound in water pipes that occurs when a faucet or solenoid valve (controlling water flow) closes suddenly to halt the water flow.

Water Softener A tank in which water is filtered through various chemicals to soften it (remove minerals).

Welded Wire Mesh Wire reinforcing for concrete slabs or walls that has been prefabricated into a mesh of wires welded together at their intersection points.

Wythe A thickness of a masonry wall.

Bibliography

MANUALS

Charles G. Ramsey and Harold R. Sleeper, *Architectural Graphic Standards,* various editions. John Wiley & Sons, New York.

1982 Building Construction Cost Data, updated yearly. Robert S. Means, Inc., Kingston, Mass.

Building Design Handbook. Wire Reinforcement Institute, McLean, Va.

Building Estimator's Reference Book, updated periodically. Frank R. Walker, Publishers, Chicago.

Manual of Steel Construction, revised periodically. American Institute of Steel Construction, Chicago.

CATALOGS AND MISCELLANEOUS DATA SHEETS

Catalog on Hardware Items, revised periodically. Stanley Hardware, New Britain, Conn.

Catalog on Timber Connector Items, revised periodically. The Simpson Company, San Leandro, Calif.

Engineering News-Record, weekly magazine published by McGraw-Hill Publishing Company, New York.

1982 Estimating Guide published by Painting and Decorating Contractors of America, Falls Church, Va.

Standard Reinforcing Bar Chart. Concrete Reinforcing Steel Institute (CRSI), Schaumberg, Ill.

Sweet's Catalogs (published yearly) Reference 6.4b/AL. Alpine Engineered Products, Inc., Pompano Beach, Fla.

Tech Facts (TF 501). Wire Reinforcement Institute, McLean, Va.

Various Estimating Forms, updated periodically. Robert S. Means, Inc., Kingston, Mass.

Index

ABS (acrylomitrile butadine styrene) pipes, 161–162

Access road, 19

Accordion doors, 130–131

Actual length of rafter, 65, 67

Adapters for piping, 141

Adhesive:
  for ceramic tile, 108, 115
  for resilient flooring, 110

Adjustable jack posts, 40

Air chambers to prevent water hammer, 146

Air-conditioning, 92, 175–176, 181, 182–183, 185–186, 196–197, 200
  energy conservation tips, 171
  room-size units, 183
  split system, 182–183
  see also Heating

Air filters, 182

Aluminum:
  siding, 83, 102
  windows, 131

American Plywood Association, 5

American Society for Testing Materials (ASTM), 60

Anchor bolts, 37, 118

Angle valves, 142

Antisiphoning valves, 155

Appliances, 190, 196
  built-in, and specialty items, 207–210
  see also specific appliances

Architect, 37

Architectural Graphic Standards (Ramsey and Sleeper), 5

Asbestos, 23

Asbestos roof shingles, 74

Asphalt-impregnated fiberboard, 59

Asphalt resilient flooring, 110

Asphalt roof shingles, 74

Attic fan, 201

Attic wiring, 197

Awning lock, 133

Awning windows, 78, 131, 132, 133, 134
  rotary gear operator, 133, 134

Baby Norman face brick, 36

Backfilling, 20, 21, 23, 25, 164, 205

Backhoe for earthwork operations, 20, 21, 22

Backup studs, 57

Balloon-frame construction, 56–57

Bar hanger box support, 190, 196

Basement:
  floors, 103
  installation of foundation drain tiles, 23, 24
  masonry piers for, 39
  notching floor joists for piping installation, 152–154
  waterproofing foundation walls, 21–24
  windows, 131, 132
  wiring, 197

Base molding, 96

Bathrooms:
  accessories, 108
  carpeting, 109
  flooring, 97, 98
  plumbing fixtures, 146, 147, 156–157. See also individual fixtures
  roughing-in diagrams, 154
  specialty items, 209

Bathtubs, 146, 147, 156–157, 165
  faucets, 157, 165
  traps, 159

Beam lintel sash, 34

Bearing posts for floor framing, 43, 44, 45, 51–52

Bedrooms, 209

Bentonite for waterproofing, 23

Bevelled siding, 83, 84

Bifolding doors, 96

Birdsmouth, 65, 66

Bituminous coatings for foundation walls, 23

Block flooring, 113, 114

Blowers for heating/cooling system, 183, 185

Board of health, county, 163

Boiler water to heat domestic hot water, 147

Bond beam, 34, 35

Bond forms, 4

Bonding, 4

Books on construction, see Reference sources

Box sills, 48, 53

Bracing for exterior floor frames, 57

Brass pipes, 140

Bricks for masonry piers, 39–40

Brick veneer, 37, 38

245

Brick veneer (*Continued*)
  as exterior wall finish, 83–87
  face brick sizes, 36
Brick walls, 34–39
  anchor bolts for, 37
  concrete and burned clay elements, 34–35
  determining number of bricks needed, 35
  exposures and patterns, 37, 38
  methods for estimating costs of, 35
  size of face bricks, 35
Bridging, 44, 50, 51, 53, 119–120
Building Design Handbook, 31n
Building Estimator's Reference Book, 124
Building paper, 75, 77
Built-ins and specialty items, 207–210
Bulldozer for earthwork operations, 19, 20, 21, 22

Cabinet door pull, 135
Cabinets, 97, 208, 209
  hardware for, 135, 136
Cable TV connection, 208, 209
Capillary joints for piping, 141
Carpeting, 97, 109–110
Casement windows, 78, 131–132, 133, 134
  hinge, 134
  rotary gear operator, 133, 134
  sash lock, 133, 134
Casing nails, 122
Cast-iron pipes and fittings, 160–161
Catalog on Hardware, 126n
Catalog on Timber Connector Items, 122n
"Cathedral" type ceilings:
  glue-laminated girders as rafters for, 44–45
  rafters and roof deck construction, 66–68
Caulking doors and windows, 171, 207
Ceilings:
  access panels, 207
  framing, 62
  interior, 91–95, 103, 104–105, 228
  painting, 103, 104–105
Ceramic tile:
  flooring, 98, 114–115
  as wall covering, 108, 109
Checklist for estimating costs, 6, 7
  for exterior painting, 102
  for interior painting, 103–104
Check valves, 142, 143
Chimes, 208
Chimneys, 174–175
  accessories, 205
Circle, calculating the area of, 9–10
Cisterns, 140
Clapboard siding, 83, 84
Clay brick, 35. *See also* Brick walls
Clay Institute, 5
Clay-tile roof covering, 74–75
Cleanouts, 160, 162
Clean-up, final, 211
Clearing and grubbing, 20
Clock outlets, 192

Closet hardware, 136, 137
Closet shelving and/or rods, 96
Clothes dryer, 156, 192
Clothes washer, 146, 147, 158
Coal heat, 170, 171, 172, 175
Collar beam, 65, 67
Common bond pattern, 38
Common nails, 122
Common rafters, 64
Completion date penalties, 211
Computations needed in estimating, 8–11
Concrete:
  cost of stripping the forms, 33
  curing of, 33
  field-mixed, 33
  ready-mix, 33
Concrete block, 34–35
  plain, walls, 34–35
  reinforced, walls, 35
  sizes and shapes, 34
Concrete brick, 35. *See also* Brick walls
Concrete floors, 103, 104
Concrete work, 29–33, 223–224
  basic computations needed in estimating, 8–9
  composition of concrete, 29
  concrete, 33
  formwork, 29–30, 31
  reinforced steel, 30–33
Conduction, 170
Conduit nipples, 201
Construction loads, 30
Construction materials, *see* Materials of construction
Construction methods, 3
  knowledge of required, 3
Contingencies, estimating costs of, 6
Contract for construction, 4
Convection, 170
Cooling coil, 175, 182, 186
Copper sweat-type fittings, 160
Copper tubing, 140–142, 144, 154, 161, 164
  fittings for, 141–142
  see also Pipe(s)
C- or channel-shaped steel members, 46, 47
Cork resilient flooring, 110
Corner beads, 92, 93
Corner braces, 125
Corner concrete block, 34
Cornerite, 92
Cornice boards, 76
Corporation cock, 144
"Costing books," 4, 6, 7
Countertops, kitchen, 97
County board of health, 163
County building codes, 139
Couplings for pipes, 141, 142
CPVC (chlorinated polyvinyl chloride), pipes, 161–162
Crane, mobile, 47
Crawlspace:
  installation of foundation drain tiles, 23, 24

plumbing plan, sample, 143, 144
  trap doors, 207
  waterproofing of foundation walls, 21–24
Cripple jacks, 64
Cross connection, 155
Curb cock, 144
Curing of concrete, 33
Cushioning for carpeting, 109, 110
Cut stone veneers as exterior wall finish, 87

Dead bolt lock, 130
Decorating:
  exterior painting and staining, 101–102
  floor coverings, 97–98, 108–115
  interior painting and varnishing, 102–104
  interior wall coverings, 104–108
  problems, 115–116
Dehumidifier, 181
Dirt-leg connection, 156
Dishwasher, 201, 208
Disposal, 201, 209
Doorbells, 208, 210
Door closer, automatic, 131, 133
Door knob, 135
Door knockers, 131, 210
Door pulls, 131
Doors, 58
  energy conservation tips, 171
  exterior, 79–80, 81, 82, 102, 125–131, 171,
    210, 227
  garage, 79–80
  hardware, 125–131, 132, 133
  interior, 95–96, 97, 103, 125–131, 171, 227
Door stops, 131, 132
Double bullnose single sash, 34
Doubled joists, 48–49
Double-hung windows, 78, 131, 132, 133, 134
  sash lift, 134
  window lock, 134
Downspout brackets, 77
Downspout drain lines, 24, 164
Downspouts, 76–77, 102, 163, 164
Drain pipes, 159, 160–162
  fittings for, 160–162
Drain tiles, foundation, 23, 24, 26, 164
Draperies, 171, 201
Drapery rods, 208, 209
Drawer hardware, 135, 136
Drawer pull, 135
Drawings, 4, 190
Drill bits, 201
Driveway, 19
Dryer, see Clothes dryer
Drywall construction, 93–95, 98
Ductwork for heating-cooling system, 92, 175,
    176, 177–179, 181, 183–185
  extended-plenum system, 181, 184
  radial system, 181
  work sheet and estimate sheet, 177–179
Duplex receptacle, 191
Dust, filtering out, 182

Dutch bond pattern, 38
DWV (drain-waste-vent) system, 159–165

Earthwork operations, 17, 221–222
  backfilling, 20, 21, 23, 25, 164, 205
  basic computations needed in estimating, 8–9
  downspout drain line, 24
  earth movement, 19
  excavating and related equipment, 20–21
  installation of foundation drain tiles, 23, 24, 26
  problems, 25
  summary, 25
  swell factors, 19
  volume calculations, 17–19
  waterproofing, 21–24
Elbow fittings for pipes, 141, 142
Electrical work, 92, 185, 189–201
  details to be noted, 196–201
  electrical legend, 192
  procedure for estimating, 190–195
  sample estimate sheets, 193–194, 198–199
  styles of estimating, 189–190
    detailed take off method, 190
    outlet method, 190
    square-foot method, 189
Electric drill, 152
Electric heat, 170, 171, 172, 174, 175, 201
Electric hot-water heater, 146, 147
Electric precipitators, 182
Electric resistance heating, 172
Electrolysis, 154
Energy conservation, 171
  insulation, 89–91, 98, 99, 171
  shower head, 157
Engineering News-Record, 7
Engineering services, 211
English cross pattern, 38
Environmental Protection Agency, 163
Epoxy adhesives, 115
Epoxy mortar, 115
Equipment, 6
  availability of necessary, 3
  for earthwork operations, 17, 19, 20–21
  see also specific types of equipment
Estimating the cost of a construction project:
  approximate *vs.* detailed, 5
  basic computations needed in, 8–11
  common errors in, 212–214
  conclusion, 215–216
  decorating, 101–116
  earthwork, 17
  electrical work, 189–201
  estimator's qualifications, 12
  forms used in, 12–14
  foundation work, 29–42
  hardware, 117–137
  heating, ventilating, and air-conditioning, 170–
    186
  house framing, 43–71
  insulation, 89–91, 98
  interior finishes, 91

Estimating the cost of a construction project
   (*Continued*)
  introduction to, 3–6
    checklists for estimator, 6, 7
    labor costs, 5, 6
    material quantity take off, 5
    other items adding to total cost, 6
    questions estimator considers before bidding,
      3–4
    reading and interpreting construction docu-
      ments, 4–5
  knowledge of costs, 6–8
  miscellaneous materials, 204–211
  plumbing, 139–169
  roofing and exterior finish materials, 73–88
  summary sheets, 213, 214–215
  see also Estimator
Estimator:
  checklists for, 6, 7
  forms used by, 12–14
  knowledge of costs, 6–8
  labor cost estimate, 5, 6
  material quantity take off, 5
  other items adding to total cost, 6, 207–210
  qualifications of, 12
  questions to consider before bidding, 3–4
  reading and understanding of construction doc-
    uments by, 4–5
Evaporating coil, 175, 182, 186
Excavation, 20–21, 163–164
Exhaust fans, 182, 183, 200, 209, 210

Face brick sizes, 36
Family room, 208
Faucets:
  bathtub, 157, 165
  clothes washer, 158
  garage mixing, 146, 147, 158
  kitchen sink, 158
  lavatory, 158
Federal Housing Administration, 147, 149, 185
Fence brackets, 125, 126
Fiberboard, asphalt-impregnated, 59, 60
Fiberglass:
  insulation, 90–91
  -reinforced forms for concrete, 30
Field personnel, 210
Field stone veneer as exterior wall finish, 87
Filtering of the air, 182
Financing, 4
Finish hardware, 117–118, 125–137
  for doors, 125–131
    folding doors, 130–131
    hinges, 126–127, 128
    locksets and latchsets, 127–130
    screen and storm doors, 131
    sliding doors, 130
    special trim hardware, 131, 132, 133
  miscellaneous, 135–137
  for windows, 131–134
    operating devices, 133, 134
    trim items, 133–134

Finishing nails, 122
Finish plate, 192
Fireplace, 171, 205
Fittings for pipes:
  draining pipes, 160–162
  water-distribution pipes, 141–142, 149–152, 153
Fixed sash windows, 78, 131
Flemish bond pattern, 38
Flitch-plated beam, 44, 46, 122
Floor(s):
  concrete, 103, 104
  framing, *see* Floor framing
  painting or varnishing, 103, 104
  wood, 97–98, 103, 104, 111–114
Floor coverings, 97–98, 108–115
Floor framing, 43–54
  bearing posts, 43, 44, 45, 51–52
  bridging, 44, 50, 51
  floor girders, 43, 44–47
  floor joists, 44, 47–51, 52
  problems, 71
  second-floor, 53
  subflooring, 44, 51–52
  summary, 52–54
  underlayment, 44, 51
Floor girders, 43, 44–47
  joining floor joists over, 49, 50
  wooden ledger on, to support joists, 49, 50
Floor joists, 44, 47–50, 52–53
  attachment of subflooring to, 51
  notching, for piping, 152–154
Floor register, 180
Flues, 174–175, 215
Folding doors, hardware for, 130–131
Foot board measure (fbm), 54
Forms:
  for concrete work, 29–30, 31
    stripping, 33
  estimator's, 12–14
Form ties, 30, 31
Foundation drain tiles, installation of, 23, 24, 26
Foundation piers, 39
Foundation walls, 164
  waterproofing, 21–24
Foundation work:
  brick walls, 35–39
  concrete block, 34–35
  concrete work, 8–9, 29–33
  masonry piers, 37, 39–40
  problems, 41–42
  steel posts, 40
  transferring load from posts, 40–41
  wooden posts, 40
Framing anchor, 123
Framing the house, *see* House framing
Frank R. Walker, Publishers, 7, 14, 124
Front-end loader for earthwork operations, 19,
    20, 21, 22
Frost line, 144
Furnace, 156, 165, 171–176, 182–183, 184, 200
  filters, 171
  flue or chimney for, 174–175

see also Ductwork for heating-cooling system
Fuse box, 185

Gable construction, 58–59
Gable roof, 63
Galvanized iron pipes, 140
Galvanized steel pipes and fittings, 160, 161
Gambrel roof, 63
Garage:
  doors, 79–80
  floors, 103
  specialty items, 209
Garage mixing faucet, 146, 157, 158
Garbage disposal, 201, 209
Garden wall bond pattern, 38
Gas company, 156
Gas heat, 170, 171, 172, 174, 175
Gas hot-water heater, 146, 147, 175
Gas meter, 156, 165
Gas piping, 155–156, 163, 165
Gas shutoff valves, 156
Gate valves, 142–143, 147
Gauging plaster, 93
General estimate sheets, 12–13
General overhead sheets, 13–14
Gin-pole type hoist, 47
Glazed tiles, 109
Globe valves, 142, 143
Glossary, 235–241
Glue-laminated girders, 44–45
Gooseneck, 144
Grader, 20
Gravel filter bed, 24, 25
Gravity-type furnace, 176
Groating for ceramic tile, 108, 115
Ground clamps, 191, 197
Ground-fault-interrupting (GFI) breaker, 200
Ground lug, 191, 197
Ground strip, 92, 93
Guide Specifications of the American Institute of
    Architects, 4
Gutter boards, 76, 77
Gutters, 76, 77, 102, 163
  accessories, 77
Gypsum plaster sheets, 93

Hacksaw blade, 201
Handrails, 207, 208
Hardware, 117–137
  finish, 125–137
    for doors, 125–131, 132, 133
    miscellaneous, 135–137
    for windows, 131–134
  rough, 117, 118–125
Hardwood floors, *see* Wood flooring
Header (brick exposure), 37
Header joists, 48
Headers for wall openings, 57, 58, 60
Hearth, 205
Heating, 170–181
  distribution, 180–181
  economy tips, 171

facts about, 170
systems, 170–181
  comparison of, 172
  down-flow furnace, 173, 183
  horizontal furnace, 173–175
  sample first floor HVAC plan, 176
  special considerations for, 183–185
  up-flow furnace, 171–173, 182–183
  work sheet and estimate sheet for ductwork,
    177–180
  zoned, 171, 183–185
  see also Air-conditioning
Heat pumps, 172, 176, 183
Herringbone bridging, 50, 51
Hinges, 126–127, 128, 134, 135
Hip jacks, 64
Hip rafters, 64
Hip roof, 63
Hollow bottom bond beam, 34, 35
Hollow chimney block, 34
Hopper windows, 131, 132, 133
Horizontal-sliding window units, 78, 79, 131,
    132, 133, 134
Hot-water heaters, 143, 146–147, 156, 162, 185
Hot water heating system, 172
House drain, 160, 165
House framing, 43–71
  floors, 43–54
  problems, 71
  roofs and ceilings, 62–71
  walls and partitions, 54–61
House sewer, 160, 165
House trap, 160
H-shaped steel members, 46, 47
Humidifier, 171, 181
Humidistats, 181
Humidity control, 181
Hurricane ties, 123
HVAC (heating-ventilating-air conditioning), 50,
    170–186
  cooling, 175–176, 181, 182–183
  distribution system, 180–181, 183
  filtering, 182
  heating, 170–181
  humidity control, 181
  special installation considerations, 183–186
  ventilation, 182
Hydrating of concrete, 33
Hygrostats, 181

Inspections, 165, 200
Instant hot-water unit, 201
Insulation, 89–91, 98, 171
  for pipes, 144, 148–149
  ''R'' value of, 90–91
Insulation Board Institute (IBI), 59
Insurance, 6
Intercom and/or built-in music systems, 201, 208,
    209
Interior finishes, 91–100
Invitation to bid, 4
I-shaped steel members, 46, 47

Jalousie windows, 131, 132–133
Joint tape and compound, 94–95
Joist and rafter roof construction, 68, 69
Joist hangers, 49, 50, 118–119
Jumper cable, 191, 197
Junction boxes, 92
Junction box outlet, 192

Kitchen, 208–209
    cabinets and counters, 97
    carpeting, 109
    exhaust ducts, 182, 184
    flooring for, 97, 98
    sink, 146, 147, 158
Kitchen hood, 192, 209

Labor costs, estimating, 5, 6, 210
Labor force, 232–234
    availability of, 3
    conditions affecting, 6
Lap siding, 83, 84
    painting and staining, 101–102
Latchsets and locksets, 127–130
Lathing and plaster, 92–93, 98
Lavatory, 97, 147, 157–158
    faucets, 158
    traps, 159
Lawn sprinkler systems, underground, 154–155,
        161
Lead pipes, 140, 162
Legal fees, 210
Lever-type operators for windows, 133
Licenses, 6, 211
Lift check valves, 142
Lighting, 201, 210. *See also* Electrical work
Lightning rods, 201
Lime, 93
Line length of rafter, 65, 67
Linoleum resilient flooring, 110
Lipped door hinge, 135
Living room, 208
Loading and hauling of excavated material, 20
Local building codes, 139, 164, 184, 185, 189,
        190
Locksets and latchsets, 127–130
Louvered doors on closets, 96
Louvers, 80–81, 210
L-shaped steel members, 46, 47
L straps, 125
Lumber, 225–232
    foot board measure (fbm), 54
    forms for concrete, 30
    sheathing for roofs, 65, 69
    sheathing for walls, 59, 60
    standard dressed (S4S), sizes, 45

Magnetic catches, 135
Mailboxes and chutes, 210
Major ridge, 64
Manholes, 164
Masonry piers, 37, 39–40
Material quantity take off sheets, 12

Materials of construction, 3
    material quantity take off, 5
Metal bridging, 44, 50, 51, 53, 119–120
Metal doors, 96
Metal joist hangers, 49, 50, 118–119
Metal tie-down plates, 122, 123
Meter socket, 197–200, 201
Microwave oven, 201
Milk boxes, 210
Millwork, 95–97, 98, 225–230
Minor ridge, 64
Mixer, countertop built-in, 201
Molding, 96, 103, 107, 228–230
Mortar, 34, 35, 83, 86–87, 108
Mosaic tiles, 109, 114
Muntin bars for windows, 134

Nails, 122–124, 201
National Blank Book, 14
National Electrical Code (NEC), 189, 190, 196–
        197, 200, 201
National Society of Professional Engineers, 4
Needle valves, 142
No-hub pipe and fittings, 161
Norman face brick, 36

Oil heat, 170, 171, 172, 174, 175
Oil hot-water heaters, 147
1/4 pitch (slope of roof), 62, 63, 64
Outlet boxes, 92, 190, 195
Ovens, 192, 208–209. *See also* Range
Overhang, 65, 66
Overhead costs, 6, 210–211
    general overhead sheets, 13–14

Painting:
    exterior, 101–102
    interior, 102–104
Painting and Decorating Contractors of America,
        102
Paneling, wood, 107–108
Panning, 184
Parquet floors, 98, 111, 113, 114
Pattern bonds, 37, 38
Paver tiles, 109, 114
Permits, 6, 211
    for electricity, 200
    for plumbing, 139–140
Personal shower, 159
Phillips-head wood screws, 124
Pilaster block, 34
Pipe(s):
    drain, 24, 26, 160–162
    gas lines, 155–156, 163, 165
    for HVAC ductwork, *see* Ductwork for heating-
        cooling system
    for storm sewers, 163
    vent, 159, 165
    waste, 160, 165
    water-supply, 163–164, 165
        estimating components needed, 149–152,
            153

fittings, 141–142, 149–152, 153
   installation, 152–154
   insulation, 144, 148–149
   materials for, 140–141, 155
   minimum sizes for, 149
   risers to fixtures, 146, 147, 148, 152
Pipe clamps and supports, 201
Pitch of roof and sheathing required, 69–71
Pivot hinge, 135
Plank flooring, 98, 110–111, 112
Plaster, 92–93, 98
Plastic:
   fittings, solvent-welded, 160
   forms for concrete, 30
   pipes, 155, 161–162
   siding, 8
Plastic polyethylene tubing, 155, 161
Plates, 57
Platform-frame construction, 54–56
Plumb cut, 65, 66
Plumbing, 139–169
   distribution system, 140–158
      cross connection, 155
      estimating materials needed, 149–152, 153
      gas piping, 155–156, 163, 165
      installation, 152–154
      pipe insulation, 144, 148–149
      piping, 140–141, 163–164, 165
      plumbing fixtures, 156–158, 165
      source of water, 140
      summary, 165–166
      underground lawn sprinkler systems, 154–155
      valves, 142–143
      water supply, 143–148
   rough-in, 92, 152, 165
   sewage disposal, 159–165
      installation, 162
      piping, 24, 26, 159, 160–162
      sample sanitary isometric diagram, 159
      sewage treatment, 162–163
      special installation instructions, 163–165
      storm sewers, 163
      summary, 166–189
Plumbing contractor, timing of, 164–165
Plumbing fixtures, 146, 147, 156–158, 165. *See also individual fixtures*
Plywood:
   -boxed girders, 139
   clips, 125
   exterior, painting and staining, 101
   forms for concrete, 30
   sheathing for exterior walls, 57, 59, 60
   sheathing for roofs, 65, 66, 71
   sheets for siding, 83–84, 86, 105
   subflooring, 51–52
Pollen, filtering out, 182
Polyethylene tubing, 155
Portiere columns, 39
Portland Cement Association, 5
Post anchors, 125, 126
Post and beam caps, 125, 126

Posts:
   load carried by, transferring, 40–41
   steel, 40
   wooden, 40
Pressure-reducing valves, 142
Previous projects, reference to, 4, 5
Profit, 6, 211
Progress reports, 211
Projected windows, 131, 132
Proposal (or bid) form, 4
Protection of finished work, costs of, 211
Public sewer, 160, 162–163, 164
Pushbars for windows, 133
PVC (polyvinyl chloride) pipes, 161–162, 163
Pythagorean Theorem, 11

Quarry tiles, 109, 114

Radiant heating system, 172
Radiation, 170
Radiators, 172
Rafter construction with sheathing, 62–66
Rafters and roof deck construction, 66–68
Ramsey, Charles G., 5
Range, 156, 165, 192, 196–197. *See also* Ovens
Receptacle plate, 191
Reference sources, 5
   on costs, 6, 7
   for estimator's forms, 14
   for specifications, 4
Registers for heat/cool air distribution, 180–181
Reinforced concrete block walls, 35
Reinforcing steel, 30–33
   costs associated with, 32–33
Resilient flooring, 97, 110
Ridge rafter connector, 125
Rim joists, 48
Ring-shanked nails, 122
Rise, 63, 64
Risers to plumbing fixtures, 146, 147, 148, 152
   sample hot- and cold-, diagram, 147–148, 159
Roads, access, 19
Robert S. Means, Inc., 7, 14
Robertson-head wood screws, 124
Rock, removal and transporting of, 20
Rocklath, 92, 93
Roller catch, 135
Roman face brick, 36
Romex mounting staples, 201
Romex wiring method, 190, 191, 196, 197
Roof coverings, 73–76
   determining amount needed, 75–76
Roof framing, 62–71
   problems, 71
   rafter and sheathing, 62–66
   rafters and roof deck, 66–68
   roof sheathing, 65, 69–71
   roof trusses, 68–69, 231
Roofing felt, 75, 77
Roof shapes, 63
Roof shingles, 73–75, 77
Roof truss clips, 123

Roof trusses, 68–69, 231
Rotary gear operators for windows, 133
Rough hardware, 117, 118–125
    anchor bolts, 37, 118
    joist hangers, 49, 50, 118–119
    metal bridging, 44, 50, 51, 53, 119–120
    miscellaneous metal framing accessories, 125
    nails and wood screws, 122–124
    truss splice plates, flitch plates, and tie-down
        plates, 44, 46, 121–122, 123
Rough sills, 57
Rowlock, 37
Rubber resilient flooring, 110
Run, defined, 62–63
Running bond pattern, 38
Rustic tiles, 114

Safety valves, 142
Sanding:
    of floor, 103
    of wood trim, 103
Screen and storm doors, 131, 171, 210
Second-floor framing, 53
Security vision glass, 131
Seismic ties, 123
Semi-concealed hinge, 135
Septic disposal field, 163
Septic system, on-site, 139
Septic tanks, 163, 164
Service cock, 144
Service-entrance ground connection, 191, 197
Service mast, 197, 200
Sewage disposal, 159–165
    installation, 162
    piping, 24, 26, 159, 160–162
    sample sanitary isometric diagram, 159
    sewage treatment, 162–163
    special installation instructions, 163–165
    storm sewers, 24, 163, 164
    summary, 166–169
Sewage-ejector pump, 164, 201
Sewage treatment, 162–163
Sewers, permit for, 140
Sheathing:
    for roofs, 65, 69–71
    for walls, 59–61
Sheathing lumber, 59, 60
Shed roof, 63
Shelving, 96, 103, 208, 209
Shingles, roof, 73–75, 77
Shiplapped sheathing boards, 60, 61
Shoring, 30, 33
Shower, 147, 157, 165
Shower head, 157
Shutters, 102
Siding, see Wall finishes, exterior
Silicone grout, 108
Single bullnose double sash, 34
Single-hung windows, 78, 131, 132
Slate shingles, 74–75
Sleeper, Harold R., 5
Sliding doors, 96

hardware for, 130
Sliding window units, horizontal-, 78, 79
Slope of the roof, 62, 63
Slotted-head wood screws, 124
Smoke detectors, 201
Smoking, 182
Snow melting, 201
Social Security, 6
Soffits, 102
Soil stack, 154, 157, 160, 162
Solar collectors for domestic hot-water heating,
    147
Solar heating system, 172
Soldered joints for piping, 141
Soldier, 37
Solenoid valves, 146
Solid bridging, 50, 51
Solid header, 34
Span, defined, 62
Specialty contractor, 7–8, 20, 164
Specialty items, 207–210
Specifications, 4
Spigot, 161
Spikes and ferrules, 77
Splash blocks, 77, 164
Sprinkler systems, underground lawn, 152–153
Square-edged sheathing boards, 60, 61
Staining, exterior, 101–102
Staircase angle, 125
Stairs, 205–207
Stair treads, 110
State building codes, 139, 189
Steam heating system, 172
Steel:
    doors, 79, 81
    forms for concrete, 30
    members for floor girders, 46–47
    painting galvanized, siding, 102
    pipe columns, 40
    posts, 40
        transferring load from, 40–41
    reinforcing, 30–33, 35
    sheets for siding, 83, 102
    tods, 30–31, 32–33
Storm and screen doors, 131, 171, 210
Storm sewers, 24, 163, 164
Storm windows, 171, 210
Stove, see Range
Strap bridging, 50, 51
Stretcher (brick exposure), 37
Stretcher concrete block, 34
Strip flooring, 97–98, 113–114
Stucco exterior wall finish, 83
    painting, 101–102
Styrofoam insulation, 90
Subcontractors, 4, 8
Subflooring, 44, 51–52, 53, 97, 98
Summary sheets, estimate, 213, 214–215
Sump pump, 24, 201
Suppliers, local, 3
Surveying services, 211
Swell factor in excavation, 19

Swing check valves, 142, 143
Switch plates, multigang, 192

Tail joists, 48
Tees for piping, 141, 142, 147
Telephone outlets, 201, 208, 209
Testing costs, 211
Thermostat to regulate central heating system, 170, 171, 181, 183
Thresholds, 110, 115
Tie-down plates, 122, 123
Time for preparing estimate of costs, 3
Time to complete project, effect on cost estimates of, 6
Toilets, 143, 147, 157, 160, 162, 182, 184
    traps, 159
Toilet seat, 157
Tongue & grooved sheathing boards, 60, 61
Trade organizations, publications of, 5
Trap doors, 207
Traps, 159, 160
Triangle:
    area of a, 11
    hypotenuse of a, 10–11
Trimmer joists, 48
Trimmers, 57
Truss splice plates, 121
T straps, 125
Tub, *see* Bathtubs
TV antenna system, 201, 208, 209

Underground lawn sprinkler systems, 152–153
Underlayment for floors, 44, 97, 98
Unions for piping, 141, 156
Unit rise, 63, 65
Unit run, 63, 65
Unit span, 63, 65
Utility companies, 89
    tie-in costs, 211
Utility room, 207, 209

Vacuum system, central, 201
Valley jacks, 64
Valley rafters, 64
Valves for water pipes, 142–143
Vanities, *see* Lavatory
Varnishing, interior, 102–104
Ventilation, 170, 182
    louvers for, 80–81
    when painting or varnishing, 103
Vent pipes, 159–160, 165
Vent stacks, 159–160
Vertical sliding windows, 131, 132, 133
Vertical tongue-and-grooved boards for exterior wall finish, 83, 85
Vinyl adhesive, 106
Vinyl asbestos resilient flooring, 110
Vinyl resilient flooring, 110
Vinyl siding, 83, 102
Vinyl wall coverings, 105–107
Visqueen, 23
Vitreous tile pipe, 161, 163

Wall finishes, exterior, 83–87, 225
    brick veneers, 84–87
    cut stone veneers, 87
    estimating quantity of materials needed, 87
    field stone veneers, 87
    lap siding, 83, 84, 101–102
    painting and staining, 101–102
    plywood sheets, 83–84, 86, 101
    problem, 88
    stucco, 83, 101–102
    vertical tongue-and-grooved boards, 83, 85
Wall-floor register, 180
Wall framing, 54–59
    additional, needed, 58–59
    estimating procedures, 57–58
    exterior walls, 54–56
    interior partitions, 57, 58
    problems, 71
    sheathing (covering) the wall, 59–61
Wallpaper, 105–107
Wall register, 180
Walls and ceilings, interior, 91–95, 207, 228
    coverings for, 104–108
    drywall, 93–95, 98
    lathing and plaster, 92–93, 98
    painting, 103, 104–105
Wall section, 39
Wall studs, 57, 60
    for gable construction, 58–59
Warm-air system, forced, 171–181
    down-flow furnace, 173, 183
    horizontal furnace, 173–175
    registers for heat distribution, 180–181
    up-flow furnace, 171–173, 182–183
Washing machine, *see* Clothes washer
Waste, removal of, 20
Waste pipes, 160, 165
Wasting of excavated earth, 19
Water:
    cross connection, 155
    distribution system, 140–158
    estimating materials needed, 149–152, 163
    installation, 152–154
    permit for, 140
    pipe insulation, 144, 148
    piping, 140–141, 163–164, 165
    plumbing fixtures, 156–158
        source of water, 140
        summary, 165–166
        underground lawn sprinkler systems, 154–155
        valves, 142–143
        water supply, 143–148
    sewage disposal, 159–165
        installation, 162
        piping, 159, 160–162
        sample sanitary isometric diagram, 159
        sewage treatment, 162–163
        special installation instructions, 163–165
        storm sewers, 163
        summary, 166–169
    softeners, 140, 146, 201

Water (*Continued*)
  tap-in charge, 140
Water closet, 143, 157
Water hammer, 146
Water main, 143, 144
  drain valve, 146
Water meter, 144–146, 191
Waterproofing, 21–24
Water service entrance lines, 155
Water storage tank, 164
Water tap, 144
Weatherstripping, 171, 207
Welded wire mesh (or fabric), 31–32
Wells, 139, 140, 155, 164
  pumps, 201
Western or platform-frame construction, 54–56
Wheat paste, 106
Windows, 58, 77–79, 102, 103, 210
  energy conservation tips, 171
  hardware for, 131–134
    operating devices, 133, 134
    trim items, 133–134, 227

Wiping, 162
Wire baskets, 77
Wiring, *see* Electrical work
Wooden posts, 40
  transferring load from, 40–41
Wood flooring, 97–98, 111–114
  painting, 103, 104
  varnishing, 103, 104
Wood paneling, 107–108
Wood sash jamb, 34
Wood screws, 124, 201
Wood shake roof shingles, 74
Wood trim, 87, 102, 226–230
  around doors and windows, 96, 227
  baseboards, 96
  painting and varnishing, 102–103
  sanding, 103
Wood windows, 131
Workmen's Compensation insurance, 6
Wrought iron pipes, 140

Zoned heating and cooling system, 171, 183